Soviet Perspectives on International Relations

1956-1967

BY WILLIAM ZIMMERMAN

PRINCETON, NEW JERSEY

PRINCETON UNIVERSITY PRESS 1969

L.C. Card: 68-56326

Soviet Perspectives on International Relations, 1956-1967 *is published under the auspices of the Russian Institute and the Institute of War and Peace Studies, Columbia University. The Russian Institute promotes research in the social sciences and the humanities as they relate to Russia and the Soviet Union. The Institute of War and Peace Studies, in addition to its interest in problems of American foreign relations and national security policy, is currently sponsoring theoretical and empirical investigations in international relations and comparative politics.*

Printed in the United States of America
by Princeton University Press

Preface

THE pages that follow represent an effort to combine two interests, one in international relations theory, the other in Soviet foreign policy, in a way which may prove beneficial to our understanding of both areas of inquiry.

In the conception and writing of this book I have been greatly aided by the counsel of Professors Alexander Dallin of Columbia's Russian Institute and William T. R. Fox of Columbia's Institute of War and Peace Studies; their interest, time, and criticisms are gratefully acknowledged. The faults which remain in this book are my own; there would have been others had I not benefited from their penetrating comments. I should also like to thank the Inter-University Committee on Travel Grants for having made it possible for me to spend a semester in the Soviet Union during 1966—thus providing the opportunity to meet Soviet scholars and to gain access to dissertations on deposit in the Lenin Library in Moscow.

Finally, I should like to thank my wife, Barbara, not only for having contributed materially to the substance and intelligibility of this inquiry, but also for having borne with me during the many metamorphoses through which this manuscript has passed.

William Zimmerman

Ann Arbor, Michigan
June 1968

Contents

Soviet Perspectives on International Relations 1956-1967

Chapter One: Introduction

IN THE traditional Marxist scheme of things, the revolutionary unity of theory and practice was predicated on a calculus whose central focus was the socio-economic system of capitalism operating within the political context of the European nation-state. To Lenin's credit, several of his works (most obviously, *Imperialism: The Highest Stage of Capitalism*) written prior to the Bolshevik seizure of power in 1917 amounted to an effort, *inter alia,* to adapt revolutionary tactics to account for the technological, economic, and political changes in the second half of the 19th century and the beginning years of the 20th, which resulted, in Leninist terminology, in the transformation of capitalism into a world system. Once the revolution had occurred in Russia alone, moreover, the imagery of the fundamental conflict almost perforce had to change from that of a struggle waged within the state between the dominant but moribund capitalists and the emerging proletariat to one taking place in the horizontally structured environment of international politics. Vertical, class, and economic concepts were transposed and adjusted to account for the basically horizontal, international, and political arena in which the Soviet leaders engaged their class enemies. In such a world—where the proletariat and the Soviet Union, while not identical, were nevertheless inseparable—Stalin's transformation of "proletarian internationalism" into a concept asserting the hegemony of Soviet interests constituted a logical adaptation. For the Bolsheviks in power, "capitalism" became a system of states, as well as a global socio-economic formation.[1]

[1] Cf. Alexander Dallin, "The Soviet Stake in Eastern Europe," *The Annals,* Vol. 317 (May 1958), pp. 138-39; Alfred G. Meyer, *Leninism*

These doctrinal adaptations notwithstanding, the role of international relations in the appraisal of the "world historical process" that prevailed in the Soviet Union in the years preceding Stalin's death in 1953 was essentially a derivative and subordinate one. Priority in determining the "course of social development" was accorded "the development of productive forces, the class struggle, those internal processes in the realm of economics and politics taking place in each country."[2] After Stalin's death,[3] however, and especially in the years following the Twentieth Congress of the Communist Party of the Soviet Union in 1956, a striking transformation in Soviet thinking

(New York: Praeger, 1962); Zbigniew K. Brzezinski, *The Soviet Bloc: Unity and Conflict* (Cambridge, Mass.: Harvard University Press, 1960), pp. 382-402; and Brzezinski, *Ideology and Power in Soviet Politics* (New York: Praeger, 1962), pp. 97-140.

[2] Akademiia Nauk SSSR, Institut Mirovoi Ekonomiki i Mezhdunarodnykh Otnoshenii [hereafter AN IMEMO], *Mezhdunarodnye otnosheniia posle vtoroi mirovoi voiny* [International Relations Since the Second World War] (Moscow: Gospolitizdat, 1962), Vol. I (1945-49), p. vi.

A slightly abridged English version of the illuminating introduction to the first volume may be found in "The Nature and Specific Features of Contemporary International Relations," *International Affairs* (Moscow) [hereafter *International Affairs*], No. 10 (October 1962), pp. 93-98.

[3] Strictly speaking, harbingers of the "post-Stalinist" change in Soviet thinking may be detected at the 19th C.P.S.U. Congress in 1952 and in Stalin's *Economic Problems of Socialism in the U.S.S.R.* See, in particular, Marshall D. Shulman, *Stalin's Foreign Policy Reappraised* (Cambridge, Mass.: Harvard University Press, 1963).

On the period after Stalin's death see Herbert S. Dinerstein, *War and the Soviet Union* (New York: Praeger, 1959), passim.

In 1963 the editors of *International Relations Since World War II* blamed "the cult of the personality" specifically for having "impeded development of Marxist-Leninist theory in questions of international relations." AN IMEMO, *Mezhdunarodnye otnosheniia . . .* , Vol. II, pp. 55-56, italics added.

about the influence of international relations on the course of history occurred. Rather than its previously secondary and derivative place, international relations acquired a central position in Soviet thinking, primarily as a result of the perceived consequences of general war in the nuclear age[4]—a comprehension exemplified by the terse declaration to the Chinese that "the atomic bomb does not observe the class principle."[5] Since "*the fate of millions of people has in the past never depended in such measure as in our time on the solution of basic international problems and first of all the problems of war and peace*"; because "*the question of war and peace is the basic question of our times*";[6] Soviet commentators declared, "*the role of international relations in the life of human society has grown sharply.*"[7] Therefore, "no serious scholarly analysis whatsoever of the trends of international development in the contemporary epoch is possible without due consideration of

[4] The divergence in perception between the Soviet military leadership and Khrushchev is discussed in my "Sokolovskii and His Critics: A Review," *Journal of Conflict Resolution*, Vol. VIII, No. 3 (September 1964), p. 323. A more general discussion of military attitudes may be found in Thomas W. Wolfe, *Soviet Strategy at the Crossroads* (Cambridge, Mass.: Harvard University Press, 1964); and Roman Kolkowicz, *The Soviet Military and the Communist Party* (Princeton, N.J.: Princeton University Press, 1967).

[5] *Pravda*, July 14, 1963.

[6] The phrases are those, respectively, of AN IMEMO, *Mezhdunarodnye otnosheniia* . . . , p. vi, italics in original, and the Program adopted by the Twenty-second Congress. For an English translation of the latter see Charlotte Saikowski and Leo Gruliow, eds., *Current Soviet Policies IV* (New York: Columbia University Press, 1962), p. 13, italics in original. While the Program became somewhat passé after the Twenty-third Congress, the particular sentiment cited above continues to be frequently expressed in Soviet commentary.

[7] AN IMEMO, *Mezhdunarodnye otnosheniia* . . . , p. vi, italics in original.

the increased role of international relations and its new laws of development."[8]

The metamorphosis in Soviet perspectives on international relations since 1956 is the subject of this book. It is concerned with the much greater Soviet interest in the study of international relations, as well as with the evolution in Soviet perspectives on international relations.

Several motivations underlie this study. It was prompted in part by an assumption that an elite's perspectives on the international system affect its selection of policy alternatives. Therefore, analysis of the organizing constructs and hypotheses of a state's decision-makers is relevant to the interpretation and prediction of a state's foreign policy, particularly at the levels of middle- and long-run policy orientation, where the selection of policies is most likely to affect behavior. For instance, one is well on his way to ascertaining Cuba's place in Soviet priorities by having analyzed Soviet thinking about the "national-democratic state" and the "export of revolution and counterrevolution." It was further assumed that the study of the international relations perspectives of Soviet decision-makers provides a valuable supplement to the direct analysis of behavior by making it more possible to appraise the relative significance of past events for present and future behavior. The intellectual cheesecloth through which decision-makers filter the facts influences the determination of which lessons taught by "history," "experience," or "life" will be learned.

Specifically, the present inquiry is intended to have a direct bearing on three themes which dominate the Western litera-

[8] *Ibid.* Cf. Stanley H. Hoffmann, ed., *Contemporary Theory in International Relations* (Englewood Cliffs, N.J.: Prentice-Hall, 1960), p. 4: international relations "have become in the twentieth century the very condition of our daily life."

ture on Soviet foreign policy: the relevance of Marxist-Leninist ideology to post-Stalinist foreign policy; second, the motif of continuity and change;[9] and third, "spontaneity and consciousness." This study offers an opportunity to evaluate the capacity of Soviet international relations observers to perceive international reality and, consequently, to determine whether and to what extent ideology retains a relevance for Soviet analysis. Focusing on Soviet international perspectives has permitted an appraisal of the extent to which we may properly assert that "current Soviet attitudes and images have not evolved far from their Bolshevik antecedents," and therefore that the terms "Bolshevik" and "Soviet" can be used "almost interchangeably."[10] Moreover, by comparing Khrushchevian and post-Khrushchevian perspectives, I have been able to relate the findings of this inquiry to the Khrushchev period in Soviet foreign policy. It is hoped that this study will permit a tentative judgment as to whether—as one limiting case—the Khrushchev years were an idiosyncratic episode or, on the other hand, whether Khrushchevism, as the Chinese and some Western specialists assert, is a larger phenomenon rooted in the changed international environment and the Soviet Union's changed position in the international system and/or the transformation of the Soviet system.[11] Does politics—and with it, consciousness—still so shape the Soviet system that a "dynas-

[9] See especially Ivo. J. Lederer, ed., *Russian Foreign Policy* (New Haven, Conn.: Yale University Press, 1962).

[10] Nathan Leites, *Kremlin Thoughts: Yielding, Rebuffing, Provoking, Retreating*, Memorandum RM-3618-ISA (Santa Monica, Calif.: The RAND Corporation, 1963), p. iv.

[11] The argument has been developed most fully by Vernon Aspaturian, in R. Barry Farrell, ed., *Approaches to Comparative and International Politics* (Evanston, Ill.: Northwestern University Press, 1966), pp. 212-87.

tic" framework remains the most profitable viewpoint for assessing Soviet foreign policy?

In addition to the above concerns, the present inquiry into Soviet international relations perspectives was prompted by an impression, shared by many specialists, that the Western literature on international relations has been excessively ethnocentric and has given insufficient attention to the development of the study of comparative international politics. The present study is intended to illuminate one path for escaping our "culture boundness." Rather than a direct response to the call of William and Annette Fox for "the comparative study of multiple sovereignty systems,"[12] my investigation pursues a somewhat different tack. In it, the modern international system is held constant and its perception by the international relations commentators in the Soviet Union, the other of the world's two superpowers, is treated as a variable. Necessarily, complete cultural transcendance is not to be achieved by scrutinizing the flowers and weeds of only one other garden of theory, however unusual its soil and climatic conditions.[13] To guard against any prediposition to assume the correctness of a view shared by Soviet and American scholars, further comparisons of international relations perspectives, beyond the limits of this study, would be desirable. Nevertheless, it is hoped that a beginning has been made here by providing the material for a typology of international relations perspectives which suggests the potential of further efforts to compare international relations perspectives.

[12] William T. R. Fox and Annette Baker Fox, "The Teaching of International Relations in the United States," *World Politics*, Vol. XIII, No. 3 (April 1961), p. 359.

[13] The garden-of-theory metaphor is that of William T. R. Fox; see Fox, ed., *Theoretical Aspects of International Relations* (Notre Dame: University of Notre Dame Press, 1959), p. 41.

Sources, Scope, and Method

This study benefited from interviews graciously granted me by Soviet specialists during my visits to the Soviet Union in 1962 and 1966, and from the opportunity while there to gain access to unpublished dissertations on deposit in the Lenin Library in Moscow. It should be emphasized, however, that the study is based primarily on published Soviet materials. Of these materials, attention was devoted primarily to the following: the specialized, more or less scholarly, international relations journals, *Mirovaia ekonomika i mezhdunarodnye otnosheniia* [*The World Economy and International Relations*][14] and *Mezhdunarodnaia zhizn'* [published in English as *International Affairs*], as well as *Voprosy istorii* [*Problems of History*]; the C.P.S.U. Central Committee's "theoretical and political organ," *Kommunist*; the "theoretical" organ (published in Prague) of the Soviet wing[15] of the world communist movement, *Problemy mira i sotsializma* [*Problems of Peace and Socialism*], issued in Canadian and British editions as *World Marxist Review*; books authored by researchers at the Institute of World Economy and International Relations of the Academy of Sciences, and to a lesser extent at the Moscow State Institute of International Relations; the major C.P.S.U. and international communist documents; and major speeches of government and Party officials active in foreign policy-making.

Attention to these materials reflects a judgment that on the basis of their sophistication and/or authoritativeness they offered

[14] Hereafter, *Mirovaia ekonomika.*

[15] As *Kommunist* declared in 1963, "the ideological platform of . . . *Problems of Peace and Socialism* is creative Marxism-Leninism." "Mezhdunarodnaia tribuna kommunistov" (International Forum of Communists), *Kommunist,* No. 4 (March 1963), p. 94.

the greatest possibility for insight into the ratiocinations of the Soviet political mind. In turn, the decision to use both authoritativeness and sophistication as criteria for inclusion and exclusion is based on an awareness that since 1956 in the Soviet Union the study of international relations has been the concern both of specialists in the institutes and of decision-makers at the apex of the state and Party structures. Indeed, one of the major consequences of the Soviet reevaluation of the role and significance of international relations has been the recognition that international relations questions are sufficiently *complex* to warrant attention by specialists, and that specialists, to the extent that their research is policy-oriented, have a major role to play in the analysis of questions concerning international relations. As the now-deceased A. A. Arzumanian, the first director of the Institute of World Economy and International Relations, stated in 1962, it is the task of international relations specialists "immediately to inform the higher [state] organs of the results of research undertaken," inasmuch as the "value of research in the area of contemporary international development is determined by the extent to which . . . [it becomes] operational."[16] At the same time, it was firmly asserted that the social sciences, including international relations, were too *important* to be the exclusive domain of the specialists. As Leonid F. Il'ichev, in 1963 a Party Secretary and major spokesman on ideology, said: "The development [of social science] is not the monopoly of separate scientific collectives and scholars but the business of the whole Soviet people, the

[16] A. A. Arzumanian, "Vazhnye voprosy razvitiia mirovoi ekonomiki" [Important Problems of the Development of the World Economy], *Vestnik Akademii Nauk SSSR* (hereafter *Vestnik*), No. 8 (August 1962), p. 15.

whole party, its theoretical [general] staff—the Central Committee of the C.P.S.U."[17]

Even with the materials utilized in this study—selected so as to exclude from consideration those Soviet materials which most evidence the aroma of *agitprop* and are influenced by immediate tactical and polemical considerations—there remains the epistemological question central to most research on the Soviet Union: the nature of the inferences that may properly be derived from overt Soviet sources.

It might even be contended that there is a prior question, namely, whether one should give serious attention to overt Soviet statements. This is a less troublesome issue. In certain cases[18] we have evidence indicating that there is a correspondence between overt Soviet sources and the content of materials of more restricted circulation. We know that communist leaders take seriously what other communist leaders say. One classic instance of this phenomenon was the furor caused by the famous Molotov statement in 1955, that in the Soviet Union "the foundations of a socialist society have already been built."[19] The Sino-Soviet conflict provides another

[17] Leonid F. Il'ichev, "Metodologicheskie problemy estestvoznaniia i obshchestvennykh nauk" [Methodological Problems of the Natural and Social Sciences], *Vestnik*, No. 11 (November 1963), pp. 3-46, at p. 13. After Khrushchev's ouster, Il'ichev was shunted over to the Ministry of Foreign Affairs.

[18] Raymond Garthoff, in a comparison of Soviet military journals designed for circulation among the general staff with those of less restricted circulation, discerned no striking differences in content. *Soviet Strategy in the Nuclear Age* (New York: Praeger, 1958), p. 270. Cf. also the materials in the Smolensk Archive. For a description, see Merle Fainsod, *Smolensk Under Soviet Rule* (Cambridge, Mass.: Harvard University Press, 1958).

[19] On the Molotov formulation and the general role of differing

illustration of this point; the reader of the major statements is struck by the extent to which the opposing sides are polemicizing against what the other side has or has not said.

It remains therefore to consider problems which arise in attempting to make the leap from the printed Soviet record to the "real" views of Soviet international relations commentators. Briefly, the Western scholar has to determine to *what extent*, and in *what manner, which* statements emanating from *which* sources are credibly representative of the international relations perspectives of *which* persons or identifiable groups. This is no mean task.

A determination has to be made of the tactical and polemical circumstances surrounding the appearance—and demise—of a particular remark and the consequences such self-serving motives have for the validity of any inferences which may be derived. In general, one is well advised to manifest an air of skepticism toward statements obviously emitted in a manipulative or otherwise self-serving context. At the same time, one need not preclude totally the use of such statements in making certain inferences. It is possible that a position or formulation conspicuously favoring an actor's own interests may nevertheless constitute the "real" perspective of that actor. Only a test against foreign-policy behavior will provide a measure of the value of such statements, and even then the action may have stemmed from different motives. Thus, for example, prior to 1962 the Soviet press frequently gave vent to the formulation that a direct military confrontation between the United States and the Soviet Union would "inevitably escalate," a notion many Western specialists regarded as tactically inspired to

---

ideological formulations in internal Soviet power struggles, consult Robert Conquest, *Power and Policy in the U.S.S.R.* (New York: St. Martin's Press, 1961), p. 268 and passim.

impinge upon United States maneuverability. Soviet behavior in the Cuban crisis, however, suggests that the formulation very likely constituted the genuine views of the regime as well. Some inferences, moreover, about Soviet international relations perspectives may be gleaned precisely from discerning Soviet assumptions concerning the manner in which Soviet interests are best served. Again, in any political process tactical statements and formulations often have a curious way of becoming, over time, the *real,* i.e., operational, positions of groups. Finally, the tactical or polemical motivation prompting the *timing* of certain statements may not adversely alter the degree of correspondence between overt statements and real views of the persons or groups propounding such views. Indeed, the connection between declaratory and real positions or perspectives may become clearer in the process of a polemic, thus aiding the outsider in his effort to derive inferences. Certainly, for instance, the West now has a better idea of the perspectives of the Soviet ruling group as a result of their polemic with the Chinese. Under some circumstances, even the well-known device of compartmentalizing audiences, with its obvious implications of the contrived nature of a public posture,[20] permits some insight into international relations perspectives. This point was well illustrated by an article written in March 1961, at a time when there was little firm evidence that disarmament had become a major issue between the Chinese and the Russians. In the English-language version, the author, Nikolai Talenskii, is quoted as having declared, "To preserve peace we must kill war. There is no other way. And to kill

[20] Cf. "O taknazyvaemykh tekhnicheskikh problemakh razoruzheniia" [Concerning the So-called Technical Problems of Disarmament], *Mezhdunarodnaia zhizn'*, No. 3 (March 1961), p. 85; and "The Technical Problems of Disarmament," *International Affairs,* No. 3 (March 1961), p. 60.

war we must liquidate the machinery of war, all the means of waging war. In other words, we must have general and complete disarmament. *I often wonder how some people fail to grasp this elementary idea*." The Russian-language version conspicuously omitted the italicized sentence. Evidently, if there are some postures that must be maintained to all or certain audiences, the regime may also consider it imperative that certain audiences clearly perceive the extent to which certain messages do correspond to the regime's views.

A second problem associated with the interpretation of Soviet statements related to the difficulty of ascertaining which views a particular statement may be taken to represent—those of an individual, an identifiable group within the Soviet Union, or the official position of the regime. To infer policy-relevant perspectives directly from overt sources was an achievement usually accomplished only after the fact during periods of Soviet history when the dictates of *partiinost'* were most manifest. There have been many spokesmen in Moscow for some time now, who operating along narrow channels, emit divergent signals on various matters of fundamental import. As a result, it has become increasingly difficult to identify *who* speaks as the voice of Moscow on *which* subjects.

The difficulties are amply illustrated by a book which received considerable attention in the West: *Military Strategy,* edited by Marshal V. D. Sokolovskii and others. It bears all the traditional earmarks of a significant source for insights into the "Soviet political mind." Thus when *Military Strategy* was first published in 1962, its main author, Sokolovskii, was a Marshal of the Soviet Union, a C.P.S.U. Central Committee member, and a former Chief of the General Staff. The book itself was depicted by its authors as the first study "in the open Soviet military literature" since 1926 to give the Soviet reader "a general understanding of military strategy." Other Soviet sources repeated this theme and made other efforts to emphasize the book's significance to potential readers.

On examination, however, *Military Strategy* turns out not to be an official position constituting the culmination of a stage in the dialogues within the military and between the military specialists and the political generalists. Instead, the book must be seen as part of an ongoing debate over matters of high policy, as an effort on the part of a major segment of the military establishment to enhance its chances of favorable treatment in the allocation of resources and the scope of decision-making by the military. Within the parameters set by the late Marshal Rodion Malinovskii's speech at the Twenty-second Congress of the C.P.S.U., as Thomas Wolfe of the RAND Corporation has noted, "the volume represents, in a sense, a point scored for the military side of the argument by getting the military viewpoint on the record in the form of the first comprehensive exposition of the new doctrine."[21]

These caveats notwithstanding, it is possible to identify some authors, usually because they combine relative sophistication with political position, whose statements bear closest scrutiny as evidence of official thinking. Certain persons, for instance, have virtually monopolized particular issues throughout the post-1956 period. Thus on four occasions in the past decade,

[21] In this regard, see in particular the introduction to V. D. Sokolovskii, ed., *Soviet Military Strategy* (Englewood Cliffs, N.J.: Prentice-Hall, 1963), analyzed and annotated by Herbert S. Dinerstein, Leon Gouré, and Thomas Wolfe [hereafter RAND, *Soviet Military Strategy*], pp. 33-34 and passim. Cf., also, Zimmerman, "Sokolovskii and His Critics," p. 323. For a post-Khrushchevian Soviet book critical of *Military Strategy*, see N. V. Pukhovskii, *O mire i voine* [Concerning War and Peace] (Moscow: Izdatel'stvo "Mysl'," 1965). The book was published under the auspices of the C.P.S.U. Higher Party School.

"M. Marinin"[22] (probably a pseudonym for Ia. S. Khavinson, the editor-in-chief of *Mirovaia ekonomika*) has had his name affixed to major statements summarizing the Soviet view of the global distribution of power. I. M. Lemin has played a similar role in the interpretation of "intra-imperialist contradictions." A. Sovetov—another pseudonym—has been perhaps the name most consistently associated with major articles treating the ramifications for Soviet foreign policy of changes in the foreign policies of the "imperialist" powers. During the Khrushchev period, similarly, articles signed by persons of the stature of an Arzumanian, Talenskii, Lemin, or V. G. Korionov were properly treated as reflecting much more than just the private views of the author. (Regrettably, the relative authoritativeness of Soviet commentators is subject to alteration over time—yet another complication to be borne in mind in assessing Soviet commentary.) Again, while it may not always be possible to distinguish those statements which diverge from consensus positions, sometimes one cannot help detecting them (e.g., when the editorial board of *Mirovaia ekonomika* felt constrained to declare that "several positions in the present article are the personal viewpoint of Academician E. S. Varga."[23]) Still, all things considered, one is left with considerable misgivings about the ability to connect (or not connect, as the case may be) statements made by international relations commentators—political generalists and second-level specialists alike—to the Soviet political process, and is consoled only partially by the good company kept.

[22] Inasmuch as the name "Marinin" was also used during World War II, it may constitute a quaint element of continuity with the Stalin era.

[23] "Teoreticheskie problemy ekonomiki 'obshchego rynka'" [Theoretical Problems of the Economy of the 'Common Market'], *Mirovaia ekonomika*, No. 10 (October 1962), p. 49.

A methodological consideration of another sort also proved a major impediment to analysis—namely, the fact that even in the West, where international relations scholarship is vastly more advanced than in the Soviet Union, there exist strong elements of uncertainty about the content of the study of international relations. One does not find ready-made a well-articulated body of principles or hypotheses about the process of international relations against which Soviet international relations perspectives can be measured. "Whether because the subject is new or because the world is changing rapidly, there are few acknowledged classics which every serious American student of international relations will be expected to have read: there are as yet no Paretos or Durkheims, no Marshalls or Keyneses, no Bagehots or Diceys."[24]

Disputes over the definition of the scope of international relations abound.[25] In part, this has been evidenced in the controversy over the relation of international relations to political science and sociology, or even in extended hassles over the proper name for the study. In part, the controversy has been a product of confusion over the range of social phenomena to be subsumed under the study of international relations. The latter difficulty is inherent, to a considerable extent, in the vastness and nebulousness of international relations as a "thing in itself." Urban G. Whitaker, Jr. has calculated that "if individuals rather than States [are] considered the basic actors in international relations . . . a study of the whole field . . . would involve nearly 4½ quintillion bilateral relationships."[26]

[24] Fox and Fox, "The Teaching of International Relations," p. 349.

[25] For evidence of disagreement in the Soviet Union as to whether international relations is a discipline, see below, p. 45.

[26] "Actors, Ends, and Means: A Coarse-Screen Macro-Theory of International Relations," in James N. Rosenau, ed., *International Politics*

Confronted with such a welter of data, some scholars have been tempted—and have attempted—to make "too audacious a synthesis,"[27] an ordering and simplification of the data which has involved dispensing with crucial features of the baby's anatomy along with the bathwater. Such a propensity, for instance, may be observed in the writings of those who regard themselves as forming a realist[28] school, of whom Hans J. Morgenthau[29] is the most renowned. Others (here Quincy Wright, in his *The Study of International Relations*, immediately comes to mind) have gone to the opposite pole. Wright's truly fertile "imagination may picture a twelve-dimensional

---

and Foreign Policy (Glencoe, Ill.: The Free Press of Glencoe, Inc., 1961), p. 444.

[27] Alfred Grosser, "L'étude des relations internationales, spécialité américaine?" *Revue française de science politique*, Vol. vi, No. 3 (July-September 1956), p. 639.

[28] Dwight Waldo (*Political Science in the United States of America* [Paris: UNESCO, 1956], Chap. 5) has observed that the political scientist who does not regard himself as a realist (in a looser sense than Professor Morgenthau uses the term) is a *rara avis*. For a political scientist, choosing to be called an anti- or a nonrealist is rather like accepting the label *Menshevik*.

It is useful to distinguish between the realist *school* which leans heavily on neo-orthodox doctrinal assumptions concerning the flawed nature of man, and others whose realism is derived from an analysis of the social context in which politics, and particularly international politics is carried on. For William T. R. Fox, the former are doctrinal realists, the latter empirical realists. "Les fondements moraux et juridiques de la politique étrangère américaine," in J. B. Duroselle, ed., *La politique étrangère et ses fondements* (Paris: A. Colin, 1954), pp. 278-90. See also John H. Herz, *International Politics in the Atomic Age* (New York: Columbia University Press, 1959), pp. 231ff. and Kenneth N. Waltz, *Man, the State, and War* (New York: Columbia University Press, 1959), for similar distinctions using other nomenclature.

[29] The Morgenthau position is stated in *Politics Among Nations* (New York: Knopf, 1960), 3rd edn., pp. 3-97.

semi-opaque cheese, within which maggots crawl around, the larger ones representing states with the government at the head and the people at the tail; they vaguely perceive each other as they approach, often changing direction in response to primitive instincts and urges, to sophisticated patterns and policies, and to deliberate appraisals of purposes and powers,"[30] but frankly my mind boggles at the prospect.

Fearing the Scylla of reductionism and Charybdis of eclecticism, most international relations specialists have shown greater timorousness than Morgenthau or Wright, and have plied safer, more restricted waters. In the process, substantial sophistication has been achieved by dissecting and analyzing major features (such as nationalism) characteristic of the modern nation-state system, or of more nearly universal applicability (the balance of power and the occurrence of war).

The plethora of approaches is symptomatic of a science that is still developing. The merits of viewing international relations as a field, plan, equilibrium, organization, or community have been discussed at length.[31] Attention has been given to the alternative consequences of adopting the perspectives of individual actors or that of the international system.[32] In short, Western international relations theorists, in their impatience for answers, have not always agreed on the questions, with the result, as Stanley Hoffmann has remarked, that "theories of international relations are like planes flying at different altitudes and in different directions," with little link-

[30] Wright, *Study of International Relations* (New York: Appleton-Century-Crofts, 1955), p. 546.

[31] For a survey see *ibid.*, pp. 481ff.

[32] J. David Singer, "The Level-of-Analysis in International Relations," *World Politics*, Vol. XIV, No. 1 (October 1961), pp. 77-92; and "International Conflict: Three Levels of Analysis," *ibid.*, Vol. XII, No. 3 (April 1960), pp. 453-61.

age between the soaring "speculative works" and the more "earthbound" empirical studies.[33]

What is perhaps the most promising device for linking general and partial theories—the comparison of international systems—also seemed suitable as an organizational construct for analyzing international relations perspectives. Indeed, a framework whose central focus is "diplomatic constellations, or historical situations," which attempts "to identify the main variables of each such system and discover the dynamics of change from one system to another,"[34] has particular relevance for the study of *Soviet* perspectives. Those professing to be Marxist-Leninists have traditionally assumed that each historical period has its own laws of development. The primary concern has always been with the main content of the current historical period. As a result, more was to be gained by detailing the generalizations Soviet observers deem applicable to international relations in the post-World War II period—or a

[33] "International Relations: The Long Road to Theory," *World Politics*, Vol. xi, No. 3 (April 1959), p. 348.

[34] Hoffmann, ed., *Contemporary Theory*, p. 174. Efforts to supply such a linkage have included Morton Kaplan's attempt in his *System and Process in International Politics* (New York: John Wiley & Sons, 1957) to construct a typology of real and hypothetical international systems; Richard Walker's dissertation, *The State System of Ancient China* (Hamden, Conn.: The Shoestring Press, 1953); Adda B. Bozeman's *Politics and Culture in International History* (Princeton, N.J.: Princeton University Press, 1960); two stimulating essays by George Modelski, "Agraria and Industria: Two Models of the International System," *World Politics*, Vol. xiv, No. 1 (October 1961), pp. 118-43, and *The Communist International System* (Center of International Studies, Woodrow Wilson School of Public and International Affairs, Research Monograph No. 9, Princeton: Princeton University Press, 1960); and Joel Larus, ed., *Comparative World Politics: Readings in Western and Pre-Modern Non-Western International Relations* (Belmont, Calif.: Wadsworth Publishing Co., Inc., 1964).

part thereof—than by a search for trans-systemic and trans-temporal hypotheses. The former strategy made it possible to ascertain the extent to which a preoccupation with qualitative change, with phasing and periodization,[35] remained a central feature of Soviet thought. Moreover, such a decision had the merit that it insulated the study from the charge of "bourgeois objectivism" to which an attempt to elucidate Soviet thinking about international relations "generally" might be subject.

Within a systemic framework it is possible—drawing on the proposals for structuring the study of international relations advanced by American specialists in recent years[36]—to pose a series of questions, a paradigm, to serve as the basis for portraying the international relations perspectives of any individual or group, in this instance, those of Soviet commentators.

These questions relate to (a) the structure of a given international system, (b) the behavior of the participant actors, and (c) the processes that influence the rate and direction of change over time in the system. With respect to Soviet perspectives on the structure of the international system, the study attempts to obtain answers to the following questions: In the

[35] On periodization in Russian historiography, generally, consult Konstantin F. Shteppa, *Russian Historians and the Soviet State* (New Brunswick, N.J.: Rutgers University Press, 1962) and Leo Yaresh, "The Problems of Periodization," in Cyril E. Black, ed., *Rewriting Russian History* (New York: Praeger, 1956).

Readers desirous of evidence of Soviet preoccupation with periodization should follow the debate on periodization of Soviet foreign policy that took place largely in the pages of *International Affairs* and which culminated ultimately in the publication of M. E. Airapetian and G. A. Deborin's *Etapy vneshnei politiki SSSR* [The Stages of USSR Foreign Policy] (Moscow: Sotsekizdat, 1961). For a Western analysis see Shulman, *Stalin's Foreign Policy Reappraised*, pp. 255-57.

[36] I have drawn freely and most heavily from the series of questions posed by Hoffmann, ed., *Contemporary Theory*, pp. 179-84.

Soviet view, what polities are conceived to be the major international actors? what is the "shape" of the power "pyramid" envisaged in a given international system?[37] how many "essential" actors[38] are seen to participate in the system? what is the perceived power disparity (and how is it measured) between the essential actors thought to be? what, in the Soviet perspective, is the "relationship of major tension,"[39] the main contradiction? how pervasive, in the Soviet view, are its reverberations throughout the system?

The section on the behavior of the units focuses primarily on the changing Soviet appraisal of the state, the United States, whose behavior most influences the Soviet calculus concerning the transformation of the international system. The questions to be asked there pertain primarily to motives and, to a lesser extent, capabilities. Are American decision-makers motivated by goals of self-extension, self-preservation, or self-abnegation?[40] If the United States' motives are thought to be extensional, are they seen as involving a desire to put an "essential" actor, especially the Soviet Union, out of business? What impact, if any, does the American domestic socio-political order have on foreign policy behavior? Is goal-con-

[37] Cf. A.F.K. Organski, *World Politics* (New York: Knopf, 1958), passim, especially pp. 326-33. Organski, however, postulates an invariably shaped pyramid.

[38] Kaplan, *System and Process*, p. 22, suggests this term as a substitute for Great Power.

[39] Wolfers, "The Pole of Power and the Pole of Indifference," *World Politics*, Vol. IV, No. 1 (October 1951), pp. 39-63, reproduced in Wolfer's *Discord and Collaboration* (Baltimore, Md.: The Johns Hopkins Press, 1962), pp. 81-102, especially p. 101. The "main contradiction" in Soviet Marxist-Leninist writings serves fundamentally the same purpose. I waive for the moment the question of whether there must be *a* main contradiction; see below, pp. 161-62.

[40] Wolfers, *Discord and Collaboration*, pp. 91-100.

sensus within the elite of the United States assumed, or would alteration in leadership, in the Soviet perspective, alter the goals pursued? How, in Soviet perspective, do capabilities influence American motives? What environmental features do Soviet commentators assume will provide constraints on and opportunities for optimizing capabilities? What are the areas of policy choice open to American decision-makers, in the Soviet view, and to what extent can policy choice affect capabilities?

These two sets of questions, one from an essentially static macro-perspective, the other from an essentially static micro-framework, make up the necessary backdrop for analyzing the Soviet appraisal of processes and patterns common to most international systems as they are manifested in international relations of the post-World War II period. Undoubtedly the most important single pattern is the occurrence of violence. Why, in Soviet thinking, do wars occur? What kinds of violence do Soviet observers foresee as most likely to occur in the international system? How, from the Soviet vantage point, can the resort to violence be minimized? Some sort of a balance-of-power process appears to characterize almost all international systems; in what fashion and to what extent, in the Soviet view, is it a feature of the system under scrutiny? What do Soviet commentators conceive to be the integrative and disintegrative patterns in the present international system? From these processes comes the main impetus to the tendency of systems toward stability or away therefrom; in the Soviet estimation, what is the rate and direction of change in the international system? What characteristics of previous systems do Soviet commentators maintain can be eliminated from consideration as possibilities for, the present system or its successors?

The final issue of these considerations is that (following the discussion in Chapter 2 of the emergence of international relations as a discipline in the Soviet Union) in the theoretical chapters which begin with Chapter 3, attention has been devoted primarily to the Soviet perception of the structural elements of the contemporary international system. Chapter 3 identifies the actors in the international arena and seeks to trace changes in the Soviet perception of these actors. Chapter 4 is given over to a consideration of the changing Soviet thinking about the hierarchical pattern of the present international order. Chapter 5 analyzes the distribution of power, in the Soviet view, between the two world powers and systems. American foreign policy behavior, however, is the focus of Chapter 6, while process is the theme of Chapter 7. Against a backdrop of Western writings on the balance of power as system and policy, an effort is made to depict the evolution in Soviet thinking about two tasks which in the atomic era have proved to be inextricably interrelated and contradictory; survival—with its corollary of international system maintenance, and revolution—which necessitates system transcendence. Finally, Chapter 8, the conclusion, assesses the implications of the evidence mustered in Chapters 2 through 7 for the explanation and prediction of Soviet foreign policy.

Chapter Two: The Emergence of International Relations as a Discipline

THE phenomenal postwar proliferation of books, journals, courses, and research institutes devoted to international relations in the United States prompted Alfred Grosser in 1956 to wonder whether the study of international relations was an American specialty.[1] Had he been writing in 1956 about the other superpower, the Soviet Union, he might well have observed that the conspicuous avoidance of the study of international relations was one of the characteristic features of academic inquiry in that country.

During the intervening years, one of the major dimensions of the changed Soviet appraisal of international relations consisted in the greatly enhanced interest in the study of international relations by specialists in the institutes of the Academy of Sciences. For them, international relations has become a legitimate area of inquiry. In the Soviet Union the study of international relations has come to be viewed as a relatively autonomous discipline. There emerged, during the years of Khrushchev's tenure in power, moreover, a new, younger generation of social scientists interested in questions pertaining to international relations, who showed a striking propensity, by previous Soviet standards for methodological and conceptual innovation. These dramatic trends in the study of international relations are traced and analyzed in this chapter.

[1] Grosser, "L'étude des relations internationales, spécialité américaine?" pp. 634-51. Since the publication of Professor Grosser's article, the spate of scholarship has continued unabated and, if anything, has quickened. For a more recent discussion see William T. R. Fox and Annette Baker Fox, "The Teaching of International Relations in the United States," pp. 339-59.

CHAPTER TWO

To the Twentieth Congress

It is not precise to say that prior to 1956 there was no international relations literature in the Soviet Union. In the broadest sense, there was. After all, there were the pronouncements of that "coryphaeus" of human wisdom, Joseph V. Stalin, who in his uniquely didactic style had struggled with several major questions of contemporary international politics—war and peace,[2] bipolarity, patterns of cohesion and disintegration among states. In the postwar period Stalin's most relevant contribution was *Economic Problems of Socialism in the U.S.S.R.*,[3] written in 1952 just prior to his death, in which he took issue with some (unidentified) comrades who argued that the Leninist theory of the inevitability of wars had become obsolete.

Moreover, while Stalin lived, there were a few studies written by diplomatic historians and international lawyers which had at least a tangential bearing on international relations. Even in the days when the strictures of *partiinost'* were most manifest, publications of diplomatic historians like Eugene Tarle and of international lawyers like Eugene Korovin and Feodor Kozhevnikov occasionally warranted examination.

In the years between Stalin's death in 1953 and the Twentieth C.P.S.U. Congress in 1956, military and strategic thought, pallid as it was by Western standards, stood out against a background of other Soviet disciplines that might conceivably contribute insights into the international political

[2] Frederic S. Burin, "The Communist Doctrine of the Inevitability of War," *American Political Science Review*, Vol. LVII, No. 2 (June 1963), pp. 334-55, examines Stalin's views on the causes of war.

[3] For a provocative interpretation of *Economic Problems of Socialism* see Robert C. Tucker, *The Soviet Political Mind* (New York: Praeger, 1963), pp. 20-34.

process. The perceived need to rethink the nature of war in light of the development of atomic weapons gave impetus to a recrudescence in military thought. It was, in fact, largely in military matters—but more in strictly military matters than in those dealing with international relations—that the consequences of the cult of the personality were aired prior to the Twentieth Congress.

Only in one other area of inquiry, what in Soviet parlance is called Eastern studies (which in the 1950s embraced Asia, Africa, and Latin America), were there minimal signs of vigor before the Twentieth C.P.S.U. Congress.[4]

There were no contributions from the two disciplines, political science and sociology, which in the West have been most concerned with international relations. There were, strictly speaking, no political scientists or sociologists (of course, international economists existed as a group, but they had generally been in bad graces since the Varga controversy in 1947). The study of politics in the Soviet Union,[5] unlike

[4] In 1962 I. I. Potekhin, until his recent death an influential Soviet Africanist, argued that Africa should not be subsumed under the rubric "the East" now that colonialism was virtually at an end. "Africa is Africa," he observed tautologically; "it is not a continuation of imperialist Europe and it is not the East." A distinct anti-Chinese thrust may be discerned here: was Potekhin intimating that neither the "East wind" (China) nor the "West wind" would prevail in Africa? ("Narody Azii i Afrika—brat'ia" [The Peoples of Asia and Africa—Brothers], *Aziia i Afrika segodnia* [Asia and Africa Today], No. 3 (March 1962), p. 4.) Potekhin made no mention of Latin America. See Walter Z. Laqueur and George Lichtheim, *The Soviet Cultural Scene: 1956-1957* (New York: Atlantic Books Ltd., 1958), pp. 237-55.

[5] For two Western estimates of political science in the Soviet Union (unfortunately already dated), see Gordon Skilling, "In Search of Political Science in the U.S.S.R.," *The Canadian Journal of Economics and Political Science*, Vol. xxix, No. 4 (November 1963), pp. 519-29 and Bohdan R. Bociurkiw, "The Post-Stalin 'Thaw' and Soviet Po-

that in the United States, had not extricated itself from legal studies,[6] a subordination which for other European countries, as W. A. Robson has pointed out, has resulted "invariably . . . in a narrow, inadequate and distorted conception of the subject."[7]

As for sociology, its status in the Soviet Union was nil. "There is no Soviet counterpart of Western sociology," Leopold Labedz could write in 1956. Despite the fact that in all Western accounts Marx is regarded as one of modern sociology's founders, the word "sociology" was always modified by the pejorative "bourgeois" in Soviet commentary. Academically its subject matter was largely subsumed under philosophy. There were no sociology departments nor institutes of sociology. (Moscow State University had a Chair of Sociology until 1924.) Practically, the purview of sociology was coopted by

---

litical Science," *The Canadian Journal of Economics and Political Science*, Vol. xxx, No. 1 (February 1964), pp. 22-48.

[6] A modest, symbolic step toward Western notions of political science may have been taken in 1960 when the Institute of Law became the Institute of State and Law. See "O reorganizatsii Instituta Prava v Institute Gosudarstva i Prava" [Concerning the Reorganization of the Institute of Law into the Institute of State and Law], *Vestnik*, No. 8 (August 1960), p. 116.

In 1963 Leonid Il'ichev told a session of the Presidium of the Academy of Sciences that "the question of studying specific spheres of politics deserves . . . attention": ". . . class relations at home and abroad, bourgeois parties, the communist and workers' movement, the democratic movement, public opinion, propaganda, the state (*not on the plane of constitutional and administrative norms, as it is studied by legal science, but on the plane of its real activities* [*zhivoi deatel'nosti*]) and, last, international relations." "Metodologicheskie problemy estestvoznaniia i obshchestvennykh nauk" [Methodological Problems of the Natural and Social Sciences], *Vestnik*, No. 11 (November 1963), p. 43, italics added.

[7] Robson, *The University Teaching of Social Sciences: Political Science* (London: UNESCO, 1954), p. 16.

the Academy of Social Sciences attached to the Central Committee of the C.P.S.U.[8]

The situation in international relations scholarship per se was especially inadequate. One gains an impression of almost total quiescence from the speeches made at the Twentieth Party Congress. An examination of statements made by participants in the round of *kritika i samokritika* (critique and self-critique)[9] which appeared on the pages of *International Affairs* (in 1956 the only Soviet journal dealing specifically with international relations) in the aftermath of the Twentieth Party Congress, produces the same effect.

The minimal research being conducted was oriented primarily to the past. Scholars apparently retreated to the pre-Soviet period, an area in which their work was less likely to attract undue attention from the Party. To many, obscurantism must have seemed the better part of wisdom. Suggestive of the research preoccupations of Soviet scholarship were several of the titles of proposed topics, which according to S.

[8] Labedz's article, on which the above draws heavily, is reproduced in Laqueur and Lichtheim, *The Soviet Cultural Scene*, pp. 185-201, at p. 185. See also George Fischer, *Science and Politics: The New Sociology in the Soviet Union* (Ithaca, N.Y.: Center for International Studies, Cornell University Press, 1964).

[9] See especially E. Korovin et al., "A Letter to the Editors," *International Affairs*, No. 12 (December 1956), p. 98; I. Ivashin, "Comments on 'A Letter to the Editors,'" *International Affairs*, No. 1 (January 1957), p. 164; "Review of Letters," *International Affairs*, No. 1 (January 1957), pp. 160-61; and I. Galkin, "The Duty of Soviet Scholars," *International Affairs*, No. 2 (February 1956), p. 133.

For Western commentary see Vernon V. Aspaturian, "Diplomacy in the Mirror of Soviet Scholarship," in *Contemporary History in the Soviet Mirror*, ed. John Keep and Liliana Brisby (New York: Praeger, 1964), pp. 243-85 and Alvin Z. Rubinstein, *The Soviets in International Organizations: Changing Policy toward Developing Countries, 1953-1963* (Princeton, N.J.: Princeton University Press, 1964), pp. 289-317, especially 298ff.

Maiorov[10] (a Gospolitizdat official responsible for international affairs literature), were submitted at this juncture to Gospolitizdat: "Essays on the History of International Relations in the Years 1763-1870" and "The Foreign Policy of the Jacobin Republic of 1793-1794" (from the Department of Contemporary History at the Moscow Potemkin Pedagogical Institute); "International Relations in the 1870's" and "Russian Foreign Policy During the Unification of Germany (1866-1870)" (from the Byelorussian Lenin State University); "The Polish Question and the Diplomatic Struggle in Europe at the End of the 1850's and the Beginning of the 1860's" and "The Role of Austro-Hungary in Unleashing the First World War" (from the Modern History Department of Leningrad University).

Recruitment of new cadres in the social sciences generally —and specifically in areas dealing with international relations—had dwindled to nearly nothing. At the Twentieth Party Congress Anastas Mikoyan asked, "Who[m] do we have, after all, to engage in a serious study of [capitalism's contemporary state]?"[11] The answer was as obvious as the question was rhetorical: virtually no one. According to Maiorov, "not a single post-graduate submitted or even prepared a thesis in Soviet foreign policy" in 1956 for the Institute of History of the Academy of Sciences.[12] "Training of post-graduates in the field of international relations has stopped . . ." asserted I. Galkin, dean of Moscow State University, "at a time when we are in dire need of research workers in the historiography of modern history, international relations, prob-

[10] "Review of Letters," p. 160.

[11] Leo Gruliow, ed., *Current Soviet Policies II: The Documentary Record of the 20th Communist Party Congress and its Aftermath* (New York: Praeger, 1957), p. 87.

[12] "Review of Letters," p. 161.

lems of scientific socialism, and other vital branches of history."[13] "There are almost no educational establishments to train qualified propagandists in the field of international affairs,"[14] declared I. Ivashin of the C.P.S.U. Central Committee's Higher Party School.

The one journal dealing with international relations (*International Affairs*)[15] was an organ of the "popular All-Union Society for the Dissemination of Political and Scientific Knowledge, and not of the Academy of Sciences. What materials *were* being published on international questions in the Soviet press amounted to "dull and stereotyped" "popular booklets" or articles which were (as one participant in the pattern of *kritika i samokritika* said of an article written by Eugene Korovin,) "evidentally composed in a hurry," and which were "nothing but a compilation of sentences and facts over a period of 40 years."[16] Four of the leading specialists in the study of international relations—including Korovin—were not exaggerating when they wrote, ". . . new and original scholarly works of research are not being published. . . . Actually no monographs on the basic problems of world affairs are available."[17]

And small wonder. Aside from any consideration of qualitative standards, there were not even the most rudimentary boundary markers indicating the existence of a legitimate area of inquiry. There were no required courses in interna-

[13] Galkin, "The Duty of Soviet Scholars," p. 133.

[14] Ivashin, "Comments," p. 164.

[15] Even *International Affairs* had only been published since 1954, although as Aspaturian (in Keep and Brisby, *Contemporary History*, p. 244) points out, a journal of the same title was published in the 1920s by the People's Commissariat for Foreign Affairs.

[16] Ivashin, "Comments," p. 164.

[17] Korovin, "Letter to the Editors," p. 98.

tional relations,[18] no textbooks, "no reference books dealing with political parties, and government bodies,"[19] "no yearbooks of world events,"[20] no institutes concerned specifically with the study of international relations.[21]

The Twentieth Congress

Thus international relations studies were essentially starting from scratch in 1956. The major impetus to the legitimation of international relations as an area of inquiry came at the Twentieth Party Congress. Part of this impetus was indirect, in that the Twentieth Congress provided an atmosphere in the Soviet Union more conducive to intellectual honesty, although, it should be noted, international relations, unlike history, played no part in the post-Congress thaw. More directly, the impetus was supplied by the critique of Soviet social sciences, including international relations, undertaken by

[18] Ivashin, "Comments," p. 164.

[19] Korovin, "Letter to the Editors," p. 98.

[20] *Ibid.*

[21] The Institute of World Economy and World Politics was disbanded after World War II as one of the results of the famous Varga controversy. N. A. Voznesensky had sharply criticized the institute's leading light, Eugene Varga, for the views he expressed in *Changes in the Economy of Capitalism as a Result of the Second World War.* (Varga's "rightist" error was that he had foreseen the possibility of a postwar capitalist recovery.) Varga's disgrace resulted in the absorption of the Institute into the Institute of Economics, then headed by Voznesensky, and the termination of the Institute's journal, *Mirovoe khoziaistvo i mirovaia politika.* (A survey of these events may be found in Robert Conquest, *Power and Policy in the U.S.S.R.*, pp. 80-89.) Voznesensky was subsequently purged by Stalin. Ironically Varga survived and lived until 1964, when as an octogenarian he died of natural causes.

There did exist, however, the Moscow State Institute of International Relations (closely associated with the Soviet Foreign Ministry), which served as a center for training foreign service cadres.

members of the dominant Khrushchevian faction of the Presidium, who encouraged, and stressed the need for, greater work by specialists in areas related to international relations.

An especially prominent role in this was played by Anastas Mikoyan.[22] He had harsh words for the Soviet "study of capitalism's contemporary state"—the quality of which, he observed, was "sadly lacking." In particular, he expressed regret that "the Institute of World Economy and World Politics . . . [had been] done away with"—an observation which, in effect, rehabilitated the Institute and conveyed the implication that it or something like it should be created. On Soviet "Eastern Studies," his remarks were equally pointed. He ridiculed the work being done in the Academy of Sciences by noting that, whereas "the whole East has awakened," the Institute of Eastern Studies of the Academy of Sciences "was still dozing," and questioned the appropriateness of having undertaken "the liquidation of the 130-year-old Moscow Institute of Eastern Studies, particularly . . . at a time when our ties with the East were increasing and strengthening, a time when the expansion of our economic, political, and cultural ties with the countries of the East had brought about a tremendous rise in the Soviet people's interest in that area, and in the need for people who know the Eastern countries' languages, econnomics, and culture." Mikhail Suslov similarly urged specialists to "consider the supreme criterion of their work to be life, [not] statements by authority,"[23] and Dmitry Shepilov charged them—along with "literary artists, [and] all our workers in the sphere of socialist ideology"—to make it their "task . . . to imbue our people with proletarian internationalism, with friendship of peoples and intolerance of all forms

[22] Gruliow, *Current Soviet Policies II*, p. 87.
[23] *Ibid*, p. 79.

of slavery, oppression, colonialism, national and racial discrimination."[24]

Several concerns seem to have animated the dominant Presidium faction to encourage at this particular time an increased scholarly interest in international relations. The key members of the Soviet ruling group may have felt a need to legitimate the general rightward turn in Soviet foreign policy, which found its expression in both the intensification of Soviet foreign policy activities on several diplomatic fronts (the "spirit of Geneva," the Bulganin-Khrushchev jaunt through Asia) and in doctrinal innovation, for example, the reconsideration of the inevitability-of-war doctrine. As a result, from the regime's vantage point, it was no longer tolerable to omit from the research plans of institutes and universities such topics as

> relations among Socialist countries, the present-day relations among capitalist states, the role and importance in international relations of countries that have overthrown the colonialist yoke and taken the road of independent development . . . the role of international organizations (UNO, democratic organizations of women, youth, or peace supporters), . . . the development of international communist and labour movements, the problems of proletarian internationalism. . . .[25]

Moreover, the ruling faction in the Presidium seems to have concluded that the credibility of the new policies could not be enhanced merely by requiring the ideologues to engage in the traditional Soviet practice of substituting new facts for old ones; rather, even for the narrow purposes of internal propaganda, a broader factual presentation was required.

In addition, Mikoyan emphasized the contribution of re-

[24] *Ibid*, p. 72.

[25] Statement by S. Maiorov, "Review of Letters," p. 160.

search to policy-making. It was "not enough" in his view for the specialists merely to affirm that "the course of history indicates that in the present stage of imperialism . . . all Marxism-Leninism's basic tenets are invariably confirmed." Instead, they should concern themselves with "when, where, to what degree, and how this takes place."[26]

The members of the dominant faction may also have been motivated by a concern for high political stakes, particularly in the case of Asian studies. Throughout 1955 and into 1956 there was, in the words of Laqueur and Lichtheim, "a distinct hiatus between the Soviet Government's efforts to improve relations with Asian and African political leaders, and the tone of writing favoured by the more or less scholarly [Soviet] journals" which "continued to subject the Soviet Government's Asian and African interlocutors to criticism and abuse in the approved orthodox manner."[27] Many Orientalists, it would seem, were not favorably disposed to the direction being taken in Soviet foreign policy and, perhaps, may have been linked to Molotov or at least sympathetic ideologically with his views. (Others may simply have assumed that the foreign policy initiatives were strictly tactical and short-run, and wished not to be found in an awkward position when the "progressiveness" of the national bourgeoisie would once again be downgraded.) The most persuasive evidence that high politics was involved was provided by the January 1956 issue of *Sovetskoe vostokovedenie* [Soviet Eastern Studies], publication of which was delayed four months (sent to press on April 2, 1956). When it finally appeared, the old editorial board had been replaced and the lead editorial contained a strong hint that persons in Eastern Studies had been

[26] Gruliow, *Current Soviet Policies II*, p. 72.

[27] Laqueur and Lichtheim, *The Soviet Cultural Scene*, p. 238.

sympathetic to Molotov's views. Thus "sectarian mistakes" and "dogmatism" were discerned, and the editorial criticized the prevalent "misunderstanding of the character and depth of the contradiction between the forces of imperialism and domestic reactionaries and the forces of national progress in the non-socialist countries of the East."[28]

At the same time, other dominant themes of the Twentieth Congress—specifically (a) the stress on the need to reinvigorate the ideology as an instrumentality for mass mobilization by overcoming the ideology's "considerable detachment from life"[29] and (b) the concern evidenced about the general misallocation of resources through "the absence of coordination,"[30] "harmful parallelism,"[31] and the misdirection of research "to the past, into history, at the expense of present-day problems"[32] —suggest that the inclination to change was related to several traditional Soviet concerns. In particular, the impulse to increase the "coordination" of research and the desire to enhance the regime's ability to use ideology as an instrument of mass manipulation, undoubtedly played a major role in the initial encouragement of interest in 1956 in international relations-related matters.

Thus for some, the chief complaint about works dealing with international relations was that the "themes of monographs [were] not, as a rule, related and . . . not based on a uni-

[28] "XX s"ezd kommunisticheskoi partii Sovetskogo Soiuza i zadachi izucheniia sovremennogo Vostoka" [The Twentieth Congress of the Communist Party of the Soviet Union and the Tasks of Studying the Modern East], *Sovetskoe vostokovedenie*, No. 1 (January 1956), pp. 3-12, especially 7.

[29] "Party propaganda," Suslov declared, "has . . . begun to lose its militant Bolshevik spirit." Gruliow, *Current Soviet Policies II*, p. 79.

[30] *Ibid.*, p. 52.

[31] *Ibid.*

[32] *Ibid.*, p. 79.

fied plan of research";[33] that "the research [was] not directed and coordinated";[34] that the Ministry of Higher Education was not planning and directing "departmental research" but merely limiting "itself to the collection of annual plans drawn [up] by universities" which the Ministry "files . . . away."[35] Similarly, for old ideological *apparatchiki* like Ivashin it was cause for concern that *International Affairs* did not have a section "in aid of the lecturer and propagandist"[36] and that the journal "fairly frequently" published articles "without regard for whom they are written."[37]

Laying the Foundations: 1956-1962

The first big step taken after the Twentieth Congress that encouraged the study of international relations for those below the apex of the Party and the government apparatus was the announced reconstitution in April 1956 of the Institute of World Economy and International Relations of the U.S.S.R. Academy of Sciences. A brief statement in *Pravda* noted that the Presidium of the Academy of Sciences had approved "the structure of the new institute"; declared that the Institute "will publish a monthly magazine entitled, *World Economy and International Relations*"; and summarized the Institute's assigned area of purview; to wit, "the study of the laws of

[33] "Review of Letters," p. 161.

[34] Galkin, "The Duty," p. 133.

[35] *Ibid.*

[36] Evidently the specialists were initially able to withstand the pressure to harness *International Affairs* so directly to the propaganda purposes of the regime, for in March 1958 it was possible for the editors to assert that "some readers do not clearly understand the journal's purpose. They suggest a satirical section, *a section for lecturers*, etc." "Readers Discuss Our Journal," *International Affairs*, No. 3 (March 1958), p. 124, italics added.

[37] Ivashin, "Comments," p. 164.

development of present-day capitalism, of the economies and policies of individual countries, of mutual relations between the two world . . . systems—capitalist and socialist—of questions relating to the new role of Asian countries in world economy and policy, etc."[38]

Apparently the activities of the Institute of World Economy and International Relations remained rather inconspicuous for more than a year. Not until July 1957 did it become a matter of public record that the institute had initiated operations in August 1956, and that in September 1956 Varga had presented a paper on the Suez situation.[39] Similarly, it was not until the publication of the March 1957 issue of *International Affairs* that mention was made of a series of meetings held in the fall and early winter of 1956, at which foreign lecturers were heard. Also, for some reason, the Institute did not begin publication of its monthly journal, *Mirovaia ekonomika i mezhdunarodnye otnosheniia*, until July 1957.

Evidence of immediate responses in 1956 to the decisions of the Twentieth Congress was decidedly meager in areas touching on international affairs. In the December 1956 issue of *International Affairs* the letter (to which reference has already been made) signed by four leading figures in Soviet social science—Korovin, A. Guber, N. Liubimov, and A. Manfred—appeared, which initiated the public airing of the situation in international relations. In that letter the four specialists drew attention to the fact that those concerned with inter-

[38] *Pravda*, April 24, 1956, translated in *Current Digest of the Soviet Press* (hereafter *Current Digest*), Vol. VIII, No. 17 (June 6, 1956), p. 21.

[39] I. Glagolev, "Nauchnaia zhizn'" [Scholarly Life], *Mirovaia ekonomika*, No. 1 (July 1957), p. 156. Mention was made of the Institute in *Vestnik* in November 1956. See "O zadachakh i strukture Instituta Vostokovedeniia" [Concerning the Tasks and Structure of the Institute of Eastern Studies], *Vestnik*, No. 11 (November 1956), pp. 104-105.

national relations were not among the "Soviet scholars . . . successfully overcoming the negative consequences of the personality cult"; "The social sciences dealing with world affairs appear to be reacting very slowly to the lead given by the Twentieth Congress. We are of the opinion that the necessary stimulation of research work on the study of current world affairs is proceeding too slowly."[40]

The torpor was not surprising. Whereas the historians, who had a journal and were already acknowledged as constituting a separate specialty, quickly responded to the more tolerant post-Congress atmosphere, obviously a certain lead time was involved in stimulating study in an area virtually lacking in cadres, lacking an academic journal, and not yet really recognized as a separate discipline. Moreover, there was some evidence that the proposal to create an Institute of World Economy and International Relations was not greeted with unmitigated enthusiasm by representatives of all "social sciences dealing with world affairs." Specifically, the remarks of V. Shurshalov and G. Zhukov, "members of the staff of the International Law Department of the Institute of Law," suggested a certain uneasiness on the part of some international lawyers about the role of the new Institute: "The establishment of the Institute of World Economics and International Relations," Shurshalov and Zhukov cautioned, "does not remove the necessity for an independent research centre to study the problems of international relations."[41]

Thus the length of time between the Twentieth Party Congress, at which Mikoyan had regretted that the old Institute of World Economy and World Politics had been "done away

[40] Korovin, "Letter to the Editors," p. 98.

[41] "Summary and Discussion," *International Affairs*, No. 5 (May 1957), p. 136.

with," the announcement in April 1956 of the establishment of the Institute of World Economy and International Relations, and the appearance of the institute's journal in July 1957 can be explained without reference to that power struggle being waged within the highest echelons of the Communist Party, which culminated in the rout of the anti-Party group (a "minority" of seven) by the "majority" of four, at the June 22-29, 1957 Plenum of the Central Committee. One assumes, however, that the precise timing of the appearance of the institute's journal was related to these high-level events, since the first number of *Mirovaia ekonomika i mezhdunarodnye otnosheniia* went to press on July 5, that is, less than a week after the June Plenum.

In 1956 Mikoyan and other partisans of the Khrushchev faction in the Presidium apparently conceived the international relations dimension of the Institute of World Economy and International Relations' research to be within the context of "the study of capitalism's present state," about which Soviet scholars were "seriously lagging"; they expected that the institute would be primarily a research center for economists. The editorial charge in 1957 to the members of the Institute of World Economy and International Relations similarly called on *economists* to fulfill the tasks the Twentieth Party Congress had set for them by studying the capitalist economy.[42]

In view of the Marxist-Leninist commitment to the interrelation of economic and political factors, there was nothing exceptional in presuming international relations expertise of economists; accordingly, at the outset, economists appear to have predominated overwhelmingly in the cadres recruited

[42] "Nashi zadachi" [Our Tasks], *Mirovaia ekonomika*, No. 1 (July 1957), pp. 3-6.

to staff the institute. However, the topic matter handled in the ensuing years was more indicative of a "scientific center bringing together specialists in world affairs in our country," the creation of which Korovin and others had declared a question "worthwhile discussing."[43] From the very first issues of the institute's journal the institute was as preoccupied with international relations as with economics—of individual countries or of the world economy generally.

The attitude was similarly, if contradictorily, prevalent that international relations was largely the domain of the historian.[44] The course offered in international relations at the major universities was taught in the history department. International relations, in the sense in which the historians were using it, meant *diplomatic history* and was basically synonymous with direct interstate relations, an attitude more appropriate to a nonrevolutionary period when "international politics was 'made' in [the foreign offices of] London, Paris, Washington, Berlin,"[45] or to the period of socialism in one country.

It was also much more appropriate to the period prior to the Twentieth Congress, when "topicality" [*aktual'nost'*] was

[43] Korovin, "Letter to the Editors," p. 98. See also the summary and discussion in No. 5 (May 1957), *International Affairs*, pp. 135-37, in which a number of participants in the round of self-debasement and mutual recrimination specifically related the Korovin proposal to the institute. The general tenor of the remarks was that the establishment of the institute was only a "*first . . . step*," italics in original.

[44] For example, the specific remark to that effect, written in 1962 in AN IMEMO, *Mezhdunarodnye otnosheniia . . .* , Vol. 1, p. xxvi: "Formerly, international relations was studied mainly by historians . . . ." See, too, Il'ichev's complaint in 1963, directed against the approach of "our historians" to the study of international relations. Il'ichev, "Metodologicheskie problemy . . . ," p. 43.

[45] AN IMEMO, *Mezhdunarodnye otnosheniia . . .* , Vol. 1, p. viii.

avoided, than to the period after 1956 when topicality[46] became the order (literally) of the day.

Under these circumstances, it was natural that international relations should increasingly have come to be regarded as a distinct field of inquiry. The mere reestablishment of the Institute of World Economy and International Relations placed it in 1957-58 further along the gradations of official sanction than two other "new" social sciences, to which only in the last years of the Khrushchev regime was belated atten-

[46] See the blunt remarks of Boris N. Ponomarev (a Party Secretary largely concerned with international communist affairs):

"Comrades! The great variety of tasks standing before Soviet scholars . . . makes it imperative to raise the questions of the *topicality* of the subjects of historical research.

"The complete groundlessness of the concepts—still not completely eliminated—that for the study of modern history there are supposedly not sufficient quantity of sources accumulated in the archives, is apparent. Such assertions do not, will not, withstand criticism. . . . . The problem of topicality . . . is determined first of all by those tasks which stand before our Party and the world revolutionary movement."

"Zadachi istoricheskoi nauki i podgotovka nauchno-pedagogicheskikh kadrov v oblasti istorii" [The Tasks of Historical Science and the Preparation of Scientific-pedagogical Cadres in History], *Voprosy istorii*, No. 1 (January 1963) pp. 3-35, at pp. 21-22, italics added.

See also, *Vsesoiuznoe soveshchanie o merakh uluchsheniia podgotovki nauchno-pedagogicheskikh kadrov po istoricheskim naukam* [All-Union Conference on Measures of Improving the Preparation of Scientific-pedagogical Cadres in the Historical Sciences] (Moscow: Izdatel'stvo "Nauka," 1964), pp. 11-54, and the discussion which follows, passim; and the remarks by Maiorov, a Gospolitizdat official ("Review of Letters," p. 160), who strongly suggested a link between possible publication and "topicality."

At the same time, it should be stressed that while the regime strongly encouraged "topicality," genuine diplomatic history also became more possible, since greater access was granted to archival materials, etc., and the regime seemed less intent on imposing politics on the past in all spheres.

tion devoted in the Soviet Union—sociology and social psychology.[47]

One indication of this emergence of international relations from a peripheral matter for economists or historians to a separate field was the upgrading accorded to the term *mezhdunarodnik* (literally, if awkwardly, *internationalist*) in the last years of the Khrushchev era. (The term actually is an old one which, often preceded by *iurist* [jurist], initially denoted international lawyers.) In the first few years after the Twentieth Party Congress, the appropriate scholars in the Academy of Sciences were referred to as economists or historians. *Mezhdunarodnik*, at this time, referred to activists as disseminators of the Party line on international matters to the masses in the Kolkhozes, etc. Thus, in a discussion of the contributions being made by *Mirovaia ekonomika*, I. M. Liadov, a lecturer of the Moscow Party *oblast'* committee, observed that the journal "had fully justified itself." It was, he said, "an academic publication . . . , but nevertheless found its readers not only among scientific workers but also among propagandists, speaker-*mezhdunarodnikov*, lecturers." Similarly A. A. Mishin of Moscow State University declared at the same meeting: "We use this journal not only as lecturer-*mezhdunarodniki* but as people engaged in scholarly work. The journal is valuable not only for economists but for representatives of the juridical and other social sciences as well."[48]

[47] For Western comments on recent developments in Soviet sociology, see George Fischer, *Science and Politics: The New Sociology in the Soviet Union*; Paul Hollander, "The Dilemmas of Soviet Sociology," *Problems of Communism*, Vol. XIV, No. 6 (November-December 1965), pp. 34-46; and Leopold Labedz, "Sociology as a Vocation," *Survey*, No. 48 (July 1963), pp. 57-65.

[48] "Khronika" [Chronicle], *Mirovaia ekonomika*, No. 9 (September 1958), pp. 151-52. Note the strikingly divergent perspectives with

By 1962, however, the *Mirovaia ekonomika* editorial calling for the fulfillment of the tasks outlined in the Twenty-second Party Congress was directed to "economists and *mezhdunarodniki*."[49] Similarly, in 1963, *Mirovaia ekonomika* introduced a forum in which specialists were given greater leeway to express their own views. It was a forum for economists and *mezhdunarodniki*. Here the term had come to be applied as a term of reference to specialists in a distinct area of inquiry (apart from, in this case, economics) who were researchers in an institute of the Academy of Sciences—that is, to a much more exalted kind of Soviet ideologue. Moreover, international relations was no longer the domain of "mainly historians" as it was "formerly": "Now the joint efforts of historians, economists, [international] lawyers, and specialists in military affairs are required."[50]

---

respect to the function of the journal. For other examples of the use of *mezhdunarodnik* to connote propagandist, see the report of a one-day conference on the German problem, organized by the Institute and the Moscow city branch of the Society for the Dissemination of Political and Scientific Knowledge (under Agitprop): "Nauchnaia zhizn'" [Scientific Life], *Mirovaia ekonomika*, No. 2 (February 1959), p. 147; R. Grigor'iants, "Nauchnaia zhizn'," *Mirovaia ekonomika*, No. 2 (February 1960), p. 155; and "Khronika," *Mirovaia ekonomika*, No. 2 (February 1959), p. 151.

[49] "XXII s"ezd KPSS i zadachi dal'neishego izucheniia problem mirovogo razvitiia" [The Twenty-second Congress of the CPSU and the Tasks of Further Studying the Problems of World Development], *Mirovaia ekonomika*, No. 3 (March 1962), p. 6.

For other examples of the use of *mezhdunarodnik* to signify a specialist, see V. Granov, "Mezhdunarodnaia tema v populiarnoi literature" [The International Theme in Popular Literature], *Kommunist*, No. 2 (January 1961), p. 122 and N. Palgunov, "Bibliotechka vneshnei politiki SSSR" [The Little Library of the Foreign Policy of the U.S.S.R.], *Mirovaia ekonomika*, No. 5 (May 1963), p. 151.

Mezhdunarodnik continues, however, to refer to propagandists as well.

[50] AN IMEMO, *Mezhdunarodnye otnosheniia. . . .* , Vol. 1, p. xxvi.

Even more important, international relations in 1961-62 began to be described publicly as a "young science arising 'at the intersection' of a number of social sciences,"[51] with its boundaries demarcated. In a manner highly reminiscent of Quincy Wright, who describes international relations as a synthetic discipline drawing on the insights of eight already recognized disciplines,[52] the introduction to *International Relations Since World War II* (published in 1962) defined international relations in the following manner: "*the aggregate of economic, political, ideological, legal, diplomatic, military ties and interrelations between peoples, between states and systems of states, between the basic social, economic and political forces and organizations acting in the world arena.*"[53]

[51] *Ibid.*

[52] This point, as Soviet observers would say, is not merely of theoretical interest. There is evidence which seems persuasive that members of the international law fraternity fought against giving recognition to international relations as a discipline presumably because it would downgrade the place of international law—and international lawyers. One major piece of evidence pertains to an extended attack by G. I. Morozov, *Organizatsiia ob"edinennykh natsii* [The United Nations Organization] (Moscow: Izdatel'stvo IMO, 1962), on those Western specialists like Wright who speak of international relations as a synthetic discipline. The term international relations, Morozov declared, is "by no means adequate . . . [for adoption] in the Soviet Union" (p. 56). Morozov, moreover, was particularly exercised by the fact that in Wright's enumeration the study of international organization and international law are way down on the list (*ibid.*, p. 57), and argued that international law properly understood can deal with all the range of issues incorporated in Western conceptions of international relations (*ibid.*, p. 58). In the light of the definitions advanced by Inozemtsev and subsequently by the Institute of World Economy and International Relations, one may assume that the developments being described in the present chapter were the brunt of Morozov's complaint. See, too, a similar attack addressed largely to Hans Morgenthau, by D. B. Levin, *Diplomatiia* [Diplomacy] (Moscow: Sotsekiz, 1962), pp. 45-46.

[53] AN IMEMO. *Mezhdunarodnye otnosheniia . . .*, Vol. 1, p. xxvi.

Other indications of a developing discipline could be seen in the improved technical competence evinced by the writings of Soviet international relations specialists. The minimal prerequisites of informational sources not available in 1956 were created. There was extensive diversification of subject matter. Many of the most glaring "memory holes" were filled in. Knowledge of Western materials and techniques advanced. The vilification of Western scholars, an atavistic residue of the heavy irony of Bolshevik polemics, tapered off somewhat, and the resort to vicious *ad hominem* arguments were less frequent.

Before 1956 a Soviet citizen, unless he was among those privileged to have access to Western sources, interested in engaging in international relations research, would have been confronted by insuperable obstacles (even allowing for the limitations of a totalitarian environment) by virtue of the absence of the most rudimentary source books. By the early sixties the absence of "the material bases" for research had been largely overcome. Factual information—to be sure, often still mendaciously selected and distorted—covering the gamut

---

A year earlier, at the time of the Twenty-second Congress, N. N. Inozemtsev, deputy director of the Institute and editor-in-chief of the textbook, utilized a somewhat different formulation: "International relations represent the aggregate of the economic, legal, ideological and military contacts and ties between classes and nations in the world arena, between states and systems of states, between the main economic formations and their alliances, between the most influential political forces and organizations." ("Results and Prospects of the Development of International Relations," *International Affairs*, No. 11 [November 1961], p. 15.) Although in each instance the passage was followed by an assertion that "*class relations* play the cardinal, determining role . . ." (italics in original), the 1962 wording appears to have the effect of playing down the emphasis on class relationships.

of international relations was now available from a number of sources. Yearbooks[54] covering world events became routine. The Institute of World Economy and International Relations (as of 1964 on a quarterly basis) published reviews of the international scene and statistical reports on the economies of nonsocialist countries. Documentary collections (especially two promising series, *Vneshniaia politika Rossii XIX i v nachale XX veka* [The Foreign Policy of Russia in the 19th and Beginning of the 20th Century] and *Dokumenty vneshnei politiki SSSR* [Documents of the Foreign Policy of the U.S.S.R.]) multiplied, and major treaties and United Nations resolutions were reproduced in Soviet journals and press with fair regularity. International front organizations, international economic organizations, the Organization of American States, and the United States Congress were just a few of the institutions for which there were available book-length accounts which provided descriptions of the historical background and the formal framework of the institution.[55] In 1961 a bibliog-

[54] Yearbooks include the *Ezhegodnik bol'shoi sovetskoi entsiklopedii* [Yearbook of the Large Soviet Encyclopedia] (Moscow: Izdatel'stvo AN SSSR); AN IMEMO, *Mezhdunarodnyi politiko-ekonomicheskoi ezhegodnik* [International Politico-Economic Yearbook] (Moscow: Gospolitizdat) (the 1962 and subsequent versions have a minor title change, *Mezhdunarodnyi ezhegodnik: politika i ekonomika*); and *Sovetskii ezhegodnik mezhdunarodnogo prava* [The Soviet Yearbook of International Law] (Moscow: Izdatel'stvo AN SSSR).

[55] For the institutions cited in the text see N. N. Ul'ianova, *Mezhdunarodnye demokraticheskie organizatsii* [International Democratic Organizations] (Kiev: Izdatel'stvo AN UkSSR, 1956); *Mezhdunarodnye ekonomicheskie organizatsii* [International Economic Organizations] (Moscow: Izdatel'stvo IMO, 1960); B. I. Gvozdarev, *Organizatsiia amerikanskikh gosudarstv* [The Organization of American States] (Moscow: Izdatel'stvo IMO, 1960); and Anatoly Gromyko, *Kongress SShA: Vybory, organizatsiia, polnomochiia* [The Congress of the U.S.A.: Elections, Organization, Powers] (Moscow: Izdatel'stvo IMO, 1957).

raphy of Soviet international relations writings[56] listed at least one book dealing with all the countries of Europe (except Yugoslavia!) and North America, most of the then existing nations of Africa and Asia, and half those of Latin America. Two fairly comprehensive bibliographies were published[57] and newly revised and updated editions of the *Politicheskii slovar'* and *Diplomaticheskii slovar'* were issued. Moreover, the bibliographies appended to a number of books, especially the multi-tomed "generalizing" works, were, by previous Soviet standards, quite impressive.[58]

In addition to the readier accessibility of raw, unadorned, pedestrian facts, extensive diversification of subject matter—suggested by several items in the preceding paragraph—occurred. Matters that before had been either left entirely to the leadership or perhaps touched on in pamphleteering, became in the early 1960s subject to considerable scrutiny by scholars. The increasingly public demonstration of technical sophistication and specificity with regard to the consequences of a third world war was a striking example. The amount of published materials dealing with relations among socialist countries, especially economic relations among Eastern European countries participating in the Council for Economic Mutual Assistance, was much larger. The United Nations was another area.[59] There were book-length studies (often surprisingly

[56] V. N. Egorov, comp., *Mezhdunarodnye otnosheniia* [International Relations] (Moscow: Izdatel'stvo IMO, 1961).

[57] V. N. Durdenevskii, *Sovetskaia literatura po mezhdunarodnomu pravu* [Soviet Literature on International Law] (Moscow: Gosiurizdat, 1959); and Egorov, comp.

[58] For example, AN IMEMO, *Mezhdunarodnye otnosheniia*, Vol. I, pp. 711-33 and Vol. II, pp. 694-712; and V. A. Zorin et al., *Istoriia diplomatii* [History of Diplomacy], Vol. I (Moscow: Gospolitizdat, 1959), pp. 824-65.

[59] See Alvin Z. Rubinstein, "Selected Bibliography of Soviet Works

knowledgeable, others rather dismal) of the International Labor Organization, the International Court of Justice, the International Atomic Energy Association, UNESCO, and the Food and Agricultural Organization—as well as the veto and collective security.[60]

The filling in of the most glaring Orwellian memory holes is amply illustrated by the striking contrast provided by two volumes dealing with international relations in the 1945-59 period, the first published in 1958 and edited by a notorious Stalinist, G. A. Deborin,[61] the second the aforementioned 1962 textbook. Alexander Dallin has described the first book as

---

on the United Nations, 1946-1959," *American Political Science Review*, Vol. LIV, No. 4 (December 1960), pp. 985-91.

[60] S. A. Ivanov, *Mezhdunarodnaia organizatsiia truda i profsoiuznoe pravo v kapitalicheskikh stranakh* [The International Labor Organization and Trade Union Rights in Capitalist Countries] (Moscow: Izdatel'stvo AN SSSR, 1959); S. B. Krylov, *Mezhdunarodnyi sud organizatsii ob"edinennykh natsii* [The International Court of the United Nations] (Moscow: Gosiurizdat, 1958); V. Lorin, *Mezhdunarodnoe agentstvo po atomnoi energii* [International Atomic Energy Agency] (Moscow: Gosiurizdat, 1957); M. Negin, *Organizatsiia ob"edinennykh natsii po voprosam prosveshcheniia, nauki i kultury* [The United Nations Educational, Scientific and Cultural Organization] (Moscow: Izdatel'stvo IMO, 1959); I. Ornatskii and M. Pan'nikov, *FAO—organizatsiia ob"edinennykh natsii po voprosam prodovol'stviia i sel'skogo khoziaistva* [FAO—The United Nations Organization for Food and Agriculture] (Moscow: Izdatel'stvo IMO, 1959); N. A. Ushakov, *Printsip edinoglasiia velikikh derzhav v organizatsii ob"edinennykh natsii* [The Principle of Unanimity of Great Powers in the United Nations] (Moscow: Izdatel'stvo AN SSSR, 1956); and V. K. Sobakin, *Kollektivnaia bezopasnost'—garantiia mirnogo sosushchestvovaniia* [Collective Security—a Guarantee of Peaceful Coexistence] (Moscow: Izdatel'stvo IMO, 1962).

[61] G. A. Deborin, ed., *Mezhdunarodnye otnosheniia i vneshniaia politika Sovetskogo Soiuza, 1945-1949gg.* [International Relations and the Foreign Policy of the Soviet Union, 1945-1949] (Moscow: Izdatel'stvo IMO, 1958).

"blatantly mendacious. . . . It contains nothing on the Stalin-Tito split, on Soviet demands on Turkey, or on the Soviet-Iranian crisis. It describes the Nazis in their attack on the U.S.S.R. as a tool of American imperialists and landlords, and Point Four as a form of American aggression."[62]

On the other hand, the later volume (published after the attacks on Stalin at the Twenty-second Party Congress) took a different tack. In the Stalin-Tito dispute the 1962 textbook apportioned blame about equally to Stalin and Yugoslavia (Tito was not once mentioned by name in the book) for the split and for relations between 1949 and 1953.[63] Apropos of Turkey, it acknowledged that, while there were "well-founded considerations and motives" (including the Soviet Union's "legitimate anxiety" for its security in the Black Sea) underlying Soviet relations with Turkey, there had also been "mistaken diplomatic actions, a result of the cult of Stalin," of which "a large share of the responsibility rests with Molotov." "The worsening of Soviet-Turkish relations," the authors observed, "was provoked by the proposal to re-examine the regime of the Black Sea straits concluded at Montreux in 1936." The advancement by Georgia and Armenia of territorial pretensions "inflamed the atmosphere," they added; "this was used by Turkish reactionary circles and foreign imperialism to intensify anti-Soviet and anti-Communist hysteria, for inducing Turkey into the military bloc headed by the U.S.A. under

[62] Alexander Dallin, "Recent Soviet Historiography," in Abraham Brumberg, ed., *Russia Under Khrushchev* (New York: Praeger, 1962), p. 487n.

[63] AN IMEMO, *Mezhdunarodnye otnosheniia . . .* , Vol. 1, pp. 103-104, 139-40. The Soviet Union's "consistent and persistent struggle" for the "just demands of Yugoslavia" in the Trieste issue was asserted on p. 514.

the pretext [sic] of obtaining [Turkey's] security."[64] Again, the Soviet-Iranian crisis was by no means completely passed over. Instead, the volume contained a moderately detailed account which mentioned: the raising "in the UN of the question of 'Soviet interference in the internal affairs of Iran' "; the withdrawal of Soviet troops; "the rout of the democratic forces"; the rupture in trade relations, "from 24% of the Iranian trade turnover in 1945-46 to 0.8% in 1948-49."[65] Remarks made by then Sen. Harry S Truman and by Sumner Welles before the United States entered the war were cited to show that "the genuine goals of the bourgeoisie" were to have "the Soviet Union and Germany bleed each other white in order to create suitable conditions for the domination by American and English imperialists."[66] But the contention was no longer made that Hitler was acting as a lackey of the United States in starting the war. Finally, on Point Four the tone was somewhat modified. It was denied that the United States initiated the program for disinterested and humane reasons and asserted that the "facts show that American 'aid' to underdeveloped countries was accompanied by interference in their domestic and foreign policy, a violation of their sovereignty. Such 'aid' serves as a means of pressure based on the calculation that these countries would remain in the future economically dependent on imperialism and first of all on American monopolies."[67] However, Point Four was not specifically branded an act of American aggression.

Knowledge of Western sources and techniques also showed improvement. Major steps to provide translations of Western

[64] *Ibid.*, p. 255.
[65] *Ibid.*, pp. 257-59.
[66] *Ibid.*
[67] *Ibid.*, p. 372.

scholarly writings were undertaken. This tendency was manifest primarily in the area of military and strategic policy.[68] William W. Kaufmann, ed., *National Security and Military Policy*; Klaus Knorr, *The War Potential of Nations*; Pierre Gallois, *Stratégie de l'âge nucléaire*; Henry Kissinger, *Nuclear Weapons and Foreign Policy*; Bernard Brodie, *Strategy in the Missile Age*; Maxwell Taylor, *The Uncertain Trumpet*; and Robert Osgood, *Limited War*—were all translated into Russian.[69] A handful of books of first magnitude in areas

[68] The translation of Western strategic literature has not been without incident. It is a measure of the task involved in rearranging expectations among Soviet elites concerning Western attitudes that the translation of W. W. Kaufmann, *Military Policy and National Security*, was condemned in a Central Committee resolution of June 4, 1959 because it "might cause harm to the politico-ideological education of the workers." *Voprosy ideologicheskoi raboty* [Questions of Ideological Work], (Moscow: Gospolitizdat, 1961), p. 275. A partial translation of the resolution is contained in "Policy Documents," *Survey*, No. 41 (April 1962), p. 172.

The continuing nature of the struggle may be illustrated by the translation in toto of Bernard Brodie's *Strategy in the Missile Age*. While the introduction, as well as many other overt Soviet sources, mendaciously intimated that Brodie's study defended preventive war, anyone wishing to find out Brodie's views need only skip the introduction and simply read the accurate Russian translation.

That such artifices have been employed has been admirably demonstrated by the statement of an anonymous Czech literary figure in "The Art of Survival," *Survey*, No. 51 (April 1964) p. 82:

"In the case of 'questionable' Western literary works to be translated into Czech, the method of submitting them for approval with an introduction criticizing . . . the author's lack of ideological insight, has worked wonders. Especially when written and signed by notorious dogmatists, the forewords (nobody reads them anyway) have made it possible for works by Beckett or a William Blake or a Valéry to be translated and published. . . ."

[69] [W. W. Kaufmann, ed.], *Voennaia politika i natsional'naia bezopasnost'* [Military Policy and National Security] (Moscow: Izdatel'stvo

other than strategy were also translated, for example, A.J.P. Taylor's *The Struggle for Mastery in Europe*, as were a number of memoirs by participant observers. Reviews in *International Affairs, World Marxist Review*, and *Mirovaia ekonomika* contributed to publicizing the positions of Western specialists. Herman Kahn, John Herz, Amitai Etzioni, Ernst Haas, Thomas Schelling and Morton Halperin, and George Kennan[70] were among those reviewed. A few Soviet

Inostranlit, 1958); Klaus Knorr, *Voennyi potentsial gosudarstv* [The War Potential of Nations] (Moscow: Voenizdat, 1960), introduction by A. N. Lagovskii; P. Gallois, *Strategiia v iadernyi vek* [Strategy in the Nuclear Age] (Moscow: Voenizdat, 1960), condensed translation with an introduction by N. A. Lomov; G. H. Kissinger, *Iadernoe oruzhie i vneshniaia politika* [Nuclear Weapons and Foreign Policy] (Moscow: Izdatel'stvo Inostranlit 1959), condensed translation with an introduction by S. N. Krasil'nikov; B. Brodi [Brodie], *Strategiia v vek raketnogo oruzhiia* [Strategy in the Missile Age] (Moscow: Voenizdat, 1961), introduction by V. M. Mochalov; M. Teilor [Taylor], *Nenadezhnaia strategiia* [An Unreliable Strategy] (Moscow: Voenizdat, 1961), introduction by M. A. Mil'shtein; Robert E. Osgood, *Ogranichennaia voina* [Limited War] (Moscow: Voenizdat, 1960), intro. by V. V. Mochalov.

For further titles see the (unfortunately incomplete) appendix to the RAND translation of V. D. Sokolovskii, ed., *Voennaia strategiia* ("Appendix II: Western Military Works Available in the Soviet Union") in RAND, *Soviet Military Strategy*, pp. 530-33.

[70] See Iu. Sheinin's review of Kahn's *On Thermonuclear War*, in *Mirovaia ekonomika*, No. 5 (May 1962), pp. 147-52 and of *Thinking About the Unthinkable*, in *ibid.*, No. 1 (January 1963), pp. 141-44. Also: V. Pechorkin, "About Acceptable War," *International Affairs*, No. 3 (March 1963), pp. 20-25; Iu. Krasin and I. Kurbatkin, review of Herz's *International Politics in the Atomic Age*, in *Mirovaia ekonomika*, No. 5 (May 1960), pp. 143-46; I. Glagolev, review of Etzioni's *The Hard Way to Peace*, in *Mirovaia ekonomika*, No. 10 (October 1962), pp. 142-44; K. Vladin, review of Haas's *The Uniting of Europe*, in *International Affairs*, No. 1 (January 1959), pp. 133-35; Y. [Iu.] Fadin, "Philosophy of a Moribund World," *International Affairs*, No. 4 (April 1962), pp. 95-98, which reviews Schelling and Halperin's *Strategy and Arms Control*; G. Anatolyev [Anatol'ev] and B. Ma-

specialists achieved a greater awareness of American materials while working at the United Nations, in Washington, or, as in the case of N. N. Iakovlev, studying in the United States.

All things considered, therefore, the improvement in the status of international relations studies in the Soviet Union was appreciable during the years 1956-62. But like rate-of-growth statistics expressed in percentages of a negligible base point, the impression becomes tarnished when other comparative criteria are interjected.

When contrasted with criteria other than the state of international relations studies before the Twentieth Party Congress, the technical competence of many Soviet specialists and their knowledge of Western sources left much to be desired. The grossest kinds of factual errors still appeared. It is problematical whether in the 1960s many Soviet specialists would have written, as the old ideological warhorse Professor P. N. Fedoseev did in 1957, that "after [Nicholas] Spykman other American sociologists came forward with arguments in favour of the ideology of force. Their number included John Dewey, James Burnham, Grayson Kirk, Harold Lasswell, former U.S. Secretary of the Treasury Hans [sic] Morgenthau, and many others"[71]—although as recently as 1965, according to one Soviet scholar, other Soviet specialists were still confusing Henry and Hans Morgenthau. On the other hand, to encounter a reference to "former Chief of Staff of the American army, General Z. [Zachary?] Taylor"[72] in a book whose au-

rushkin, "Through the Distorting Glass: Review of Kennan's *The Decision to Intervene*," *International Affairs*, No. 1 (January 1959), pp. 104-105.

[71] P. Fedoseyev [Fedoseev], "Sociological Theories and the Foreign Policy of Imperialism," *International Affairs*, No. 3 (March 1957), p. 12.

[72] Boris Dmitriev [B. Piadyshev], *Pentagon i vneshniaia politika SShA* [The Pentagon and U.S. Foreign Policy] (Moscow: Izdatel'stvo IMO, 1961), p. 155.

thor otherwise demonstrated an acquaintance with American sources, is equally disconcerting. It would unfortunately be an all too simple matter to multiply these examples.[73]

At the level of methodological techniques, Soviet international relations lagged far behind other *Soviet* social sciences. One searches in vain, prior to 1962, for a public manifestation of efforts on the part of international relations specialists to bring to bear any device from among the panoply of mathematical approaches which have been applied by other social scientists. Soviet international relations studies at this juncture paled in contrast not only with Western interest in, for instance, game theory and communications theory, but even with that of other branches of Soviet social science. There was no indication that international relations specialists regarded electronic computers as a valid research aid, as did at least three Soviet scholars (Iu. G. Kosarev, E. V. Evreinov, and V. A. Ustinov) whose fields were ancient history. If there were counterparts in international relations to the mathematical marginalists, L. V. Kantorovich and V. V. Novozhilov, in Soviet economics, they did not reveal themselves publicly.

Moreover, the emergence of international relations as an area "at the intersections" of other social sciences involved certain costs. Along with the emergence of international re-

[73] Cf. the timid recognition by V. G. Trukhanovskii, editor-in-chief of *Voprosy istorii*, of the unpreparedness of Soviet historians:

"In American and English journals, articles appear in which the blunders of our historians are rather often noted. The cause of these blunders is first of all the insufficiently deep knowledge of the material by several authors. When inaccuracy is allowed, then our argument is turned against ourselves. We do not need 'strong words' in the struggle with our opponents. Strong argument is needed and we can have it since historical truth is on our side."

"Vsesoiuznoe soveshchanie istorikov" [All-Union Meeting of Historians], *Voprosy istorii*, No. 2 (February 1963), p. 17.

lations into a status of its own, it was, at the same time, increasingly "collectivized" and politicized. Collectivization was expressed in three ways. The specialists were brought together in Moscow, the "production center."[74] They were obliged to deal increasingly with present-day issues, with "topicality," and therefore publication, was determined by "state interests." Finally, strenuous efforts were made to increase the number of collectively authored works.

Almost by definition, these collectivizing tendencies were steps that permitted greater control. (In light of V. D. Sokolovskii's *Military Strategy* a caveat should be entered. Collective works will obviously stifle individual initiative; they may, however, be expressions of *institutional* initiative, i.e., pressure, directed to particular members of an elite. But they do not necessarily signify inferior quality.) Directing the scholar's purview away from obscure events and to present-day matters tended partly to deprive the specialists of one of the few weapons at their disposal for coping with the Party functionary—their expertise. (Their counterparts in the physical sciences had less difficulty; it is rather implausible, in our day and age, to envisage a generalist in the Party hierarchy challenging a physicist on the compatibility of his research with the theoretical foundations of Marxism-Leninism.) In practice, prior to 1963, there were only a few indications of any proclivity to self-assertiveness on the part of international relations specialists other than the not insignificant accomplishment of having secured recognition that interna-

[74] In 1961 *Kommunist* asserted that more than ninety per cent of the social science professors and doctors in the R.F.S.F.R. lived in Moscow or Leningrad. (N. Kaz'min, "Tesnee sviazat' s zhizn'iu prepodavanie obshchestvennykh nauk v vuzakh" [Link the Training of the Social Sciences in Higher Schools More Closely with Life], *Kommunist*, No. 6 [April 1961], p. 27.)

tional relations was a legitimate area of inquiry. Suggestive in this regard is the fact that *Mirovaia ekonomika* had only one editor-in-chief, Ia. S. Khavinson, during these years of publication. (At this writing, autumn 1967, Khavinson remains the editor of *Mirovaia ekonomika.*) Its editorial policy was rarely criticized, and never in the strident tones which oblige an editorial board to acknowledge "the principled criticism" of its critics. There were no articles published for which the editors were subsequently chastened publicly for their unwisdom. Only one article, by Eugene Varga, was published in which the editors felt constrained to enter the admonishment that "several assertions of the present article are the personal opinion of Academician E. S. Varga."[75]

There was one area, however, in which the editors of the international relations journals and the social science specialists do appear to have waged a holding action for a measure of uniqueness. The specialists apparently tried unsuccessfully[76] to maintain the patina of scholarship by avoid-

[75] "Teoreticheskie problemy . . . ," p. 49. The fact that Varga was a politically rehabilitated octogenarian undoubtedly made it easier for him to express a minority view. For a brief discussion of his differences of opinion with his Soviet confrères (which involved the proper appraisal of the European Common Market) and the proximity of his views to those of the French Communist Party, see François Fejtö, *The French Communist Party and the Crisis of International Communism* (Cambridge, Mass.: The M.I.T. Press, 1967), p. 140.

[76] *International Affairs*, an organ of the Society for the Dissemination of Political-Scientific Knowledge, suffered no worse than *Mirovaia ekonomika*, an Academy of Sciences journal. Beginning with the March 1960 issue, the editors of *International Affairs* began publishing a section "in aid" to the lecturer and propagandist (a section euphemistically described in the English language edition as "Facts & Figures"). As early as 1957 Ivashin and others complained that *International Affairs* did not publish "the best lectures." At that time, it was possible for the editors to rebuff these efforts.

ing features characteristic of the consciously propagandistic journals (such as *Agitator, Politicheskoe samoobrazovanie* [Political Self-education], etc.). The editors of *Mirovaia ekonomika* encountered efforts to redefine the purpose of the journal in a way which would bring it more in line with the mass journals. M. Liadov of the Moscow *oblast'* committee, gave clearest expression to this pressure to popularize when he "declared that the issuance of the journal *Mirovaia ekonomika i mezhdunarodnye otnosheniia* had fully justified itself. The journal was an academic publication, an organ of the Institute of World Economy and International Relations, but nevertheless found its readers not only among scientific workers, but among propagandists, international affairs speakers, [and] lecturers. It is rather helpful in their lecture and propaganda work."[77]

Those, like Liadov, who saw *Mirovaia ekonomika* mainly as rendering a service to propagandists, emphasized the importance of having reviews of international developments and then, once the reviews were begun, of publishing them frequently.[78] A. A. Mishin of Moscow State University, on the

[77] "Khronika," *Mirovaia ekonomika*, No. 9 (September 1958), p. 151. The issue went to press August 19. At approximately the same time, interestingly, as the editors were holding a meeting with Moscow "readers" (July 4), the editors of *International Affairs* were meeting with their *Leningrad* "readers." ("Conference of Leningrad Readers," *ibid.*, No. 7 [July 1958], to press June 20. No exact date was given for the meeting "to discuss the issues of 1957 and the first part of 1958" [p. 127].) The meetings were held primarily to make known the Party's wish that more attention be paid to the underdeveloped countries, especially in Southeast Asia, and to the socialist countries.

[78] For documentation of the persistence of the propagandists (and professors in the peripheral cities) on the question of international reviews, see the statements by Liadov and P. P. Kolesnikov, in "Khronika," *Mirovaia ekonomika*, No. 9 (September 1959), pp. 151-52; the statements of V. A. Doguadze, S. I. Sadad, and K. N. Vaiser-

other hand, expressed a view undoubtedly more in harmony with that of the editors. The rapporteur noted that Mishin, "having pointed out that the journal had found its audiences," had reversed Liadov's description: "We use this journal not only as international affairs lecturers but also as people engaging in scholarly work. The journal is valuable not only for economists but for representatives of the juridical and other social sciences as well."[79] In view of these contrasting roles envisaged for the journal, the statement prefacing the publication of the first review of international events acquires an interesting connotation: "In connection with numerous requests by readers, the editors of the journal *Mirovaia ekonomika i mezhdunarodnye otnosheniia* contemplate carrying periodically international reviews. . . . The editors hope that such material can render assistance to lecturers, propagandists, and all who are interested in international relations."[80]

Similarly, to those with aspirations to maintain a minimal facade of scholarship, the Central Committee decree in May 1961, "on measures for improving the selection and preparation of propaganda cadres," must have come as a blow (if not a surprise). The central committee declared, *inter alia*, that "the editorial staffs of the scholarly journals, in the first place

man in "Konferentsiia zhurnala 'Mirovaia ekonomika i mezhdunarodnye otnosheniia' v Tbilisi" [Conference of the Journal 'World Economy and International Relations' in Tbilisi], *Mirovaia ekonomika*, No. 12 (December 1960), pp. 142-44; and those by A. I. Patalazhen, V. F. Brovkin, and D. K. Karmazin, "Obsuzhdeniia zhurnala 'Mirovaia ekonomika i mezhdunarodnye otnosheniia' " [Discussion of the Journal 'World Economy and International Relations'], *Mirovaia ekonomika*, No. 8 (August 1962), p. 156.

[79] "Khronika," *Mirovaia ekonomika*, No. 9 (September 1958), p. 152.

[80] A. A. Galkin et al., "Tekushchie problemy mirovoi politiki (obzor)" [Current Problems of World Politics (A Review)], *Mirovaia ekonomika*, No. 7 (July 1959), p. 3.

Questions of the History of the CPSU, Questions of History, Questions of Philosophy, Questions of Economics, and *World Economy and International Relations*, must regularly publish a section in assistance to propagandists."[81] For the editors of *Mirovaia ekonomika* the Central Committee *ukaz* only reaffirmed the Party hierarchy's position asserted by local Party functionaries, that an academic journal's *raison d'être* was largely to provide materials for propagandist *aktiv*. In fact, *Mirovaia ekonomika* had already begun providing such features. A section for answers to readers' questions became a regular feature with the No. 10 (October) issue of 1958 (a month after the meeting with Moscow "readers" had been reported). By 1962 what would be called in the United States a "man in the news" section ("People and Politics") had been introduced and the international reviews were being published on a quarterly basis. (The latter, moreover, were generally written by *Pravda* and *Izvestiia* commentators rather than Institute researchers.) One probable (and important) reason the institute members were reluctant to produce reviews on a quarterly basis is suggested by the first words of the first quarterly review: "Three months is a very short time."[82]

Under these circumstances it was not surprising that even from the regime's standpoint, cadre recruitment, as in 1956, continued to be unsatisfactory. Indeed, judging by Boris Ponomarev's December 1962 speech to Soviet historians, the

[81] "O merakh po uluchsheniiu podbora i podgotovki propagandistskikh kadrov" [Concerning Measures for the Improvement of Selection and Preparation of Propaganda Cadres], *Partinaia zhizn'* [Party Life], No. 10 (May 1961), p. 33.

[82] V. A. Matveev, V. N. Nekrasov, and E. M. Primakov, "Tekushchie problemy mirovoi politiki" [Current Problems of World Politics], *Mirovaia ekonomika*, No. 4 (April 1962), pp. 57-74.

situation had reached crisis proportions.[83] Evidently few intelligent Soviet youths were choosing careers in the social sciences, and particularly international relations—whether as scholar, diplomat, or correspondent—in preference to the safer, freer, more apolitical climes of the physical sciences. Ironically this pattern, moreover, is one which the Party actually encouraged, since the physical sciences promise more immediate payoff to the regime. According to Ponomarev's figures, no candidates' dissertations[84] were submitted in 1956, 1957, 1959, or 1960 that dealt with Latin American history; three were submitted in 1958 and one in 1961. "For almost seven years," he observed, "not one specialist on the history of Cuba has graduated from aspirant status."

"Soviet Africanists are making only the first steps," he continued. "We have definitely not prepared enough specialists on the history . . . of the countries of northern Europe." In Ponomarev's view, the situation was especially troublesome with respect to "the history of socialist countries, expecially in the peoples' democratic phase," for here, "we cannot even observe a tendency toward growth. On the contrary, the quantity of dissertations has contracted. In 1957 three were defended; in 1958, three; in 1959, two; in 1961, two; in 1962, one." Small wonder, therefore, that Ponomarev was concerned whether "the training of specialists is sufficient even to provide regular replacement of old personnel."

Thus, up to 1962, the need in the nuclear age for more sophisticated published analysis of international affairs seems to have taken a back seat to domestic propaganda considerations. Although Khrushchev was much more willing to listen to

[83] Ponomarev, "Zadachi istoricheskoi nauki . . . ," pp. 21-22.

[84] Very roughly speaking, the Russian candidate's degree requires less work than the American doctorate, the Russian doctorate more.

advice than Stalin was, and although he seemed to have some notion that several persons might possess insight, he was probably less disposed to recognize others' claims to expertise in international relations than perhaps in any other field except agriculture. In many facets of international relations, the role—or at least the public posture—of the specialist in the Institute as policy adviser and scholar continued to be secondary to his role as mobilizer, propagandist, and apologist.

The New Respectability: 1963-1967

In the last year or two of the Khrushchev tenure in power however, developments at two levels, within the political leadership and among the specialists, suggested that the prospects for technically sophisticated research in areas of high political priority to the regime might be greater than indicated by experience prior to 1963.

From within the ruling group came calls for greater attention to methodology and theory by international relations specialists. The most direct evidence was contained in Leonid Il'ichev's speech in October 1963 to the Presidium of the Academy of Sciences.[85] In that speech, Il'ichev characterized "attention to methodological questions as a symbol of progress in Soviet science" and adverted specifically to the recent development in the Soviet Union, *inter alia*, "of international relations theory." More detailed analysis, he contended, was called for in such "specific spheres of politics" as "class relations among us and abroad, bourgeois parties, the communist and worker's movements, and also democratic movements, public opinion, propaganda. . . ." Finally, in language reminiscent of a controversy settled in American political science

[85] "Metodologicheskie problemy estestvoznaniia i obshchestvennykh nauk," pp. 3-46.

a generation ago, he expressed his dissatisfaction with traditional modes of analysis of the state and international relations. The state, he asserted, needed further study, "not on the plane of constitutional and administrative norms, as it is studied by legal science but on the plane of its real activities." International relations, he continued, needed to be examined "not as the historians do, but on the plane of the burning vital questions of the day."

There are possibly two reasons for the interest shown within the ruling group in greater sophistication on the part of Soviet international relations specialists. One relates to the growing tendency by Khrushchev and some other members of the ruling group to regard Leninism as irrelevant to international politics in the atomic age. That development is treated elsewhere in this book.[86] What warrants emphasis here is that, having concluded that the Leninist unity of theory and practice had been severed, presumably forever, these alleged defenders of the faith appear to have been increasingly attracted to the potential political payoffs to be achieved by encouraging the specialists below the top echelons of the Party to engage in rigorous analysis—without great concern for doctrinal considerations—of such "burning, vital questions of the day" as the foreign policy consequences of the internal political process in nonsocialist states, Western integration, and war and peace.

They may have been encouraged in this inclination by a sense that the work of American specialists (especially with respect to strategic doctrine and perhaps operations research) had been a factor in enhancing the effectiveness of American foreign policy, the success of which was in marked contrast

[86] See below, pp. 133-35.

to the succession of foreign policy setbacks suffered by the Soviet regime.[87]

Moreover, especially in strategic matters, domestic political considerations probably figured in the calculation. One distinctive feature of the strategy dialogue in the Soviet Union in the last years of Khrushchev's tenure was that it was carried on within the military and between the military specialists and the political generalists.[88] This being a situation no leader concerned with his power position would find satisfactory for long, Khrushchev (despite his reluctance to acknowledge expertise to others in the area of international relations) may have encouraged the development of strategic expertise to prevent himself from becoming captive to the expertise of military strategists whose preoccupation was with waging war rather than with deterrence.[89]

[87] For the modest evidence in this regard see in particular G. Gerasimov, "War Savants Play Games," *International Affairs*, No. 7 (July 1964), pp. 77-82; AN IMEMO, *Dvizhushchie sily vneshnei politiki SShA* [Moving Forces of U.S. Foreign Policy] (Moscow: Izdatel'stvo "Nauka," 1965), p. 3; and I. Lemin, "Velikaia Oktiabr'skaia sotsialisticheskaia revoliutsiia i mirovaia politika" [The Great October Revolution and World Politics], *Mirovaia ekonomika*, No. 6 (June 1967), p. 10.

[88] Wolfe, *Soviet Strategy at the Crossroads*, passim.

[89] In the last years of the Khrushchev term in power there was growing evidence of strategically relevant commentary by a few nonmilitary figures. See for instance N. M. Nikol'skii, *Osnovnoi vopros sovremennosti* (Moscow: Izdatel'stvo "Mezhdunarodnye otnosheniia," 1964); Iu. Sheinin's *Nauka i militarizm v SShA*, (Moscow: Izdatel'stvo AN SSSR, 1963), as well as Gerasimov, "War Savants . . . ," pp. 77-83.

At the same time, inasmuch as the 1962 international relations textbook explicitly recognized that strategists had a contribution to make in the study of international relations, it is possible that ultimately an interplay between nonmilitary and military strategists within the Soviet Union may set off a dialogue in which keener insights into questions of war and peace may emerge. By October 1964, however, there were almost no signs of even a mechanism for such a dialogue.

There were also important developments among the specialists. In early 1963 a "forum for economists and international relations specialists" was introduced as a regular feature of *Mirovaia ekonomika.* Its establishment had the effect of symbolizing a parity between economics and international relations and of reasserting a degree of differentiation between the explicitly propagandistic journals and a journal of an institute of the Academy of Sciences. More importantly, with its creation, specialists for the first time had a vehicle in which the expression of innovative views was encouraged and in which the risk of boldness to authors raising controversial issues was considerably reduced. Because the forum articles were published on the author's responsibility, the editorial board of *Mirovaia ekonomika* felt less constrained to rebuke an author or pressure him to engage in self-criticism—even when, as at the very outset, an author published a clearly revisionist statement that produced an intense reaction from old, Stalinist political economists and Arab emigré communists.[90]

In 1963 there were transparent efforts to indicate the emergence of a younger generation of Soviet scholars, all considerably less cowed by dogma than the Arzumanians and the Vargas, and all in 1963 under 40. The device was a simple

---

For a rare example of collaboration between a military and a non-military specialist see I. Glagolev and V. Larionov "Soviet Defence Might and Peaceful Coexistence," *International Affairs,* No. 11 (November 1963), pp. 27-33.

[90] G. Mirskii, "Tvorcheskii Marksizm i problemy natsional'no-osvoboditel'nykh revoliutsii" [Creative Marxism and the Problems of the National-Liberation Revolutions], *Mirovaia ekonomika,* No. 2 (February 1963), pp. 63-68. For a Western account see Uri Ra'anan, "Moscow and the Third World," *Problems of Communism,* Vol. xiv, No. 1 (January-February 1965), pp. 1-10.

one: the editors merely indicated the birthdates of the younger contributors to the forum—G. Mirskii had been born in 1926; V. Kiselev, 1924; V. Terekhov, 1928; and V. Shastitko, 1924.

The last two years of Khrushchev's regime witnessed the appearance, actually for the first time, of a few works by specialists which were distinguished by markedly greater sophistication than that revealed in statements of political generalists. Substantive innovations, including statements directly and explicitly contravening *doctrinal* positions, appeared in the specialized international relations literature. Thus Mirskii,[91] in an article published in early 1963, significantly entitled "Creative Marxism [*not* creative Marxism-Leninism] and the Problems of National Liberation Revolutions," attempted to circumvent the impediments of class analysis *and* the dichotomic world-view[92] to the analysis of elite recruitment by calling for study of "the social elements of societies which do not go into the concept 'bourgeoisie' but in many cases play an enormous or even leading role, namely the intelligentsia and the army." Similarly indicative of efforts to reformulate a major problem in the study of international relations was a book by M. N. Nikol'skii, which, drawing on the American scholar Klaus Knorr's concept of the disposable surplus for war as a measure of a state's power in international relations, advanced the sensible suggestion that in the nuclear age Soviet power potential be calculated in terms of "*peace potential*";[93]

[91] Mirskii, "Tvorcheskii Marksizm. . . ."

[92] The Khrushchevian division of American ruling circles into "men of reason" and "madmen" suggests an effort to circumvent a class analysis of American politics; significantly, however, the *division* is still dichotomic in character.

[93] N. M. Nikol'skii, *Osnovnoi vopros sovremennosti*, p. 269, italics in original.

i.e., be evaluated in terms of deterrent, rather than war-waging, capability. Another radical—and controversial—departure from conventional Soviet thinking first articulated in the specialized international relations literature[94] involved the explicit repudiation of the famous Clausewitzian dictum and core element in Leninism, that war is the continuation of politics via other means.

Perhaps equally significantly, lengthy studies related to politically sensitive topics could be published in which, for purposes of legitimation, only token deference was tendered the writings of the founders of Marxism-Leninism. Indeed, as V. I. Kaplan's *The U. S. in the War and Post-War Years* vividly illustrates,[95] a lengthy study could be published (and favorably reviewed) which virtually ignored Lenin, Marx, and Engels. Kaplan's book, for instance, contains 1,585 footnotes; of these, there was one reference to Lenin, one to Marx alone, and one to Marx and Engels. There were, to be sure, several references to the Twenty-second C.P.S.U. Congress and to Khrushchev, although the latter, appropriately, were largely related to his visit to the U.S.

It was also evident that in the last years of Khrushchev's tenure certain Western approaches hitherto conspicuously avoided by Soviet specialists had been legitimated. In the summer 1963, for instance, there were hints in the specialized journals that interest group analysis had become a tolerated analytical tool. One S. Epstein, writing in *Mirovaia ekonomika*, reviewed favorably a Polish political scientist's (Stan-

[94] V. Gantman et al., "Tekushchie problemy mirovoi politiki," *Mirovaia ekonomika*, No. 1 (January 1963), pp. 3-23.

[95] V. I. Lan [Kaplan], *SShA v voennye i poslevoennye gody* [The U.S. in the War and Postwar Years] (Moscow: Izdatel'stvo "Nauka," 1964).

lislaw Ehrlich's) study of pressure groups, *Grupy Nacisku.*[96] A brief note appeared in *International Affairs,* which acknowledged the existence of lobbies other than ones "operated by Big Business." "Trade unions, churches, and other organizations, including the AFL-CIO, the National Farmers' Union, the American Medical Association," the author of the note informed his readers, "have their own lobbies."[97] Confirmation of the hypothesis that interest group analysis had become permissible came in the winter of 1963-64 with the publication of *Parties in the System of the Dictatorship of the Monopolies.* In the words of the authors, the study treats "the role of foreign parties, employers' unions and societies, and also other pressure groups as instruments of the subordination of the state mechanism to control by the monopolies."[98] Similarly, in July 1964 an article appeared in *International Affairs,* which demonstrated an awareness that game theory might be used by "peace-loving forces" as well as "militarists." The purpose of the article, its author, G. Gerasimov, asserted, was "not to put . . . game theory in the dock." "If anything," he stated, "I think, it [should] . . . be defended against mutilation by the militarists."[99]

Thus Khrushchev's waning months seemed to hold forth the possibility of an era in Soviet social science in which there would be a genuine possibility of technically sophisticated

[96] "Gruppy davleniia," *Mirovaia ekonomika,* No. 8 (August 1963), pp. 150-51. Ehrlich, it might be noted, argued that pressure-group analysis can be applied to socialist countries, a fact omitted by Epstein.

[97] G. Yevgenyev [Evgenev], "Lobbying in the U.S.A.," *International Affairs,* No. 6 (June 1963), pp. 93-94.

[98] AN SSSR, Institut Gosudarstva i Prava, *Partii v sisteme diktatury monopolii* [Parties in the System of Monopoly Dictatorship] (Moscow: Izdatel'stvo "Nauka," 1964), p. 3.

[99] Gerasimov, "War Savants . . . ," pp. 77-82, at p. 81.

international relations research involving short- and middle-range theorizing on topics of immediate policy relevance to the political leadership. This is not to suggest the likelihood of the kind of abstract theorizing undertaken by Morton Kaplan in *System and Process in International Politics*; abstract theorizing would seem highly unlikely. Whether from the perspective of a few years hence these developments will be viewed as harbinging a new era or as merely an idiosyncratic phenomenon—a product perhaps of the post-Cuban missile crisis atmosphere in the Soviet Union and the dissensus within the Soviet ruling group—is unclear now.

In general, the present ruling group has shown itself to be less inclined than Khrushchev to permit ideology to encumber the specialists' analysis—perhaps best exemplified by the disgrace of Trofim Lysenko and the concomitant rehabilitation of classical genetics—and more prone to tolerate the depoliticization of scholarly inquiry. Such evidence as does exist suggests that for some influential personages, interest in taking politics out of science extends even to the science of politics. Indeed, a remarkable article by Feodor Burlatskii in *Pravda* in early 1965 encouraged specialists in politics, domestic and international, to engage in the kind of lively and sophisticated dialogue that has characterized Soviet economics in recent years.[100] On the other hand, in practice, the new ruling group, out of external and presumably internal considerations, severely circumscribed the specialists' opportunity during the first 18 months after Khrushchev's ouster to comment publicly on two important substantive topics—military strategy[101] and international communist developments. Can-

[100] *Pravda*, January 10, 1965.

[101] This appears only to have been a temporary phenomenon. See V. Larionov, "Razvitie sredstv vooruzheniia i strategicheskie kontseptsii

dor about developments within the camp had been conspicuous by its absence throughout the Khrushchev years, as well, and was therefore largely a continuation of previous practice. In military matters, however, there had been evidence of the beginnings of a civilian literature on strategic matters.

In addition, many of the doctrinal innovations concerning international relations intimately associated with the Khrushchev regime have been quietly abandoned, effectively reformulated, or publicly attacked, particularly after September 1965, by members of the new ruling group or representatives of powerful Soviet sub-elites. There have been attacks by name on persons (specifically Nikol'skii and Nikolai Talenskii)[102] who gave vent to many of the novel insights of the last years of Khrushchev's tenure in office. All of this has presumably served to dampen specialists' interest in innovating.

Certainly it has been the case that the three years following Khrushchev's ouster have not seen the degree of promising creativity in evidence during 1963-64. Of the innovative materials that have appeared, a number were completed soon after Khrushchev's removal and must properly be construed as a direct outgrowth of projects undertaken during his years as premier. Such was the case, for instance, of several Soviet analyses of American foreign policy, all of which were noteworthy for their balanced and relatively nonideological treatment of American foreign policy behavior. One of these studies drew heavily (plagiarized might be the more candid

SShA" [The Development of the Means of Armament and U.S. Strategic Concepts], *Mirovaia ekonomika*, No. 6 (June 1966), pp. 74-81.

[102] See the articles by Col. I. Grudinin in *Krasnaia zvezda*, July 21, 1966, and Col. E. Rybkin in *Kommunist vooruzhennykh sil*, cited in English translation in Roman Kolkowicz, "The Red 'Hawks' on the Rationality of Nuclear War," Memorandum RM 4899 PR (Santa Monica, Calif.: The RAND Corporation, March 1966), p. 46.

term) from the writings of Stanley Hoffmann, and another was significant for the attention (previously unnoted in Soviet commentary) it showed to public opinion as a variable shaping American foreign policy.[103]

At the same time, it has not been the case that, even discounting those works properly assigned to Khrushchev's time, the years since Khrushchev have been ones of inactivity among those in the Soviet Union concerned with international relations. In mid-1966, for instance, Gerasimov published the clearest exposition of game theory and its potential relevance to the study of international relations yet to appear in the Soviet literature.[104] Of equal significance was the fact that certain topics and doctrines which previously had been denied the specialists' purview began to be analyzed. The Stalinist definition of nationalism, which throughout the whole de-Stalinization process in the Khrushchev years went almost unchallenged, underwent a major reappraisal by Soviet historians during 1966,[105] the strenuous efforts of other Soviet his-

[103] For the former see AN IMEMO, *Dvizhushchie sily. . . .* Public opinion is stressed in E. I. Popova's dissertation published in 1966, *SShA: bor'ba po voprosam vneshnei politiki* [The USA: The Struggle Over Questions of Foreign Policy] (Moscow: Izdatel'stvo "Mezhdunarodnye otnosheniia," 1966).

[104] "Teoriia igr i mezhdunarodnye otnosheniia" [The Theory of Games and International Relations], *Mirovaia ekonomika,* No. 7 (July 1966), pp. 101-108.

[105] See, in particular, the articles by P. M. Rogachev and M. A. Sverdlin, "O poniatii 'natsiia'" [Concerning the Concept 'Nation'], *Voprosy istorii,* No. 1 (January 1966), pp. 33-48; R. F. Vinokurova, "Obsuzhdenie stat'i P. M. Rogacheva i M. A. Sverdlina 'o poniatii natsiia'" [A Discussion of the Article by P. M. Rogachev and M. A. Sverdlin, "Concerning the Concept 'Nation'"], *Voprosy istorii,* No. 2 (February 1966), pp. 169-71; and S. T. Kaltakhchian, "K voprosu o poniatii 'natsiia'" [On the Question of the Concept 'Nation'], *Voprosy istorii,* No. 6 (June 1966), pp. 211-43. Of particular interest is Kal-

torians to avert such a reappraisal notwithstanding. Moreover, in the fall of 1966 there were indications of a new candor in Soviet commentary about relations among socialist states. For the first time, an article was published that disabused Soviet readers of the notion—long a part of the conventional belief—that the communist system of states was something more than an international system.[106] As a result, it may yet prove possible for Soviet specialists to treat relations among communist states as a legitimate area of scrutiny; ultimately it may even be possible for Soviet specialists to redress what a Czech historian has characterized as the "paradoxical situation" wherein "the socialist countries [have] fallen behind . . . the Western world in the study of . . . the socialist system."[107]

From an institutional perspective, the most notable event was the appointment in 1966 (to succeed the deceased A. A.

---

takhchian's resounding declaration (in response to the efforts of one S. D. Iakubuskaia to restrict the scope of the reexamination) in favor of "free discussion." (Vinokovura, p. 170.) For a thorough Western account see Grey Hodnett, "What's in a Nation," *Problems of Communism*, Vol. XVI, No. 5 (September-October 1967), pp. 2-16.

[106] A. Butenko, "O zakonomernostiakh razvitiia sotsializma kak obshchestvennogo stroia i kak mirovoi sistemy" [Concerning the Law-governed Development of Socialism as a Social System and as a World System], *Mirovaia ekonomika*, No. 11 (November 1966), pp. 84-91. Also "Problemy razvitiia mirovoi sotsialisticheskoi sistemy" [Problems of the Development of a World Socialist System], *Vestnik*, No. 11 (November 1966), pp. 86-89. The appearance of such articles should be read in the context of Soviet-Rumanian relations. For a vigorous traditionalist rejoinder to Butenko's article see M. Savov and E. Bondarenko "Spornaia tochka zreniia" [Debatable Viewpoint], *Mirovaia ekonomika*, No. 6 (June 1967), pp. 117-120. Savov is identified as a Bulgarian.

[107] V. Kotyk, "The Problem of Historical Research on the World Socialist System," *Ceskoslovensky Casopis Historicky*, No. 3, 1965, trans. in Radio Free Europe, Czechoslovak Press Survey No. 1,689 (244), p. 2.

Arzumanian) of N. N. Inozemtsev as director of the Institute of World Economy and International Relations. Perhaps more than any other Soviet specialist, Inozemtsev has advocated the recognition of international relations as a synthetic, but autonomous, discipline drawing on the insights of several narrower, specialized areas of inquiry. He has, in addition, specifically lamented the fact that international relations and related subjects were the "step-children" of the Soviet academic family.[108] Consequently, Inozemtsev's appointment acquired considerable symbolic significance. It served as a measure of the progressive evolution of the Institute of World Economy and International Relations in the decade since 1956 away from an organization primarily composed of economists interested only tangentially in international relations, and toward an interdisciplinary center according equal weight to the study of noncommunist economics and the international market, on the one hand, and international relations, per se, on the other. It was moreover another indication of the legitimation of international relations as an area of specialist inquiry.

The appointment of Inozemtsev was followed by a lead editorial in *Mirovaia ekonomika* in mid-1967 which speaks of the tasks "before the social sciences, in particular the science of international relations," and asserts that "it goes without saying" that "the use of computers, the application of the 'theory of games,' the 'theory of probabilities' and other mathematical methods are fully expedient both in the sphere of foreign policy and in the science of international relations."[109]

For all the ambivalence of the record since October 1964 it

[108] *Pravda*, June 13, 1965. For a translation see *Current Digest*, Vol. XVII, No. 23 (June 23, 1965), pp. 14-15.

[109] Lemin, "Velikaia Oktiabr'skaia revolutsiia . . . ," p. 10.

would seem, therefore, that there continues to be interest in the Soviet Union within the ruling group, as well as among the specialists in the institutes in enhancing the study of international relations. Progress in such a politically sensitive area will naturally continue to be highly responsive to political flux, domestic and international; any projections thus must be tentative. Nevertheless, it is of considerable significance that the Soviet system has become sufficiently depoliticized that it is at least possible to speculate about a time when serious studies of international politics will issue forth from the Soviet Union with the blessing of the keepers of the faith. Were such a development to occur, the function of ideology in the Soviet system would have been radically transformed. Ideology would have ceased to be the language of analysis and become instead merely the rhetoric for legitimating a process whereby the ruling group would weigh divergent specialist appraisals—the latter being couched in terms particular to the specialists' narrow areas of inquiry. For the last years of Khrushchev's tenure in office and for the three years following his removal, however, such a prospect remained almost totally in the future. Thus, in the substantive analysis of Soviet international relations perspectives which follows, the focus has necessarily been directed to the overt declarations of both specialist and political generalist alike.

Chapter Three: The Actors

NOTHING is more important to a theory of international relations than the identification of the main actors. In Western international relations literature one traditional approach has been to treat the state as the sole international actor. States were thought to be cohesive, impermeable, and independent units of roughly equal size. The "billiard balls"—to use Wolfers' apt characterization[1]—moved about (or were moved) in a random fashion in the international arena, occasionally (or frequently) colliding with other balls. The pattern of interaction among the units, while resulting in nicks and scratches in the balls' surfaces, almost never entailed collisions of an intensity sufficient to threaten their very existence. States in this imagery could be reified without seriously obfuscating analysis. Broad-gauge generalizations about the behavior of states were asserted; states, provided the opportunity, extend themselves to acquire desired goals; states, like nature, abhor a vacuum, etc. Often these descriptive statements, expressed in the imperative voice, became maxims for behavior: if opportunity presents itself, extend the state to acquire desired goals. Protagonists of this position assumed that it was possible to advance descriptive and predictive assertions which sufficed to describe the behavior of any state.[2]

A devaluation of the billiard-ball model has taken place

[1] Arnold Wolfers, "The Pole of Power and the Pole of Indifference," in *Discord and Collaboration*, p. 82. See also his "The Actors in International Politics," in William T. R. Fox, ed., *Theoretical Aspects of International Relations*, pp. 83-106. I have used slightly different adjectives than Wolfers; his are "closed, impermeable, and sovereign."

[2] Morgenthau, *Politics Among Nations*, pp. 38-68, serves to exemplify the tendency—simultaneously, albeit contradictorily—to distinguish between status quo and imperialist power.

in recent years among Western specialists. The specialists have been impelled by changes in international politics in the twentieth century, especially in the postwar period, as well as by developments in the social sciences,[3] to reevaluate their traditional approach to international politics. Almost all Western specialists would agree that the billiard-ball model does not satisfactorily characterize the modern world and that it must be supplemented or supplanted by other approaches. Few if any Western theorists would be happy associating themselves with the assertion that all states in the postwar international system manifest billiard ball-like attributes.

"Cohesive, impermeable, and independent units of roughly equal size" must seem a curious manner of portraying states in a decolonizing, revolutionary, thermonuclear, and still essentially bipolar era. Granted, modern authoritarian regimes may be quite cohesive. Even stable democracies *may* also actually demonstrate fairly high cohesiveness when acting in international affairs. However, many of the new states—states in little more than name—are located more in the opposite direction. Impermeability, too, seems something less than a universal feature of states in the mid-twentieth century. John H. Herz[4] has stressed, perhaps too emphatically, the irrelevance of impermeability as a concept related to defense in the atomic age. Certainly the wide range of contacts across state boundaries runs counter to the notion of impermeability.[5] More importantly (Europe in the 19th century was also char-

[3] Cf. Chadwick F. Alger, "Comparison of Intranational and International Politics," *American Political Science Review*, Vol. LVII, No. 2 (June 1963), pp. 406-19; and Wolfers, "Actors in International Politics," pp. 83-106, for divergent emphases of the contribution developments in other social science fields may make with respect to the identity of the actors in a theory of international politics.

[4] *International Politics in the Atomic Age.*

[5] There is something to be said for the old functionalist argument,

acterized by high permeability in this sense—at least at the elite level), extranational actors now often participate directly in a state's decision-making process. Indeed, it has been suggested by James N. Rosenau that what is required is a major focus on the "penetrated" political system.[6] Nor have independence and equality served as useful analytic terms to describe the political attributes of legally sovereign entities in the postwar period. Finally, in contrast with the billiard-ball model, Western scholars have not expected states in the postwar period to "bounce" off each other randomly. In a revolutionary era neither affinities nor enmities are randomly allotted or readily abandoned.

There is, apparently, general agreement that if, in the present international system, aggregate socio-political entities are to be regarded as international actors, the nation-state would be one entity so treated. Moreover, among corporate actors the state occupies a paramount position, notwithstanding the efforts in 1959-60 of Reinhold Niebuhr and John Herz to accord such a status to large social aggregates—empires in Niebuhr's case, blocs in Herz's. As Stanley Hoffmann, in an essay not disposed to view charitably the contribution of Professor Morgenthau and other "doctrinaire" realists to the study of international relations, has said of "Morgenthau's 'realist' theory": it does have the merit of "focusing on the units that remain the principal actors in world affairs: the States."[7]

---

as the Russians, of all people, have learned. Stalinism as an international system, by creating socialism in one country in many countries, created conditions, once the informal control mechanisms had broken down, analogous to the Hobbesian war of all against all.

[6] Rosenau, "Pre-theories and Theories of Foreign Policy," in R. Barry Farrell, ed., *Approaches to Comparative and International Politics*, pp. 27-92.

[7] Hoffmann, ed., *Contemporary Theory in International Politics*, p. 30. The prevalence of the view that states are the main international actors is similarly exemplified by an introductory international rela-

Another matter about which there is general consensus among Western specialists is whether the state should be treated as the sole international actor. Many theorists could be mustered to defend the assertion that corporate actors other than the nation-state would be included in the present international system. Wolfers, for instance, would consider "international, supernational, transnational, and subnational corporate bodies as potential coactors on the international stage." "There is ample evidence," in his view, "to show that the United Nations and its agencies, the European Coal and Steel Community, the Afro-Asian bloc, the Arab League, the Vatican, the Arabian-American Oil Company, and a host of other nonstate entities are . . . on occasion . . . actors in the international arena and competitors of the nation-state."[8] An analogously large number of scholars would not likely entertain the notion that the state—or corporate entities generally—should function as units of analysis to the total exclusion of individuals. (That Wolfers talks about the "decision-making" and "minds of men" approaches in his discussion of individuals as actors illustrates just how little ingenuity would be required.[9]

Few Western international relations theorists would now

---

tions text by Charles O. Lerche, Jr. and Abdul A. Said, *Concepts of International Politics* (Englewood Cliffs, N.J.: Prentice-Hall, Inc., 1963). Part One is entitled "The Actors: The State in International Politics," on the evident assumption that the equation is such a commonplace as to warrant no explanation.

[8] Fox, *Theoretical Aspects of International Relations*, pp. 101, 104.

[9] One is hard put to think of a Western scholar who would assert that individuals are the sole individual actors—although Urban C. Whitaker, Jr. has said the individual is the "primary entity." "Actors, Ends, and Means: A Coarse-Screen Macro-Theory of International Relations," in Rosenau, ed., *International Politics and Foreign Policy*, p. 442.

willingly hazard many statements purporting to be of general and sufficient validity about actor (corporate or individual) behavior, except perhaps under stated specific conditions, the incidence of which is itself an important variable. The result has been the incorporation of nonstate corporate actors into many models, efforts to account for individual behavior patterns, and marked diminution in the perceived relevance for *all* states of the traditional billiard-ball imagery.

In the Soviet view, that states do not occupy an unchallenged place as the paramount actors in contemporary international relations should scarcely seem remarkable. Granted that in comparison with the traditional Marxist frame of reference there has been a steady augmentation, dating at least from the achievement of socialism in one country, in the role of states as actors, as Soviet observers adapted to operating in a horizontal, international, and political arena. Nevertheless, given the traditional Marxist-Leninist calculus, with its attendant imagery of classes as historical agents and a preoccupation with revolutionary, qualitative change, it was entirely logical for Zbigniew K. Brzezinski to declare in 1960 that "the interplay between nation-states is" in the Soviet view "merely one, and often only a formal, aspect of international affairs."[10]

If one examines Soviet international relations commentary in the years since 1956, however, one is struck by the significance which Soviet international relations commentators in fact ascribe to the place of states in the international arena. Soviet commentators write as though their perspectives have

[10] *Ideology and Power*, p. 105. The chapter from which this quote was drawn was originally published in a slightly different form as "Communist Ideology and International Affairs" in the *Journal of Conflict Resolution*, Vol. IV, No. 3 (September 1960), pp. 266-91.

in practice drawn closer to those of American commentators. Whereas American theorists are less prone to hypostatize the nation-state than previously, Soviet analyists have upgraded the role of the state in their scheme of things. This development in Soviet thought has been a phenomenon primarily associated with the last years of Khrushchev's power and the years following his removal. What follows, consequently, is intended less as counterpoint to Professor Brzezinski's observation than as a report on an aspect of a general pattern of ideological erosion, which at this writing seems clear-cut but was only emerging in 1960.

Under Khrushchev, Soviet authors occasionally gave the impression that they were using something like the billiard-ball model as a working hypothesis. Thus the influential foreign policy specialist, V. M. Khvostov, informed readers of *International Affairs* (Moscow) that "the fact that so far the U.S.A. has had to exercise restraint in encroaching on the interests of the West European countries is due to the existence of the Soviet Union. Were there no socialist camp, and above all no Soviet Union, Britain, France, Italy and other West European countries would have got more of the 'big stick' from Uncle Sam."[11] More recently, in a book issued under the general editorship of Andrei A. Gromyko, it was asserted that "the system of international relations is founded on the intercourse of sovereign states [each of] which [is] organized in the confines of a definite territory, over which a given state exercises command, that is, exclusive power [*vlast'*]."[12]

[11] V. M. Khvostov, "The Leninist Principles of Foreign Policy," *International Affairs*, No. 4 (April 1957), p. 21.

[12] Institut Mezhdunarodnykh Otnoshenii, *Mirnoe sosushchestvovanie —Leninskii kurs vneshnei politiki Sovetskogo Soiuza* [Peaceful Co-

Statements such as these, containing the intimation that states were thought of as sole international actors, were encountered comparatively infrequently. There is no question, however, that throughout the period surveyed, states were considered by Soviet international relations observers to be important international actors. Countless statements can be mustered to the effect that "the Soviet Union played a decisive role in . . .", "France, . . . Washington thought, was shirking her NATO duties too demonstratively," "the main line of American foreign policy [is] . . . , "London's policy is influenced by the growing conviction that. . . ."[13] Similarly, there is little doubt that Soviet writers typically perceived the international arena as populated by a multiplicity of corporate actors than as solely by states. The textbook, *International Relations Since World War II*, contains a succinct statement expressive of the typical Soviet observation: "*International relations is the aggregate of economic, political, ideological, legal, diplomatic, military ties and interrelationships between peoples, between states and systems of states, between the basic social, economic, and political forces and organizations acting in the world arena.*"[14]

The issues raised by endeavoring to identify the interna-

---

existence—The Leninist Course of Soviet Foreign Policy] (Moscow: Izdatel'stvo IMO, 1962), p. 227.

[13] The examples cited are from M. Airapetyan [Airapetian] and G. Deborin, "The Guiding Force of Socialist Foreign Policy," *International Affairs*, No. 11 (November 1958), p. 35; A. Galkin, "The Paradoxes of Western Foreign Policy," *International Affairs*, No. 2 (February 1960), p. 53; N. Matveyeva [Matveeva], "Present Trends in U.S. Foreign Policy," *International Affairs*, No. 4 (April 1957), p. 42; and A. Sovetov, "The Soviet Union and Present International Affairs," *International Affairs*, No. 1 (January 1966), p. 7.

[14] AN IMEMO, *Mezhdunarodnye otnosheniia* . . . , Vol. 1, p. xxvi, italics in original.

tional actors in the Soviet perspective are not, it would seem, whether states were considered the sole international actors or, at the other pole, whether states were included among the actors. At issue are (a) whether it is appropriate to ascribe to Soviet writers in the 1960s the view that states were the main actors in international politics, and (b) which other corporate entities are international actors.

States: The Main Actors?

In contemporary international relations the corporate actors most likely to rival the preeminence of the place of states are the "world systems" of capitalism and socialism. Numerous authoritative formulations taken from major policy pronouncements testify to the significance of the world systems as supranational corporate actors. For example, one of the distinguishing features of the postwar world is said to be the "emergence of socialism from within the confines of one country and its transformation into a world system."[15] "In our epoch world development is shaped by the course and results of the competition between two diametrically opposed social systems."[16] "The development of international relations in our day is determined by the struggle of the two social systems. . . ."[17] The world distribution of power is evaluated between capitalism and socialism, and between these two the major contradiction lies. "Imperialism is no longer able every-

[15] Nikita S. Khrushchev, *Report of the Central Committee of the CPSU to the Twentieth Party Congress*, trans. in Leo Gruliow, ed., *Current Soviet Policies II*, p. 29.

[16] The 1957 Moscow Declaration, trans. in G. F. Hudson, Richard Lowenthal, and Roderick MacFarquhar, eds., *The Sino-Soviet Dispute* (New York: Praeger, 1960), p. 47.

[17] The 1960 Moscow statement, in *ibid.*, p. 189, reproduced from *World Marxist Review*, Vol. III, No. 12 (December 1960), pp. 3-28.

where to dictate its will and to pursue its aggressive policy without hindrance."[18] "It is the principal characteristic of our time that the world socialist system is becoming the decisive factor in the development of society."[19]

The Soviet tendency to treat the two systems as actors originated in Marxist-Leninist ideology, and was evident mainly in the two-camp thesis; "camp" [*lager'*] and "system" are used interchangeably in the Soviet lexicon. The two-camp thesis, a transfer of the Marxist dichotomic model to the arena of international politics, has been a dominant theme in Soviet thought since the Bolshevik seizure of power. It expresses an ideologically rooted assumption that there is a characteristic tendency in phenomena, natural and social, to polarization.

The two-camp thesis is most obvious in leftist periods, in periods when Soviet attitudes are most prone to emphasize communist uniqueness and policies are most characterized by intransigence. It plays an important function in analysis during rightist phases as well. During the Khrushchev regime, for instance, the interwar period was described as one in which the competition between socialist and capitalist systems largely shaped the course and development of world events. The postwar years differed chiefly in that the socialist system had then, like the capitalist system, become a world system.[20]

[18] Editorial, *Pravda*, January 7, 1963. Trans. in *Current Digest*, Vol. xv, No. 1 (January 30, 1963), p. 6.

[19] Hudson, Lowenthal, MacFarquhar, *Sino-Soviet Dispute*, p. 178, italics in original omitted.

[20] It is perhaps for this reason that as harsh and far-ranging as Khrushchev-era comments about Stalin were, there was no criticism of Stalin's policy moves which led to the signing of the Nazi-Soviet pact. Apparently Khrushchev, had he been in Stalin's shoes, might also have overestimated the possibility that the imperialists would join against the Soviet Union and might thereby have committed the

THE BIPOLAR world seemed tailor-made for the two-camp thesis. In fact, Soviet analysts, writing prior to Khrushchev's major speech in January 1961, achieved a fairly close "fit" with reality in their treatment of the Western camp when they drew on the polarization strand in the two-camp thesis. (Prior to Khrushchev's speech, descriptive, eulogistic, and normative terms referring to the socialist camp were hopelessly intertwined—thus rendering analysis of Soviet perspectives on the socialist camp a fruitless exercise.) Distinctive features of bipolarity—in particular, cohesion and a camp's capability for international actions—were grasped. At the same time, states continued to be allotted an important role as actors. Thus the United States and Soviet Union were described as the poles to which other states in the postwar world gravitated. One author, for instance, commenting on an article written by Walter Lippmann, acknowledged that "it can be assumed that Lippmann is correct when he says that two great centres of power—the USSR and the USA—arose after the Second World War. But the main coalitions, or *to be more precise,* camps—the socialist and the capitalist—arose under different conditions."[21] Similarly, two other specialists, in a review of

---

same blunder. For a Soviet book commending the "wisdom" of the Molotov-Ribbentrop pact, see V. G. Trukhanovskii, *Vneshniaia politika Anglii na pervom etape obshchego krizisa kapitalizma* (1919-1939gg.) [English Foreign Policy in the First Stage of the General Crisis of Capitalism (1919-1939)] (Moscow: Izdatel'stvo AN SSSR, 1962), p. 383. See, by way of contrast, Edward Kardelj, *Socialism and War* (London: Methuen and Co., 1961), p. 35.

One gets the impression that the two-camp thesis is akin to the White Rabbit's watch, which, because it did not run, was exactly right twice a day: the accuracy of the two-camp thesis depends on a reality that will conveniently adapt to the model.

[21] D. Zaslavsky [Zaslavskii], "What Will Happen Ten Years Hence?" *International Affairs*, No. 6 (June 1957), p. 79, italics added.

John Herz's *International Politics in the Atomic Age,* concerning his concept of bipolarity (by which, they explained, "Herz understands the concentration of military-political might at two poles—that of the Soviet Union and the U.S.A."), only objected that it failed to go below "the surface phenomena . . . [to] the competition of two social-economic systems," and acknowledged that "of course it is impossible to deny the important influence of military technology on the international relationships of the two systems. . . ."[22]

Again, Soviet academicians vented their criticism of the Yugoslavs during the renewal of public polemics in 1958 in a way that suggested some insight into the Western camp's "unity and diversity." The Yugoslavs, it will be recalled, in their draft Program had referred to both East and West as blocs, and to both the United States and the Soviet Union as superstates.[23] The main Soviet objection to this nomenclature was quite obviously that the terms were "intended to place the U.S.S.R. and the U.S.A. on the same level and moreover to ascribe both aggressiveness and expansionism to the Soviet Union."[24] Analytically, it was objected that the Yugoslav terminology tended to "hide the genuine class content of the struggle now taking place on a world scale . . . a struggle waged, not between two rival states or even two blocs, but between the camp of socialism and peace on one side and the camp of aggression and war on the other."[25] The term "bloc," it was said, obscured "the main, the basic in the contemporary

[22] Krasin and Kurbatkin, *Mirovaia ekonomika,* p. 143.

[23] Brzezinski, *The Soviet Bloc,* pp. 318-22.

[24] N. Nazarov, "Ideinye korni revizionizma v voprosakh mezhdunarodnykh otnoshenii" [The Ideological Roots of Revisionism in Questions of International Relations], *Mirovaia ekonomika,* No. 7 (July 1958), p. 20.

[25] *Ibid.*

world: the existence of two antithetical socio-economic systems."[26] "The theory of 'two super-states,'" on the other hand, was attacked because it "denies the role and significance, the sovereignty and independence of all other countries large and small, lowers all the countries of Western Europe to a position of vassals and satellites in an American bloc."[27]

A dimension of the Soviet perspective encountered at the same time postulated a homogeneity of interest and degree of intra-bloc coordination among elites across state boundaries which amounted to assuming that the organization of the Western camp for the whole postwar period approximated the cohesion Stalin had imposed on the Soviet bloc in the period 1949-53. (That Soviet writers were at the same time maintaining the impossibility of reconciling inter-imperialist contradictions illustrates the inconsistency of the Soviet view of the Western world.)

The most intricate and elaborate effort encountered, which attempted to delineate the links among Western "ruling circles" is found in a two-part article written by A. Leonidov, appropriately entitled "The Secret Alliance of War Monopolies and Its Role in World Politics."[28] The essence of Leonidov's views was that at least with respect to the most vital issues, war and peace and the cold war, the West was a highly homogeneous system held together by inter-elite ties, which though often reflected in governmental organizations, were

[26] *Ibid.*, p. 18.

[27] *Ibid.*, p. 20.

[28] A. Leonidov, "Tainyi soiuz voennykh monopolii i ego rol' v mirovoi politike" [The Secret Alliance of War Monopolies and Its Role in World Politics], *Mirovaia ekonomika*, Part I, No. 11 (November 1958), pp. 27-46; Part II, No. 3 (March 1959), pp. 68-82. The article must have entailed a prodigious expenditure of effort; on that ground alone, the inclination is to rule out an intent solely to deceive. In some instances, no doubt, such has been the case.

based on informal, covert associations. However fanciful the underlying assumptions may be, Leonidov's conclusions warrant partial quotation as an example of the impact of the conspiracy thesis on the Soviet determination of the main actors.

> 1. The facts emphasize the existence behind the facade of the Atlantic bloc of a secret alliance of war monopolies, continuously advancing the arms race with a view to profits.
>
> 2. The alliance of war monopolies embraces all the main producers of weapons in the capitalist world.
>
> 3. All the leading oligarchical dynasties of the West: Rockefeller, Morgan, Dupont, Mellon, Rothschild, Chamberlain, . . . Krupp and others in some degree or another take part in [the alliance].
>
> 4. The general leadership of this secret alliance of war monopolists belongs in the hands of the American financial oligarchy. . . . .
>
> 9. The leading reactionary politicians of the bourgeois countries, along with the military leaders, diplomats, heads of royal dynasties, princes of the Church, bosses of the bourgeois press and powerful bureaucrats are in league with the war monopolies. . . .
>
> 10. The activity of the union of war monopolies is directed first of all at the systematic intensification of the "cold war," sabotage of the goal of disarmament, opposition to attempts to lessen international tensions, kindling enmity against the socialist world. Whatever else may be the internal contradictions among the magnates of the war industries of various countries, in this they act as one. Ultimately the activity of the secret alliances of war monopolies is directed toward the unleashing of a third world war.[29]

[29] *Ibid.*, Part II, p. 82.

To the extent that the assumptions contained in this article were dominant—they certainly were widespread—among Soviet observers in the late fifties, one may safely conclude that Soviet international relations analysts at that time assumed that capitalism as a system was one of the main actors in the international arena.

The models of Western-camp cohesion envisaged in the polarization and conspiracy strands of Soviet analysis cannot logically be reconciled. They were nevertheless entertained simultaneously. Both assumptions have roots in Soviet ideology: analysis based on the conspiracy strand seemed to represent the unthinking transfer of Soviet domestic and intra-bloc experience to the international arena. Description drawing on the notion of polarization seemed instead more an effort to describe the postwar reality in the terminology of the ideology.

Indeed, there was much to be said for the latter perspective. The concept of camp steered a middle course between coalition and bloc—"coalition" conveying the short-term alliance patterns characteristic of a multi-polar model in which states remained the sole actors; "bloc" tending to exclude the nation-state somewhat prematurely from the international scene. At the same time, unfortunately for the validity of Soviet perspectives, Leninist doctrine and Soviet experience colored the content of the term "camp," thus rendering it ambiguous. For in referring to the Western and socialist camps, Soviet spokesmen equated *socio-economic* systems and systems of *states*. In evaluating the actor capability of a supra-national corporate entity, it makes a difference, needless to say, whether the operative model is that of a socio-economic system or a system of states—particularly when, as in the late fifties, Soviet writers were using *stroi*, a Russian word denoting high integration (*gosudarstvennyi stroi,* a state system; *obshchestvennyi stroi,* social system) with equal or greater frequency in reference to the two systems than the more neutral *sistema.* To equate the two is plausible if the assumption is made that control is largely exercised through nonstate control mechanisms—the Party, the secret police, the monopoly of the means of communication, the economy. But in interstate relations this leads to exactly the kind of misconception about interstate controls for which Khrushchev justly criticized Stalin's attitude toward Tito, which, as reported by Khrushchev in his secret speech, was, " 'I will shake my little finger and there will be no more Tito.' " As Khrushchev said, Stalin could not make Tito fall because "Tito had behind him a state and a people who had gone through a severe school of fighting for liberty and independence, a people who gave support to their leader."[30] The intellectual schizophrenia which characterized Soviet views in 1956-61 could be expressed in another manner. The corporate entities being described were actors in two scenarios, international relations and the world historical process. To the outsider it is quite conceivable that the actors in the two dramas are not the same. The Soviet identification of the participants in the allegedly teleological movement of history with the actors in international relations imparted a distinctly anthropomorphic quality to the social system in the international arena.[31] At the Twenty-second

[30] Trans. in Gruliow, *Current Soviet Policies II*, p. 183.

[31] Cf. the following statements contained in, respectively, the 1957 Declaration, the 1960 Statement, and the 1961 C.P.S.U. Program: "In our epoch world development is shaped by the course and results of the competition between two diametrically opposed social systems" (trans. in Hudson, Lowenthal, and MacFarquhar, *Sino-Soviet Dispute*, p. 47); "In our time, the development of international relations is determined by the struggle of the two social systems" (*ibid.*, p. 189);

Congress of the C.P.S.U. it was "the world socialist system," perhaps symptomatically, to which credit was given as the international actor, that was becoming "a more reliable shield, protecting not only the peoples of Socialist countries, but all mankind as well from the military adventures of imperialism."[32]

Thus, in 1956-61 there persisted a curious coexistence of diametrically opposed ideas about the actors in international politics. In concrete day-to-day description, however, Khrushchev and his spokesmen in the specialized international relations journals tended more to discern states as the main actors, as illustrated by the previously cited examples.[33] Moreover, Khrushchev during this time was apparently gradually integrating into his thought and into Soviet perspectives several implications of the uniqueness of the international arena.

Some doctrinal innovations may be cited as indicating a

"Imperialism has ceased to play a dominating role in international relations and the socialist system is playing a bigger and bigger role" (trans. in *Current Digest,* Vol. XIII, No. 45 [December 6, 1961], p. 15).

[32] "Rezoliutsiia XXII s"ezda kommunisticheskoi partii Sovetskogo Soiuza" [Resolution of the Twenty-second Congress of the Communist Party of the Soviet Union], *Kommunist,* No. 16 (November 1961), p. 7. The next sentence reads: "the ever growing might of the Soviet Union and other socialist countries is an important guarantee of peace in all the world."

Khrushchev, in the Central Committee Report, stated that "the world socialist system *has become* a reliable shield . . ." (trans. in *Current Digest,* Vol. XIII, No. 41 [November 8, 1961], p. 3), and did not follow his remark with a reference to the might of the Soviet Union and other socialist countries.

Divergent resource allocation choices would seem to follow from the two formulations. See, e.g., S. I. Ploss's provocative, though extreme, article: "The Uncertainty of Soviet Foreign Policy," *World Politics,* Vol. XV, No. 3 (April 1963), pp. 455-64.

[33] See p. 81 above.

tendency on the part of Soviet observers to emphasize the place of the states as actors and seeming to adumbrate still greater emphasis. For instance, one assumption underlying the Soviet doctrine of peaceful coexistence[34] was that in conditions of *détente* between the two camps the contradictions within the Western camp would assert themselves more extensively, thereby impeding efforts to create supra-national corporate entities capable of acting internationally. In 1964, Khrushchev for the first time publicly acknowledged the cohesiveness of the socialist camp was also adversely affected by *détente*. Interestingly, in this view state action was the main motive force for increasing or decreasing supra-national actor capability, the implication being that states, at least in the West, were the main actors. Similarly, while there were forces "struggling for peace" within the Western states and in the underdeveloped countries, membership in the "*zone* of peace" was allotted to states on a unit basis only. A reflection of the recognition that in the international system the state was the effective agent (and that, given mutual deterrence, small powers counted) may be seen in elements of the rightist policy with respect to the underdeveloped countries: the importance of the national bourgeoisie, the desirability of neutrality,[35] and the assertion that colonialism had virtually ended.

[34] "Peaceful coexistence" has been discussed ad nauseam in both Western and Soviet commentary. For a Western discussion see Robert C. Tucker, *The Soviet Political Mind*, pp. 201-22 and Michael P. Gehlen, *The Politics of Coexistence* (Bloomington, Ind.: Indiana University Press, 1967).

[35] Note, in particular, the numerous attacks in 1963 against the Chinese for actions which allegedly might lead India to abandon its neutrality. E.g., R. Ul'ianovskii, "Amerikanskaia strategiia v Indii" [American Strategy in India], *Mirovaia ekonomika*, No. 5 (May 1963), pp. 27-37.

A PERCEPTIBLE adjustment in the Soviet description of the actors in international politics took place in the last years of Khrushchev's tenure in office. The adjustment was consonant with a general disposition by Soviet observers to describe the world generally, and Western foreign policy particularly, in a more sophisticated and discriminating manner.

One development of special significance to the characterization of the actor-capacity of the West was the muting of the overdeterminist, conspiratorial strand in Soviet analysis. It would undoubtedly exceed the available evidence to assert that in Khrushchev's last years in power international relations commentators completely abandoned the conspiracy theory.[36] Nevertheless, analyses such as Leonidov's, portraying the covert ties that existed between American imperialists and European imperialists, were less prominent. Even the eagerness[37] with which Soviet writers seized on the evidence of a military-industrial complex dominating American foreign policy, marshaled by Fred Cook and the late C. Wright Mills, dissipated somewhat. The heretical view was promulgated that the President of the United States was not a puppet dangling from the strings of the imperialists. Soviet commentary was less engaged in a search for bizarre and tenuous ties between imperialists, and instead more oriented to the political, institutional nexus of decision-making. Similarly, Soviet ob-

[36] See, for instance, the abridged report of a meeting organized by the Agitation and Propaganda Department of the Moscow *gorkom*, the Institute of World Economy and International Relations, and the Editorial Board of *International Affairs*: "The Ideological Struggle and Present International Relations," *International Affairs*, No. 8 (August 1963 [sent to press July 23], pp. 3-41.) Note the observation by V. V. Kortunov (p. 10) on Western propaganda: "A careful examination reveals that all this is directed from a single center. . . ."

[37] See, for instance, Bor. Dmitriev, *Pentagon i vneshniaia politika SShA*, passim.

servers, in analyzing the cohesiveness of the Western camp, looked increasingly—and with concern—to observable institutionalized links among the Western powers, instead of to "secret alliances."

> In the postwar period, fundamental *changes in relations between imperialist states* have taken place.
>
> The contradiction between socialism and capitalism—the main contradiction of the modern world—is directly affecting the transformation of these relations. The development of this contradiction in large measure determines the nature of contemporary inter-imperialist contradictions.
>
> The imperialists, in fear of the world revolutionary forces, have undertaken attempts to unite themselves. Under the leadership of the United States of America, a bloc of imperialist states was created for the struggle against socialism, the national liberation and democratic movements. The imperialist states are trying to carry out a common foreign policy course and a united military strategy through the North Atlantic bloc (NATO), created on the initiative of the American and English imperialists, as well as other related regional military blocs.
>
> *For the first time in peacetime a military coalition has been created which has a [permanent] staff, standardized weapons, and a system of training troops, [and] which works out general strategy and tactics at military maneuvers and exercise conducted on the territory of many states under the leadership of a united command.*
>
> In order to strengthen the economic underpinnings of NATO, US ruling circles are striving to unite their European partners in a 'common market.' Integration has become the banner of imperialist foreign policy. Its roots are

> in the economy and politics of modern imperialism. It reflects the process of the ever growing interweaving of the interests of monopoly capital, which due to its concentration, has outgrown national boundaries, and at the same time is striving to set up a new 'Holy Alliance' for the struggle against socialism, the workers, and national liberation movement.
>
> All these processes are connected with the further development of state monopoly capitalism. The monopolies are using state power not only to regulate the national economy in their interest. They are [also] creating supra-state and inter-state institutions in order to have a free hand with whole continents.
>
> But integration and supra-state institutions do not eliminate and do not weaken imperialist contradictions; they only give them another form and content. . . .[38]

The *shift* in the Soviet depiction[39] of the socialist camp and, by extension, the world communist movement, was equally profound. It was, in fact, commensurate with the historic developments which have rocked the socialist camp—the death

[38] AN IMEMO, *Mezhdunarodnye otnosheniia* . . . , Vol. 1, pp. xxiii-xxiv, italics added.

[39] Changes in Soviet formulations characterizing the socialist camp are inextricably bound up with political and manipulative considerations. In what follows, therefore, it should be stressed that no claim is being advanced that the symbolism utilized should necessarily be taken literally. The purpose is to emphasize the trend (and not the content) in overt formulations toward greater emphasis on state action and away from camp action. In 1960, however much Khrushchev may have doubted that the camp was monolithic, the camp still appeared sufficiently cohesive that maintenance of the public posture of monolithic unity may have made sense politically. By the end of the Khrushchev era, in all likelihood, it would not have occurred to any Soviet commentator to describe the camp as monolithic for any reason.

of Stalin, the Hungarian revolution, and the Sino-Soviet conflict. Soviet "socialist consciousness," however, distinctly lagged behind reality; it also lagged behind that of non-Soviet Marxists who were less circumspect about the implications of the Sino-Soviet conflict than the Russians were prior to 1963. So little explicit comment had in fact appeared in the Soviet press concerning the Sino-Soviet conflict prior to 1963, that as late as January 28, 1962 the usually knowledgeable Yugoslav Moscow correspondent Frane Barbieri could write in the Zagreb *Vjesnik*: "As yet no one knows anything openly in Moscow about the Soviet-Chinese clash. There are still many citizens who are not even aware of it unofficially"; significantly, the July 14, 1963 Soviet statement detailing the Soviet case in the dispute was not addressed to the Chinese but to "all party organizations, to all Communists of the Soviet Union." (As early as 1958 there had been intimations of major differences. By 1960 the careful reader of the Soviet press could discern that Mao was being bracketed with Genghis Khan and Herman Kahn.) Within the context of identifying the postwar actors, Soviet writings during Khrushchev's last years in power moved from a portrayal of the socialist camp as an international actor, monolithic, cohesive, unencumbered by antagonistic contradictions, to that of a much more loose-knit grouping of state actors. The socialist camp, lacking institutional ties and economic interdependence,[40] came to be described in 1963-64 as being at most a system of states sharing, but not necessarily linked by, a few common traits. Thus Khrushchev, at the Sixth Congress of the Socialist Unity Party of the D.D.R., declared, "the founda-

[40] As George Modelski points out, the socialist camp is characterized by a paucity of institutional ties involving all members of the camp. *The Communist International System*, passim.

tion of our unity is a common ideology—Marxism-Leninism, the principles of proletarian internationalism. The chief things that unite us are the community of class interests . . . , a correct Marxist-Leninist understanding of the international tasks of the working class and profound faith in . . . our great cause and the inevitability of the victory of socialism. . . ."[41]

The notion of a socialist commonwealth[42] was the first doctrinal evidence of a change in Soviet attitudes toward the communist camp. Initially formulated for transparent political reasons during the Hungarian crisis in 1956, the concept subsequently came to signify a series of institutional arrangements summarized by the phrase "the socialist division of labor." Implied in the concept of the "socialist division of labor"—and in the assiduous, albeit unsuccessful, efforts of the Soviet government to induce the socialist countries to participate in such a division of labor—was the recognition that the building of "socialism in one country" by *every* socialist country was incompatible with conditions under which the socialist camp could perform internationally as a single corporate actor. Consequently, after the Twenty-second C.P.S.U. Congress it be-

[41] *Pravda* and *Izvestiia*, January 17, 1963; trans. in *Current Digest*, Vol. xv, No. 3 (February 13, 1963), pp. 3-8 and No. 4 (February 20, 1963), pp. 13-20, at p. 19. The C.P.S.U. and the C.C.P. have each charged the other with violations of proletarian internationalism. See, e.g., the *Jen-min Jih-pao* editorial, August 22, 1963, attacking Soviet behavior with regard to the Sino-Indian border conflict of September 1959 as a "betrayal of proletarian internationalism." *Peking Review*, Vol. vi, No. 34 (August 30, 1963), p. 21 and B. Ponomaryov [Ponomarev], "Proletarian Internationalism—a Powerful Force in the Revolutionary Transformation of the World," *World Marxist Review*, Vol. vii, No. 8 (August 1964), p. 67.

[42] For Western analysis see Kurt L. London, "The 'Socialist Commonwealth of Nations': Pattern for Communist World Organization," *Orbis*, Vol. iii, No. 4 (Winter/1960), pp. 424-42 and Brzezinski, *The Soviet Bloc*, pp. 358-82.

came fashionable among Soviet observers to assert that "the idea of autarchy is alien to us," thus doubtless causing Stalin to turn over in his grave (newly located outside the Mausoleum).[43] For the camp to perform internationally as a single corporate actor required—with the dissipation of the informal control mechanisms—the artificial stimulation of cohesiveness through economic dependence and interdependence.

Dramatic evidence that the socialist camp no longer had the cohesiveness requisite for international actor capacity was provided by Khrushchev in his major speech of January 6, 1961. In that speech Khrushchev rejected the dictum that the socialist camp and the international communist movement must have a center. With a characteristic admixture of realism and wishful thinking he declared: "At present when there are a large group of socialist countries, each confronted with its own tasks, it is impossible to implement the leadership of the socialist countries and Communist parties from some kind of center. It is both impossible and unnecessary."[44]

In January 1961 the "dialectical unity" in Khrushchev's description of the camp had been one of realism and wishful thinking. Two years later, in January 1963, with Sino-Soviet

[43] For an illustration of such a statement see "XXII s"ezd KPSS i zadachi dal'neishego izucheniia problem mirovogo razvitiia" [The Twenty-second Congress of the CPSU and the Tasks of Further Studying the Problem of World Development], *Mirovaia ekonomika*, No. 3 (March 1962), p. 14.

A statement in 1967 to the same effect is contained in the thesis of the Institute of World Economy and International Relations, adopted on the occasion of the Fiftieth anniversary of the publication of Lenin's *Imperialism*. See "Uchenie V. I. Lenina ob imperializme i sovremennost' " [V. I. Lenin's Doctrine of Imperialism and Today], *Mirovaia ekonomika*, No. 5 (May 1967), p. 11.

[44] "Za novye pobedy mirovogo kommunisticheskogo dvizheniia" [For New Victories of the World Communist Movement], *Kommunist*, No. 1 (January 1961), p. 34.

relations at a new low after the Cuban missile crisis and the Sino-Indian border conflict, Khrushchev's speech at the Sixth Congress of the East German Socialist Unity Party bespoke a tolerance and, for our purposes, more significantly, a *recognition* of socialist camp diversity induced by realism and desperation. In that speech he acknowledged that there were 14 socialist countries, that is, that the socialist camp included China, Albania, Cuba, *and* Yugoslavia.[45] This being admitted, it is safe to assert that Soviet commentary had abandoned even the public posture of the camp as a single international actor. Khrushchev in moments of extreme optimism *might* have deluded himself that a socialist camp lacking "some kind of center" could act internationally. But most certainly, the notion of a socialist camp which includes these 14 states cannot by any standards, Bolshevik or otherwise, be reconciled with the postulate of a highly integrated system or the perception of a system as international actor.

Moreover, nationalism has been recognized as a force of immense influence in determining the behavior of some socialist states. The C.P.S.U. Program had warned that "nationalism is the basic political and ideological weapon used by international reaction and the remnants of the domestic forces against the unity of the socialist countries. . . . Nationalist prejudices . . . may be most prolonged, stubborn, fierce and insidious."[46] The warnings contained in the C.P.S.U. Program on the possible effects of nationalism, while sternly expressed, were however placid in comparison to Soviet statements in 1963-64. An article by Ponomarev, written in connection with the centenary of the First International, well illustrates the

[45] *Pravda*, January 17, 1963.

[46] Trans. in *Current Digest*, Vol. XIII, No. 45 (December 6, 1961), p. 7.

tone of these latter statements. Ponomarev discerned "traces of *abnormal, ugly relations*" between "nations born of capitalism" [which] remain for some time after the socialist revolution," and declared that "recent experience [shows] . . . that not all the Communist parties in power have proved capable of resisting nationalistic pressures. . . ." Specifically, he continued, a "petty-bourgeois wave . . . has engulfed the CPC leadership [which] has brought to the surface the froth and foam of nationalism and great-power chauvinism."[47]

A third facet of the change in Soviet symbolism was related to the prevention of general war. In 1963-64 much greater emphasis (in large part, for self-serving reasons) was placed on the Soviet Union, rather than the socialist camp or the masses, as the actor which deterred the imperialists from unleashing a third world war.[48] This change in symbolism, consonant with Khrushchev's "fetishization"[49] of modern weaponry, seemed to indicate less obfuscation in Soviet commentary than hereto-

[47] Ponomarev, "Proletarian Internationalism . . . ," p. 66, italics added. Note, also, the air of resignation in the statement by Todor Zhivkov, one of the few non-Soviet Communists who in 1963-64 could still be regarded as a Khrushchev spokesman: "Nationalism and other inimical trends will continue to exert pressure on the parties and to engender non-Marxist views. This is beyond doubt. . . . *The virus of nationalism will be with us for a long time.*" Zhivkov, "Building Communism," *World Marxist Review*, Vol. VI, No. 1 (January 1963), p. 5, italics added.

[48] See Ponomarev, "Proletarian Internationalism . . . ," p. 67; I. Glagolev and V. Larionov, "Soviet Defence Might and Peaceful Coexistence," *International Affairs*, No. 11 (November 1963), pp. 27-33; and N. Talensky [Talenskii], "Anti-Missile Systems and Disarmament," *International Affairs*, No. 10 (October 1964), p. 18.

[49] For an attack on the obsession with nuclear weapons by a major Soviet military figure, A. N. Lagovskii, published four months *after* Khrushchev's major speech on Soviet military strategy of January 14, 1960, see the introduction to the Russian translation of Klaus Knorr's *The War Potential of Nations, Voennyi potentsial gosudarstv*, p. 13.

fore generally apparent between the two arenas, the "world historical process" and international politics. If such was the case, the heuristic capacity of the atomic bomb in combination with other, primarily tactical, considerations may have contributed to greater clarity of Soviet description and greater separation of the ideological from the international-political realm.

In 1964 Khrushchev for the first time publicly recognized that *détente,* with its attendant diminution in the sensed immediacy of external threat, had produced divisiveness in the socialist camp, as well as in the Western one. Interestingly, the argument he developed in recognizing this fact paralleled that of Arnold Wolfers in his essay "The Pole of Power and the Pole of Compulsion," that the variability in behavior of corporate actors increased as they move away from "the pole of compulsion":

> When the imperialists waged an open attack against the socialist countries, resorting to blunt military threats, everyone could see and understand that the close solidarity of the socialist forces was necessary to defend the world socialist system against the encroachments of the imperialists.
>
> All of us, I daresay, have been in the woods during a thunderstorm, when people involuntarily huddle together and seek refuge from the rain under the same shelter. But when the clouds blow away, the sun comes out and people begin to disperse over the meadows. (*Amused stir in the hall, applause.*)
>
> Something like this is happening in political life. When imperialism tried to grab us by the throat, we rallied more closely to rebuff it; but now that we have warded off the

immediate threat of war, some have begun to think that the bonds of friendship can be relaxed. Moreover, the imperialists, striving to intensify such tendencies, are conducting a rather cunning policy, bringing economic weapons to bear as well.[50]

In more subtle ways, also, changes in symbolism, presumably reflecting attitudinal changes, were to be detected. No longer were *stroi* and *sistema* used interchangeably; henceforth it was only the neutral *sistema,* which could be used to characterize any system no matter how diffuse. By February 1961[51] the degree of socialist-camp cohesion so little corresponded to conventional Leninist-Stalinist norms for relations among communist states and parties that after that date the phrase, "monolithic unity," *qua* description, was abandoned in Soviet references to the camp. At the Twenty-second C.P.S.U. Congress in October 1961 Khrushchev, in his concluding remarks,

[50] *Pravda,* April 8, 1964, trans. in *Current Digest,* Vol. XVI, No. 15 (May 6, 1964), p. 10.

[51] At this juncture, i.e., shortly after Khrushchev's "state of the union" speech ("Za novye pobedy . . ."), the term "monolithic unity" was mentioned in reference to the camp in a flurry of articles and then dropped out of Soviet commentary. See the editorial "Vydaiushchiesia dokumenty sovremennosti" [Signal Documents of Our Time], *Voprosy istorii,* No. 2 (February 1961), p. 9 and A. Arzumanian, "Novyi etap obshchego krizisa kapitalizma" [New Stage in the General Crisis of Capitalism], *Mirovaia ekonomika,* No. 2 (February 1961), p. 18.

Cf. also the lead articles in *Kommunist* and *International Affairs* stressing the importance of unity without specifically employing the word monolithic; Sh. Sanakoyev [Sanakoev], "The Decisive Factor in World Development," *International Affairs,* No. 2 (February 1961), pp. 3-10; and M. Mitin, "Nerushimoe edinstvo sotsialisticheskikh stran" [The Indissoluble Unity of the Socialist Countries], *Kommunist,* No. 2 (January 1961), pp. 11-22.

used the term "monolithic solidarity," a phrase which contrasted conspicuously with the alleged "monolithic unity"[52] of the C.P.S.U. *After* 1961 "monolithic" appears to have been confined to exhortative statements. Similarly, after 1961, even "unity" and "solidarity" were rarely used descriptively, but were generally accompanied by exhortations such as "strengthen" and "consolidate."

THE REMOVAL of Nikita Khrushchev has not thus far resulted in any reversal of the trend toward giving greater emphasis to states as the major effective international agents. If anything, the available evidence suggests that the trend has intensified. The dominant, Brezhnev-Kosygin faction—Kosygin probably more than others—in the (now again since 1966) Politburo has been generally preoccupied with day-to-day tasks. This has been reflected in the general appraisal of the world scene. Whereas the analysis in Khrushchev's major speeches was generally placed in a developmental context, Kosygin and Brezhnev's major pronouncements have been conspicuous for their inattention to the nature of the epoch. Here Brezhnev's treatment of world developments in his report to the Twenty-third Congress is particularly suggestive.[53] His statement describes "the international position of the U.S.S.R." and "the foreign policy activity of the C.P.S.U." and is little more than a charting of the changes in the global political climate since the 1961 Twenty-second Congress. As a result, the confusion between the ontological realm of the world historical process and the existential arena of world politics has been at a mini-

[52] Khrushchev, *Concluding Remarks to the Twenty-second Congress of the CPSU* on October 27, 1961, trans. in *Current Digest*, Vol. XIII, No. 46 (December 13, 1961), pp. 23, 27.

[53] *Materialy XXIII s"ezda KPSS* [Materials of the Twenty-third CPSU Congress] (Moscow: Politizdat, 1966).

mum; the world historical process seems to be of decreasing relevance in the analysis of world politics. "Ultimate victory on a world scale," it is affirmed, "belongs to Socialism as the most progressive social system, which ensures the fullest development of the productive forces and their most effective use for the benefit of the whole of society. The operative word," however, it is stressed, "is *ultimate*. Meanwhile, it is the ups and downs of the struggle that in the main constitute the content of international affairs."[54] In other ways, too, the emphasis on the state and the state system has been shown. Although the matter was still a subject of dispute,[55] by late 1966 some Soviet specialists were willing and able to state the obvious about the world socialist system: that it was a world system of states—not an integrated socio-economic system—and to draw the consequent conclusions—that it was not an international actor. A detailed exposition of this argument was developed in an article by A. Butenko[56] and published in *Mirovaia ekonomika*'s forum for economists and international relations specialists. Its very title, "Concerning the Laws of Development of Socialism as a Social System and as a World System," suggests the clear separation in Butenko's mind between socialism as a social system and as a world system of states. Moreover, in his article, Butenko makes all the major points. It is incorrect, he argues, to assert that a "single eco-

[54] Sh. Sanakoyev [Sanakoev], "The World Socialist System and the Future of Mankind," *International Affairs*, No. 10 (October 1966), p. 62, italics in original.

[55] The differences of view among Soviet specialists are briefly described in "Problemy razvitiia mirovoi sotsialisticheskoi sistemy" [Problems of the Development of the World Socialist System], *Vestnik*, No. 11 (November 1966), pp. 86-89.

[56] A. Butenko, "O zakonomernostiakh razvitiia sotsializma kak obshchestvennogo stroia i kak mirovoi sistemy," *Mirovaia ekonomika*, No. 11 (November 1966), pp. 84-91.

nomic base" underlies the world system of socialism. It is, furthermore, "the laws of development of interaction among countries" that "operate" within the world socialist system, and not those "between people." "The key to [understanding] . . . the laws of development of the world socialism organized into states," he continues, "is a scientific approach to its contemporary *structure*." Adopting such a perspective—consonant (as we have seen) with the trend in the last years of the Khrushchev years—he declared that "the world system of socialism is not at all . . . a single country, a single economy, a single socio-economic organism . . . [administered] from a single center. . . . Its actual structure is complex and contradictory inasmuch as the world system of socialism is an international union of national and multi-national, self-sufficient, socialist states having their own territory, balanced economy, and separate political organization." There were indications, moreover, that Soviet observers—projecting perhaps—were increasingly ignoring the role of trans-national ties in their interpretation of the behavior of the major international actors other than the Soviet Union. In the early 1960s, under Khrushchev, the greatest attention was directed toward cultivating relations with the reasonable forces of the ruling circles within the major Western powers, especially the United States. The propensity on the part of most Soviet observers—one finding a counterpart in Soviet behavior—since 1965 by contrast has been to analyze intra-camp capitalist contradictions with a view to playing the lesser capitalist powers off against the United States.[57] In its policy prescriptions concerning the proper handling of contradictions, such an appraisal

[57] Vernon V. Aspaturian, "Foreign Policy Perspectives in the Sixties," in Alexander Dallin and Thomas B. Larson, eds., *Soviet Politics Since Khrushchev* (Englewood Cliffs, N.J.: Prentice-Hall, 1968), pp. 129-62.

was more orthodox than the Khrushchevian men of reason/madmen dichotomy. At the same time, it seems to have been prompted by an assumption that, in determining the behavior of the decision-makers acting in the name of the state, considerations of national interest took priority, a view strikingly similar to the realist school. The trend of Soviet commentary in 1965-67 seems increasingly to have been to appraise American and Communist Chinese foreign policy moves in terms of rather cynical national interests, in which calculations of trans-national class ties played little part.[58] Indeed, in 1965-67 Soviet specialists usually gave Hans Morgenthau's concept of national interest a generally sympathetic reception, faulting him only for his failure to bear in mind the internal class basis of politics.[59]

By October 1967, then, 50 years after the Bolshevik seizure of power, it appeared that from the Soviet perspective states had become the main international actors. Neither of the two camps (the chief rivals of the state for paramountcy) was thought of as sufficiently cohesive to act as a single corporate actor. *Stroi,* with its connotations of a highly integrated system, was not applied to either camp; the emphasis was put on the camps as systems of states, rather than as social systems. Soviet observers under Khrushchev, as well as during the years since his ouster, have continued Stalin's emphasis on state power and state actor capability. At the same time, they gradually extricated themselves from the Stalinist disposition simultaneously to see in both camps, states and social systems as main actors. This they did in large part as a result of ex-

[58] See below, pp. 240-41.

[59] According to Soviet scholars, one of the most credible pieces of Soviet international relations scholarship is A. Obukhov's as yet unpublished study of Hans Morgenthau and the realist school.

periencing developments within what used to be called the Soviet bloc. These developments stemmed from a contradiction inherent in Stalinism as a state system. Once the informal control mechanisms became ineffective, there was little to prevent the preeminence of state action in a bloc whose constituent members (having dutifully mimicked Soviet experience) were autarchic impermeable units. The collapse of Stalinist control patterns may be interpreted as having posed for Soviet commentators two options in their analysis of the actors in international relations. Since the Stalinist social and political system—an institutionalized expression of the transfer of class imagery to international relations—was no longer viable, the alternatives were either to treat "masses" or states as primary international actors.[60] In view of the level of development, power, and international status of the Soviet Union, it is understandable that Soviet analysts directed their focus increasingly on states.

Lesser Corporate Actors

It is not my intention in this section to undertake a complete inventory of actors or even categories of actors. Such a task would be superfluous: the Soviet preoccupation with the part played by certain subnational actors, for instance, is well known. The attention Soviet writers have paid to the allegedly direct actions (as contrasted with actions taken by a state in response to the pressures of a subgroup) of American oil companies, for example, or for that matter, "liberation fronts," is well established and scarcely warrants extensive documentation. It is also a commonplace, but an important one to bear in mind, that "peoples," "nations," and "states" have had dis-

[60] I. Lemin, "Marks i voprosy vneshnei politiki" [Marx and Foreign Policy], *Mirovaia ekonomika*, No. 5 (May 1958), p. 31.

tinct connotations for those schooled in Marxism-Leninism—at least until 1966 when contributors to *Voprosy istorii* began to reappraise the Stalinist concept of the nation.[61] Consequently Soviet commentators have been less inclined to make the ready equation of nation and state,[62] than are Western observers accustomed to a one-nation, one-state international norm, although there is some indication that Soviet observers have in practice also been given to Europo-centrism.[63]

More interesting material is to be found in the Soviet analysis of the place of international, supra-national, and trans-national actors.

The international organization that has attracted greatest attention among Soviet writers is the United Nations. Soviet commentary by elite members and their foreign policy spokesmen has consistently regarded the United Nations as an instrument, although, depending largely on whether at a given time the U.N. was construed as a tool of American imperialism or as something to be exploited by the "peace" forces, Soviet attitudes toward the U.N. have fluctuated from positive to negative evaluations of its activities. Throughout its existence, moreover, the U.N. has been viewed as a voluntary organization of independent states which best fulfills its purposes when it functions as a "broad forum." In

[61] See above, p. 71.

[62] Klaus Knorr's title, *The War Potential of Nations*, was properly translated as *Voennyi potentsial gosudarstv*.

[63] But an article by K. Ivanov ("Present-day Colonialism and International Relations," *International Affairs*, No. 9 [September 1962], p. 41) strongly suggests that in practice Soviet observers have also been guilty of Europo-centrism: "Thus, the type of 'national state' which best suited the economic interests of developing capitalism was actually a curious *exception* when capitalism was at its peak . . . in the late 18th century and the first half of the 19th century . . . ," italics in original.

the Soviet appraisal, it is, as the title of a 1963 article in *International Affairs* suggests, a rostrum, a forum, and an arena.[64] Constant, too, has been the tendency to downplay the importance of the United Nations, even when it has played a specific role. Major authoritative pronouncements virtually ignore it. It is not mentioned in the 1960 Statement of the Eighty-one Communist Parties or the Party Program adopted at the Twenty-second C.P.S.U. Congress. The single reference to the United Nations in the second edition (1962) of *Fundamentals of Marxism-Leninism* [*Osnovy Marksizma-Leninizma*] represented an increase over the first edition, in which no mention of the U.N. appears. Similarly, in what is probably the nearest counterpart to the *Osnovy* to have appeared since Khrushchev's removal, the five-volume *Socialism and Communism*, the volume which treats *The Construction of Communism and the World Revolutionary Process* finds occasion to mention the U.N. three times in more than 500 pages.[65] Soviet observers, in brief, have persistently regarded the United Nations as largely form, of little substance, an organization constituted (rightly, from the vantage point of Soviet foreign policy) so that it is structurally incapable of action against a superpower or one of its allies.

Thus Soviet description under Khrushchev and in the years 1964-67 has consistently characterized the Korean War as an American action waged "under the flag of the U.N." and utilizing its name—"behind the fig leaf of the U.N." as the Chinese Communists are wont to put it.[66]

[64] M. Lvov [L'vov], "U.N.: Rostrum, Forum, Arena," *International Affairs*, No. 11 (November 1963), pp. 10-15.

[65] AN IMEMO, *Stroitel'stvo kommunizma i mirovoi revoliutsionnyi protsess* [The Construction of Communism and the World Revolutionary Process] (Moscow: Izdatel'stvo "Nauka," 1966).

[66] E.g., *Diplomaticheskii slovar'*, Vol. I, pp. 12-14, Vol. II, p. 444;

In this instance, the Soviet predisposition to minimize the U.N.'s role was well-founded. It is obviously more precise to treat Korea as an exercise in American foreign policy than as a United Nations police action. The Congo crisis was another matter entirely. It will be recalled that in the early days of the Congo crisis, the Soviet Union, having committed itself to supporting the aspirations of the African countries, found itself obliged to support the creation of a U.N. Congo force (O.N.U.F.). Although O.N.U.F. was "an international armed force precisely of the sort that the U.S.S.R. had heretofore opposed,"[67] the Soviet leadership, given its optimistic evaluation of the world distribution of power and taking into consideration the Charter-imposed limits on the U.N., probably calculated that formation of O.N.U.F. entailed only minimal risk of unintended consequences. Apparently it did not occur to Soviet foreign policy-makers that, even if the government of a permanent member, possessed of sober second thoughts, were to withdraw support, the Secretary-General might be able to continue to implement the mandate of the Security Council. When, in fact, the Secretary-General did exactly this, the Soviet Union found itself hoist by its own petard. O.N.U.F. had become a barrier to the "forward movement of history." The United Nations, rather than serving to legitimize American action, was itself an international actor.

B. I. Bukharov, *Politika SShA v otnoshenii Kitaiskoi Narodnoi Respubliki (1949-1953gg.)* [U.S. Policy with the Chinese People's Republic (1949-1953)] (Moscow: Izdatel'stvo AN SSSR, 1958), pp. 47-74; V. K. Sobakin, *Kollektivnaia bezopasnost'* . . . , pp. 252-60; and Institut Mirovykh Otnoshenii, *Mirnoe sosushchestvovanie*, p. 89; AN IMEMO, *Stroitel'stvo kommunizma* . . . , p. 225.

[67] Alexander Dallin, *The Soviet Union at the United Nations: An Inquiry into Soviet Motives and Objectives* (New York: Praeger, 1962), p. 141.

By his action, Hammarskjold (like President Eisenhower at the time of the U-2 incident) provided the Monday-morning quarterbacks in the international communist movement with an opportunity to ridicule Soviet signal-calling. The Chinese quickly took advantage of it. "How can anybody believe that the U.N., which still remains under United States control, will stand for justice and will help the struggle against colonialism?"[68] wondered *Jen-min Jih-pao* at the time. "In the Congo as in Korea the United Nations Forces Are a Weapon of American Imperialism," another article later headlined.[69] As late as 1963 the Chinese were still bemoaning "the bitter lessons of the Congo":

> When the United Nations Security Council unanimously adopted its resolution for international intervention in the Congo, there were some people in the international communist movement who believed this to be a shining example of the international co-operation. They believed that colonialism could be wiped out through the intervention of the U.N., which would enable the Congolese people to obtain their freedom and independence. But what was the outcome? . . . We ask those who are clamouring for peaceful coexistence between the oppressed nations and peoples, on the one hand, and the imperialists and colonialists, on the other, and for 'joint intervention' in the underdeveloped areas: Have you forgotten the tragic lesson of the Congo incident?[70]

[68] *Jen-min Jih-pao*, August 22, 1960, cited in Dallin, *Soviet Union at the United Nations*, p. 169.

[69] *Jen-min Jih-pao*, February 16, 1961, cited in Dallin, *Soviet Union at the United Nations*, p. 240.

[70] "The Differences Between Comrade Togliatti and Us," *Peking Review*, Vol. VI, No. 1 (January 4, 1963), p. 16.

Thus challenged, Soviet foreign policy articulators were compelled to explain the Congo developments. Interestingly, both Soviet commentary and behavior subsequent to the Congo crisis revealed that, at least in a sense relevant to a discussion about the actors in international politics, Soviet commentators had evaluated the implications of the U.N.'s Congo role more profoundly than the Chinese. The Chinese used the incident to reiterate their contention that an affirmative answer was in order to the question, "Was the U.N. an American instrumentality?" The Soviet preoccupation was as much with the manifest capacity of the U.N. to act internationally as with the degree of U.S. influence in the U.N. For this unanticipated development did not gibe with traditional Soviet notions about the constitutent elements of international power. How could "international political organizations—being phenomena of the super-structure"[71]—act independently of the base, much less impinge on developments taking place in the base? One explanation was the conspiracy theory, the traditional, almost visceral, response of Leninists which cushions the impact of reality on ideology by providing a simplistic and satisfying key to phenomena that fail to correspond to their expectations. Ralph Bunche and Andrew Cordier were obviously being used by the State Department; the Secretariat was virtually a N.A.T.O. operation; the Secretary-General, the representative of the United States.[72]

[71] "Reshit' problemy reorganizatsii OON" [Resolve the Problem of the Reorganization of the U.N.], *Kommunist*, No. 4 (March 1961), p. 24.

[72] See Khrushchev's U.N. speech of September 23, 1960. Khrushchev, *O vneshnei politike Sovetskogo Soiuza* [On the Foreign Policy of the Soviet Union] (Moscow: Gospolitizdat, 1961), Vol. II, pp. 322-23, and his speech of October 20, 1960, in Moscow, trans. in *Current Digest*, Vol. XII, No. 42 (November 16, 1960), pp. 3-14.

However, despite the conspiracy theory, Soviet accounts did not analyze the Congo events in the same manner as the Korean events. Soviet observations revealed an assumption that the role of the U.N. in the Congo action was *substantive.* Whereas, in the depiction of the Korean War, the U.N. was seen as merely legitimating U.S. policy, Soviet commentary on the behavior of the Secretariat or the Secretary-General personally in the Congo crisis indicated that—after the fact—Soviet observers, notwithstanding their predispositions to the contrary, acknowledged that the United Nations had been an international actor in the Congo. Among the phrases encountered in Soviet accounts characterizing the behavior of the Secretariat or the Secretary-General, are "approaches," "sided," "adopted a position," "acting," and, even, "*in essence killed.*" Equally indicative was the observation of V. Poliakov which implicitly recognized that the U.N. acted independently. At least in the early days of the crisis, Poliakov contended,

> no one . . . ever denied that on more than one occasion Hammarskjold did come out with solemn declarations about his "willingness" to help the Congo without delay. But what was the net result? Instead of helping the lawful Congolese Government beat off Belgian aggression, the "U.N. Force" Command on Hammarskjold's orders, from the very start prevented the Government from exercising its sovereign rights and intervened in the internal affairs of the young African Republic. Very soon the "U.N. Force" itself became an instrument of the aggressors.[73]

[73] V. Polyakov [Poliakov], "Strange Objectivity," *International Affairs,* No. 6 (June 1963), p. 90. The article purports to be a review of Herbert Nicholas' *The United Nations as a Political Organization.* The passage should be compared with the Chinese view expressed in "The Differences Between Comrade Togliatti and Us," p. 16.

Finally, it is revealing that, even discounting the rhetoric, in one Soviet account, the Secretary-General was depicted as almost singlehandedly manning the dikes against the flow of history: "It is perfectly obvious that [Kasavubu, Ileo, and Mobutu] would not withstand for a day the tide of events, had they not received support from U.N. Secretary-General Hammarskjold and several of his aides."[74]

Indeed, the Congo events apparently prompted the Soviet leadership to reappraise the place allotted the U.N. internationally and to recognize that it had to be treated as having manifested a potential for action contrary to Soviet interests. It was with the Congo in mind that Khrushchev proposed to replace the Secretary-General with a *troika* and to alter radically the composition of the Secretariat to assure that "the activity of the U.N. executive will not be to the detriment of any of these [three] groups of states in the world."[75]

Whether in Soviet calculations the U.N. will ever again demonstrate a capacity to act independently, at least against Soviet interests, is another matter. From Soviet commentary it appears that whereas in the early sixties Soviet observers were fearful that unless steps were taken the U.N. might again act in opposition to Soviet interest, Soviet observers in the mid-sixties no longer regard such a prospect as a serious possibility.[76] They are probably correct in this judgment, largely because of the changed composition of the General Assembly

[74] L. Bagramov et al., "Tekushchie problemy mirovoi politiki—mezhdunarodnyi obzor (iiul' 1960g.-ianvar' 1961g.)" [Current Problems of World Politics—an International Review (July 1960-January 1961)], *Mirovaia ekonomika*, No. 1 (January 1961), p. 14.

[75] Khrushchev, *O vneshnei politike Sovetskogo Soiuza*, p. 329.

[76] See especially AN SSSR, Institut Istorii, *Sovetskii Soiuz v Organizatsii Ob"edinennykh Natsii* [The Soviet Union in the United Nations] (Moscow: Izdatel'stvo "Nauka," 1965), passim.

and partly as a result of Soviet actions to prevent a recurrence of the conditions which made the United Nations action in the Congo possible. To the extent therefore that the likelihood of the U.N. acting independently has decreased as a result of Soviet pressure, Soviet practice had the effect of restoring the validity of the traditional Soviet calculus. At the same time, the analytical response to the Congo events demonstrated that by the early sixties Soviet observers had escaped sufficiently from the Stalinist penchant for viewing politics in military terms[77] that they were able to realize that under certain circumstances nonstate, nonclass organizations—indeed even superstructural phenomena—could act internationally.

With reservations to be noted, a similar development transpired with respect to a major *trans-national* corporate entity as well—the Vatican. Much has been made of the attention (especially apparent since 1961) devoted to the Vatican in the Soviet press and by the Soviet government. Western observers found it fashionable to observe that Khrushchev by his behavior showed that he would answer "some"[78] or "several" to the apt, if apocryphal, question ascribed to Stalin: "The Pope, how many divisions does he have?"

The increased appreciation of the Vatican's capability to exert influence in the international arena might better be described as evidence that Khrushchev, had he been asked the above question, would have responded, "None—but does that necessarily matter?" In the Khrushchevian perspective, the absence of one or more of the factors—"material resources, manpower, and organization"[79]—that Stalin thought engendered

[77] *Sino-Soviet Conflict*, pp. 225-35.

[78] E.g., Miklos Veto, "Kremlin and Vatican," *Survey*, No. 48 (July 1963), p. 171.

[79] Dallin, *Soviet Union at the United Nations*, p. 35.

power internationally, did not preclude the Catholic Church from being an international actor. There is no evidence in the Soviet specialized press or the behavior of the post-Khrushchevian ruling group indicating any change of appraisal in this regard during the three years after Khrushchev's ouster.[80]

Of course there were readily apparent tactical motives for Moscow's interest in the Vatican—associated with the doctrines of peaceful coexistence and peaceful accession to power—which must be kept in mind. But it is significant that these tactical motives presuppose an appreciation of the Pope's ability to influence the internal and foreign policies of states. As *International Affairs* noted in 1963, "The Vatican is one of the smallest states in the world: it has a territory of only 44 hectares and a population of about 1,000. But its place in world politics is not determined by these data, but by the fact that it is the international centre of the Catholic Church."[81]

We would be giving Soviet writers more credit than they deserve if we did not note a persisting ambivalence toward the international-actor capability of the Vatican. One Soviet author, N. A. Koval'skii, for instance, having concluded that "the Catholic Church is a significant force," adds immediately "which imperialism uses in the struggle against all [that is] advanced and progressive."[82] If the latter part of this observa-

[80] See, for instance, the treatment in AN IMEMO, *Mezhdunarodnye otnosheniia posle vtoroi mirovoi voiny*, Vol. III (Moscow: Politizdat, 1965), pp. 460, 477.

[81] "How the Vatican is Run," *International Affairs*, No. 3 (March 1963), p. 114.

[82] "Vatikan nakanune Vselenskogo sobora" [The Vatican on the Eve of the Ecumenical Council], *Mirovaia ekonomika*, No. 9 (September 1962), p. 34. See also p. 43. For a longer study by the same author, see his significantly titled *Vatikan i mirovaia politika: Organizatsiia*

tion could be dismissed as mere rhetoric, we could speak more enthusiastically about the intuitive elegance of the Soviet perception of the international actors in the world arena. We cannot, however: Soviet writers have persisted in describing the Vatican as *both* instrument *and* actor. The old pejoratives may have been muted, but the overdeterministic tendency remains: to describe entities uncontrolled by Moscow as imperialist instruments. The assertion that Soviet analysts in the sixties acknowledged the capability of the Vatican to act internationally needs, therefore, to be qualified by the caution that simultaneously and contradictorily—as with the U.N. —the habitual disposition to anticipate control from a single center continued. Only an analysis of both Soviet sources and behavior permits such stress on the changing Soviet evaluation of the autonomous acting capacity of a trans-national entity like the Vatican.

With certain supra-national corporate entities the issue was much less problematical. In the case of economic organizations like the European Common Market, the significance ascribed to them was striking, particularly when compared with Lenin's view expressed in *A United States of Europe?* There Lenin merely acknowledged that "Of course, *temporary* agreements between capitalists and between powers are possible."[83] After several years of vigorous debate within the

---

vneshnepoliticheskoi deatel'nosti katolicheskogo klerikalizma [The Vatican and World Politics: The Organization of the Foreign Policy Activities of Catholic Clericalism] (Moscow: Izdatel'stvo IMO, 1964).

[83] *Sochineniia* [Works], 4th edn. (Moscow: Gospolitizdat, 1952), Vol. XXI, p. 310, italics in original. See also Brzezinski, "Russia and Europe," *Foreign Affairs*, Vol. XLII, No. 3 (April 1964), pp. 428-44; Marshall Shulman, "Bloc Reaction to the Common Market," *Problems of Communism*, Vol. XII, No. 5 (September-October 1963), pp. 47-54; and Shulman, "The Communist States and Western Integration," *International Organization*, Vol. XVII, No. 3 (Summer 1963), pp. 649-62.

Soviet specialist press,[84] perhaps within the Soviet ruling group, and certainly in the world communist movement,[85] Soviet commentary in the last years of Khrushchev's years in power showed an awareness of the international-actor capability of capitalist supra-national economic entities. "The development of state monopoly capitalism," it was concluded, "has changed the very 'machinery' of inter-state economic, political and diplomatic relations. In these [relations] agreements and deals enacted through inter-state institutions acquire ever growing weight."[86] Consequently, in Sovetov's words, "The present-day inter-imperialist struggle for markets, spheres of influence and capital investment, etc., is frequently taking the form not of a struggle between separate imperialist states, but of one between opposing imperialist economic blocs."[87] In 1962 the Institute of World Economy

[84] The debate has been particularly evident in the pages of *Mirovaia ekonomika.* Of special interest were the major appraisals in 1959 and 1962 of Common Market activities. For 1959 see the papers presented at the scientific conference, " 'Obshchii rynok' i ego rol' v ekonomike i politike sovremennogo imperializma" ['The Common Market' and its Role in the Economy and Politics of Contemporary Imperialism], No. 7 (July) pp. 108ff; No. 8 (August), pp. 104ff.; No. 9 (September), pp. 86ff.; No. 10 (October), pp. 73ff. For 1962 over half the articles in issues Nos. 8, 9, 10, 11, and 12 would need to be consulted.

[85] The West European Communists have been particularly active in educating the socialist camp comrades about the significance of the Common Market.

[86] AN IMEMO, *Mezhdunarodnye otnosheniia . . .* , Vol. 1, pp. xxiv-xxv.

[87] "Contradictions in the Western Bloc," *International Affairs*, No. 6 (June 1963), p. 7. In the same article, however, Sovetov declared:

"If what has been said [by Hallstein] is put into Marxist language, we arrive at almost the same conclusion as that drawn from the analysis given in Marxist literature before the present crisis became apparent. The clearest and most obvious cause of the present quarrel in the

and International Relations characterized the most developed of these, the Common Market, as "a new phenomenon in the development of modern capitalism,"[88] and warned that "Schemes for establishing in one form or another a 'supra-state' political association of the 'Common Market' countries with corresponding 'supra-national' agencies pose a great danger for the democratic rights of the working people, for the vital interests of the peoples of Western Europe. . . . The plans for political 'integration' are a serious threat to the independent national existence of the peoples of Western Europe."[89]

Five years later, in another set of theses,[90] the institute was still characterizing the Common Market in essentially similar terms. The Common Market, the institute declared, was one of several "new interstate forms of union" which, it acknowledged implicitly, were more than temporary alliances. Recent events, the institute contended, had "fully confirmed" Lenin's "conclusion concerning the impossibility of a union of the imperialisms of the whole world." Moreover, the 1967 theses have abandoned the practice, universal under Khrushchev, of

---

imperialist bloc is the change in the relation of forces in the *countries and inter-state groupings* belonging to that bloc."

Ibid., italics added. The term "groupings" conveys a considerably less cohesive entity than does "bloc." One wonders whether the difference in terminology is indicative of confusion, murky analysis, or ambivalence.

[88] AN IMEMO, "Ob imperialisticheskoi 'integratsii' v zapadnoi Evrope ('Obschii rynok')" [Concerning Imperialist 'Integration' in Western Europe (The 'Common Market')], supplement to *Mirovaia ekonomika*, No. 9 (September 1962), p. 4. See also *Pravda*, August 26, 1962; trans. in *Current Digest*, Vol. xiv, No. 34 (September 19, 1962), pp. 9-16.

[89] AN IMEMO, "Ob imperialisticheskoi . . . ," pp. 7-8.

[90] "Uchenie V. I. Lenina ob imperializme i sovremennost'" [V. I. Lenin's Doctrine of Imperialism and Today], *Mirovaia ekonomika*, No. 5 (May 1967), pp. 13-14.

referring to the Common Market in quotation marks,[91] a symbolic change suggesting that in the mid-sixties Soviet observers have finally absorbed the blandishments of the West European communists concerning the significance of the Common Market, and have come round to the view expressed by a Belgian communist, P. Joye, in 1962: "The Common Market is a reality," "with which we have to reckon, a reality which, in a way, is irreversible. The Common Market, it is true, may be replaced by something else, but in no circumstances will this 'something else' be a return to the situation which existed prior to 1958."[92]

Hence nonstate *institutions*, along with states, acquired new status in the Soviet international relations appraisal. Several entities manifesting rather strange traits when measured by traditional Soviet notions of power were treated as having a capacity to act internationally. Moreover, the place ascribed to such nonstate organizations as the United Nations, the Vatican, and the European Common Market seemed to reinforce a conclusion arrived at earlier in connection with the appraisal of the actor capacity of states: that in determining the international actors, Soviet commentary accorded appreciable significance to the institutional nexus. This more general development was reflective of a shift in Soviet appraisal away from a frame of reference that was highly ideological in jargon and content, to a more analytical and international-political one, which, while having ideological overtones, was neverthe-

[91] This development was adumbrated in a lead article by A. M. Rumiantsev, "Reshaiushchii faktor razvitiia chelovecheskogo obshchestva" [Decisive Factor in the Development of Human Society], *Mirovaia ekonomika*, No. 1 (January 1966), p. 6.

[92] Joye's statement was made at a symposium on "Problems of Modern Capitalism" held in Moscow from August 27 to September 3, 1962. *World Marxist Review*, No. 12 (December 1962), p. 58.

less "divorced from reality." The shift in appraisal brought Soviet actor perspectives closer to the Western post-billiard-ball consensus by focusing primarily on states and systems of states (and by assuming that the cohesiveness of state systems was a function, to a considerable degree, of intersystem tension) in a political universe populated by many types of actors.

At no time, however, was there more than a minimum of evidence to suggest that in Soviet analysis identification of the actors was sufficient for an assessment of actor behavior or the patterns of interaction among corporate entities. Soviet generalizations about the main actors remained merely the first in an extensive series of answers to questions about international relations. Unlike the billiard-ball model, these generalizations never constituted in themselves a general theory of international politics providing an answer to a single central question—how do states behave? While a gradual separation of the realm of the world historical process and the arena of world politics was to be discerned, the traditional Soviet preoccupation with class struggle and, more generally, the internal dynamics underlying foreign policy continued to obtain. Consequently, such a development was precluded. As in the Western post-billiard-ball perspective, therefore, the task of identifying those entities constituting, in Soviet perspective, the main actors was merely a preliminary step in the elaboration of Soviet international relations perspectives.

Chapter Four: The Hierarchy

IN WESTERN international relations literature we are accustomed to distinguishing five gradations of corporate actors in the postwar international order. Those in the first four have generally been designated world powers (or superpowers),[1] great powers, middle powers, and small powers. At the bottom is a fifth category of politically ineffectual corporate entities usually lacking formally independent status; these may be called "null" powers. As the nomenclature suggests,[2] differences in terms of power are considered the major standard for distinguishing between what Samuel Grafton has called the "elephants" and "squirrels"[3] in the international order.

Elephant status is often thought of as something acquired solely by virtue of power.[4] The use of such a criterion raises troublesome questions relating to the accuracy of power as an analytical tool. The political scientist finds himself at a great disadvantage vis-à-vis his zoologist counterpart because power has no common denominator: in what units is it to be

[1] A.F.K. Organski, *World Politics*, pp. 326-33, argues that there must be a single "dominant nation" in a given international order. Cf. also George Modelski's monograph, *The Communist International System*, for speculation about an international order of the future in which the Soviet Union would be the dominant power.

[2] William T. R. Fox, *The Super-powers* (New York: Harcourt, Brace, and Co., 1944), p. 4.

[3] Quoted in *ibid.*, p. 3.

[4] In what follows I have utilized the definition of power suggested by Harold Lasswell and Abraham Kaplan in *Power and Society* (New Haven, Conn.: Yale University Press, 1950): the capacity to produce a desired action from others. An actor, whether corporate or private individual, has power when it can affect in the desired manner, under certain conditions, values of another actor.

expressed? Even compared to that of the economist, the political scientist's position is an uncomfortable one. An economist gets along quite nicely by assuming that money approximates value. In international politics entities may achieve major-power status by combining a number of traits, although in a given context, possession of certain elements of power may be necessary and perhaps sufficient criteria for location on the upper rungs of the hierarchy. It should be pointed out, also, that in international relations changes of situation have a disturbing way of invalidating previously held notions of an "elephant." Finally, even when *power* is the sole standard for determining status, the task is a troublesome one, because in international politics—unlike zoology—elephants and squirrels are in a sense defined in terms of each other: vis-à-vis Liechtenstein, it has often been said, Switzerland is a great power. "Power . . . is power *over*; it is a relational concept."[5]

To the foregoing, another complicating factor must be added: major-power status is often not described as a state-of-being exclusively acquired through an actor's objective capabilities. Instead, the element of recognition, or legitimacy, is introduced into the equation. Here, great-power status is not something an actor simply has; the other great powers have to accord it[6]—usually by permitting an actor to participate in a general settlement such as a peace conference, or by allotting it a special status such as permanent membership on the United Nations Security Council.

For the decision-makers of actors in the international system, the use of nonobjective criteria in determining great-

[5] Fox, *The Super-powers*, p. 10, italics in original.

[6] Note, however, that an important distinction suggests itself: some states are so powerful that their decision-makers take decisions which effectively determine which other power aggregates are great powers. Other actors, by contrast, are "supplicants" for great-power status.

power status sometimes has considerable merit. Decision-makers in the "genuine" great powers may have expectations about an actor's future power-status, or not wish to create expectations among foreign-policy elites in other states that would adversely affect future alliances. As a result, an actor might become a great power operationally, while falling short of the objective criteria. To this extent, great powers are those actors which foreign-policy elites think of as great powers. This being the case, the specialist is well advised to apply cautiously strictly objective standards in identifying great powers.[7]

Nevertheless, there seems little doubt that some actors command and receive deference, at least with respect to certain values and certain roles, from other actors in the international order largely because of differences in relative power position, and that Western decision-makers and specialists alike think these qualitative differences in power position are readily discerned. To cite Grafton again: "Even after you give a squirrel a certificate which says he is quite as big as any elephant, he is still going to be smaller, and all the squirrels will know it and all the elephants will know it."[8]

Grafton's comment may have been especially applicable to the international system in the immediate post-World War II

[7] Two other approaches to the identification of the great powers merit mention. Morton Kaplan, in *System and Process in International Relations*, advocates defining the great powers ("essential actors") as those actors whose absence would alter the nature of the system. Second, it is at least conceivable that those entities which behave in a certain way are great powers. E. H. Carr, in *The Twenty Years Crisis, 1919-1939* (London: Macmillan Co., Ltd., 1958), p. 131, seems to have come very near this conception when he argued that "the economic weapon is pre-eminently the weapon of strong Powers." Presumably a state which failed to meet this test was not a great power.

[8] Fox, *The Super-powers*, p. 3.

period when, more than in many diplomatic constellations, the gap between elephants and others was qualitative. This was particularly true of the gap between the superpowers and all other actors, including even France and Nationalist China whose great-power status was legitimated by giving each one permanent Security Council membership, with its concomitant veto power. In the postwar hierarchy, the actors of the first rank achieved their status almost exclusively because of readily recognizable, salient differences in capabilities. Even during World War II, as Fox's *The Super-powers* attests, *before* the atomic weapon was introduced, it was possible to define the major elements distinguishing the first-rank from the second-rank powers. The superpowers had "great power plus great mobility of power."[9] They were *world* powers as measured by their interests and ability to participate in the high politics of more than one continent. In addition, for each superpower there was one geographical region clearly its domain, one region in which its voice was predominant, though not necessarily supreme. Great powers (powers of the second rank) were geographically more restricted in their commitments and capabilities; their influence was confined primarily to a single continent. It was clear that a great power would achieve its policy goals only if it were a regional partner of one or more of the superpowers. All of this disappeared with the advent of nuclear weaponry. Nuclear weapons made the distinction between superpowers and the remaining actors in the international order even more obvious than at the beginning of the postwar era. To characterize a superpower as having great power and great flexibility of power was drastically to understate its capabilities in the age of the 15-minute war.

Even if there have always been elephants as well as squirrels

[9] *Ibid.*, p. 21.

in the international order; if the standard for distinguishing among corporate actors has been predominantly power differential; if, that is, the international system has always been hierarchically ordered—it does not follow that the configuration these hierarchical patterns take in various historical periods is constant. Variations may take place in *the number of gradations* in the hierarchy. *The distribution of actors* among the gradations may fluctuate substantially. *The degree of discontinuity* between gradations may be subject to significant alteration. In addition, *the rigidity of the hierarchy* (measured by the range of values over which an actor at one qualitative level can command deference from an actor in another category) would appear to be a way the hierarchical configuration of various international systems may differ.

Moreover, since phenomena, real or prospective, which substantially affect the style of international politics are subsumed under these categories, they represent transformations in the international system from which useful typologies of international systems might be constructed. Similarly, they constitute a major facet of an appraisal of Soviet international relations perspectives. Do the international relations commentators of an unquestioned "elephant," the Soviet Union, "know" the squirrels and elephants in the postwar international environment? What *gradations* among international actors do Soviet commentators perceive and what is the *shape* of the hierarchical configuration? How *rigid*—in the sense used here—is the international hierarchy?

To THE traditional Leninist-Stalinist perspective, the very notion of nonhierarchical power relations was anathema. There was little subtlety to the conventional Bolshevik imagery; states, classes, individuals were either on top or they were not (except during historically brief moments when one actor replaced another) and values were allocated accordingly. *Which* protagonist would emerge the winner and *which* the loser, was the central question of politics. *Kto-kogo*,[10] the famous who-whom, aptly summarized this view of politics (to use the idiom of game theory) as a zero-sum game in which the whole gamut of the participants' values were at stake. With the Bolshevik seizure of power and consequent transfer of vertical class imagery to a horizontal international environment, international politics came to be viewed as differing in no way from other political relationships, and the international system was perceived as structured in a rigidly hierarchical manner.

Soviet commentary during the Khrushchev years generally followed the traditional Bolshevik wisdom in describing international relations under the dominance of capitalism, that is, before the Bolshevik revolution initiated the general crisis of capitalism. The editors of the highly authoritative *Fundamentals of Marxism-Leninism* depicted the world capitalist system as "a rigid hierarchy, secured by the actual distribution of power," with a configuration resembling a "pyramid."[11] At

[10] The standard treatment of Bolshevik attitudes is Nathan Leites, *A Study of Bolshevism* (Glencoe, Ill.: The Free Press of Glencoe, 1953).

[11] Otto V. Kuusinen et al., eds., *Osnovy Marksizma-Leninizma* [Fundamentals of Marxism-Leninism] (Moscow: Gospolitizdat, 2nd edn., 1962), p. 657. For an English language edition see Otto Kuusinen et al., eds., *Fundamentals of Marxism-Leninism*, 2nd rev. edn. (Moscow: Foreign Languages Publishing House, 1963). For other statements describing the international system as highly structured, see A. Arzumanian, *Krizis mirovogo kapitalizma na sovremennom etape* [The Crisis of World Capitalism in its Contemporary Stage] (Moscow: Izdatel'stvo AN SSSR, 1962), p. 44 and K. Ivanov, "Present-day Colonialism and International Relations," *International Affairs*, No. 4 (April 1962), pp. 36-45. Ivanov's analysis of 19th-century international relations, however, is characterized by a tendency to greater discrimination than other Soviet articles. See especially pp. 40-41.

the apex of the pyramid stood a single dominant power. The defining characteristic of the dominant power was its geographically secure position of strategic invulnerability. The invulnerability, in turn, permitted the dominant power to choose the "decisive moment of a quarrel to side with the more powerful against the weaker."[12] As a result, the dominant power operated a curious balance-of-power system in which it acted as holder of the balance in order to preserve or secure its dominant position in the international order. There were, in addition, a number of other developed, imperialist, great powers[13] engaged in a constant struggle for place and markets, impetus for which derived from a kind of law of uneven development under capitalism. Meanwhile, at the base of the hierarchy, separated by a qualitative gap, were the colonies and "semi-colonies," consisting of the "oppressed" peoples and nations, as well as the small and weak "semi-independent" states, which in accordance with the polarization tendency were being forced into dependency status.[14]

[12] E.g., I. Lemin, "Marks i voprosy vneshnei politiki" [Marx and Questions of Foreign Policy], *Mirovaia ekonomika*, No. 5 (May 1958), p. 23.

[13] Soviet authors thus far have not recognized that the three categories of states are not identical. I am not aware of any published effort to explain, for instance, why Portugal has maintained its empire while France and Great Britain have dissolved theirs. Nor have I encountered an explanation of why some industrial powers (notably Sweden) were not imperialist. Ivanov, "Present-day Colonialism . . . ," p. 40, asserts, however: "In his notes for the unfinished paper *Statistics and Sociology*, Lenin lists eleven imperialist powers which had colonies at that time . . . ; the West European countries without colonies were Switzerland, Sweden and Norway." In 1965, however, *Mirovaia ekonomika* used major sections of its August-December numbers (Nos. 8-12 [q.v.]) for a discussion of the continued existence in the contemporary world of "Metropoles Without Colonies"—a phenomenon which raises awkward questions for those still prone to treat Lenin seriously.

[14] Materials on which this paragraph is based include Ivanov,

A similar view was held of international relations within the capitalist camp in the years immediately following World War II. The United States, in the Soviet view, occupied an absolutely dominant position[15] vis-à-vis the remaining capitalist powers—even including Great Britain which, according to Soviet commentary, continued to be a great power.[16] A measure of the gap separating the United States from the Western European countries was provided by the bilateral agreements negotiated in connection with the establishment of the Marshall Plan, which "were practically identical for all countries participating in the 'Marshall Plan' . . . ,"[17] a datum of particular significance to Soviet observers who are strongly disposed to regard treaties as expressing the distribution of power between the participating parties. The corresponding allocation of values was indicated by the fact that these agreements "in essence [involved] the recognition of the United States' right not only to determine of what the goals of a given law consisted, but to decide to what extent measures undertaken by Western European countries corresponded to the law."

As with international relations in the imperialist era, hierarchical patterns within the capitalist camp were manifested in a struggle for a place in the pecking order. (A pure pecking order has as many gradations as there are actors, whereas the

"Present-day Colonialism . . ."; S. Viskov, "The Crisis of Imperialism's Foreign Policy," *International Affairs,* No. 1 (January 1962), pp. 22-23; and Arzumanian, *Krizis mirovogo kapitalizma* . . . , passim.

[15] D. Mel'nikov, "Obostrenie mezhimperialisticheskikh protivorechii na sovremennom etape" [Aggravation of Inter-imperialist Contradictions in the Contemporary Stage], *Mirovaia ekonomika,* No. 6 (June 1963), pp. 18-33, at p. 24; AN IMEMO, *Mezhdunarodnye otnosheniia* . . . , Vol. 1, p. 457.

[16] See especially the lengthy discussion, *ibid.,* p. 397.

[17] *Ibid.,* p. 583.

equally rigid polarization concept suggests only two gradations. Common to these contradictory notions is an assumption of rigid hierarchy. Since the polarization tendency must obtain only in the indefinite future, the two notions could be simultaneously entertained, with the pecking-order thesis being of greatest operational relevance to the present. Soviet writers usually have been concerned with the place of only the first half-dozen or so actors; the remaining ones are the "and others.") Numerous examples may be cited of the preoccupation with place within the capitalist camp that persisted throughout the Khrushchev years.[18] "The situation of the Western states 'according to power [*po sile*],'" one review of international developments explained to its readers, "has become different from [what it was] several years ago. The Federal Republic of Germany has changed into the leading European power, leaving behind France and conducting a bitter struggle with England *for first place* in the economy and politics of Western Europe."[19] Another article explained that the Zurich agreement, creating an independent Cyprus, "painstakingly protects the interests of England and the interests of Turkey (compared with Greece the more powerful member of the [NATO] bloc").[20] The pecking-order conception can be easily extended further, as when the impression is given that in disputes, noninvolved states side with the disputant

[18] For an example of concern voiced by a Soviet specialist lest too much weight be attached to the focus on place, however, see E. Kutnik, "Narastanie protivorechii v NATO" [Intensification of Contradictions in NATO], *Mirovaia ekonomika,* No. 2 (February 1959), p. 105.

[19] A. Galkin et al., "Tekushchie problemy mirovoi politiki (obzor)" [Current Problems of World Politics (a Review)], *Mirovaia ekonomika,* No. 7 (July 1959), pp. 19-20.

[20] I. Cheprov and Ia. Iudin, "Nesostoiatel'nost' politiki voennykh blokov" [The Bankruptcy of the Policy of Military Blocs], *Mirovaia ekonomika,* No. 4 (April 1959), p. 78.

higher in the pecking order. Such a view occasionally found expression in Soviet commentary in the early 1960s. "Every time," it was said, "West Germany has to choose between the United States and France, it prefers the U.S.A."[21]

The disposition to regard power relations as rigidly hierarchical also characterized the description of early postwar relations within the socialist camp. The Khrushchev regime persisted in being more politically sensitive about intra-camp relations than international relations generally. The degree of objectivity in descriptions of intra-camp relations suffered accordingly. Despite this, the authors of *International Relations Since World War II* virtually acknowledged the validity of Zbigniew Brzezinski's characterization of "the second Stalinist phase" as a period in which "all state treaties declined in importance, and were only used to formalize a relationship of strict hierarchical, almost feudal, subordination."[22] If we bear in mind the analysis of the bilateral agreements between the United States and the west European states, the portent of the following passage is discernible, if elliptical: "The new relations between the Soviet Union and these countries [the newly created "people's democracies"] at the base of which lay the principle of proletarian internationalism, were juridically registered and consolidated in the treaties of friendship, cooperation, and mutual aid. . . . *The content of all these treaties was almost identical.*"[23]

[21] A. Galkin, "The 'Paradoxes' of Western Foreign Policy," *International Affairs*, No. 2 (February 1960), p. 54, italics added.

[22] Brzezinski, *The Soviet Bloc*, p. 399.

[23] AN IMEMO, *Mezhdunarodnye otnosheniia . . .* , Vol. 1, p. 138, italics added. The disposition to perceive the camp as being structured, until recently, in rigidly hierarchical fashion may be demonstrated in several other ways. The long-standing tendency to view the camp as a single actor presupposed the same centrality of power; so did the

KHRUSHCHEV AND THE THIRD STAGE OF CAPITALISM'S GENERAL CRISIS

THUS Soviet commentary during Khrushchev's tenure in office, in describing international relations in the "imperialist" vein and in describing the hierarchical patterns within the two camps in the early postwar period, retained the typical Bolshevik expectation of rigid hierarchical political relationships. Such was not the perception of international relations at the present stage of world development, which in the early 1960s Khrushchev and other Soviet observers began to term a new third stage in the "general crisis of capitalism."

When compared with the attributes Soviet commentaries conventionally have ascribed to the first and second stages of that "general crisis," the third stage of the crisis of capitalism was a very curious stage, indeed. The first stage began with the October Revolution and extended to World War II. The second had its beginnings in the takeovers in eastern Europe and in Asia, the emergence of socialism from the confines of one country, and the formation of a socialist world system of states. The first and second stages had in common the fact that they were born of world war and had resulted in major revolutionary advance. And they could be dated with relative

---

formulation (of equal venerability) of the Soviet Union as head of the camp. According to Khrushchev ("Za novye pobedy . . . "), the latter formula was omitted from the 1960 Eighty-one Party Statement at Soviet insistence. For an example of that formulation well after January 1961, see A. Arzumanian, "Krizis mirovogo kapitalizma" [Crisis of World Capitalism], *Mirovaia ekonomika*, No. 12 (December), 1961, p. 5; and Arzumanian, *Krizis mirovogo kapitalizma* . . . , p. 16.

Brzezinski, *The Soviet Bloc*, pp. 380n-81n, has demonstrated the "manifest" hierarchical pattern in the order of speeches by camp leaders at major Soviet Communist Party meetings.

precision. None of this common ground held true in the Soviet description of the third stage of capitalism's general crisis.

Soviet commentators were noticeably vague in specifying when it began. The most authoritative sources of the general line—the 1960 statement, the C.P.S.U. Program, the *Osnovy Marksizma-Leninizma*, Khrushchev's January 1961 speech—avoided mention of a date altogether. However, Academician A. A. Arzumanian, then Director of the Institute of World Economy and International Relations, asserted that the new stage had its beginnings in the "mid-fifties."[24] But the most precise determination was made by M. S. Dragilev, who marked the beginnings of the new stage at "the middle and second half of the fifties"[25]—a nebulous dividing line to separate two qualitatively different historical stages. In fact, Dragilev did not intend to separate carefully the second and third stages, but instead seemed intent on running the two together, as the following exercise in dialectical gymnastics illustrates:

> It would be a mistake to represent differences between stages of the general crisis of capitalism, *especially between the second and the third*, too simply. V. I. Lenin declared that in nature and society all borders are conditional and mobile. The conditionality and mobility of borders should be borne in mind in exposing the specific character of stages in the general crisis of capitalism since several processes which characterize the new stage existed—in not as developed a a form, it is true—in the second stage, and, on the other

[24] Arzumanian, *Krizis mirovogo kapitalizma . . .* , p. 9.

[25] M. S. Dragilev, "Ob osobennosti novogo, tret'ego etapa obshchego krizisa kapitalizma" [Concerning the Unique Features of the New, Third Stage of the General Crisis of Capitalism], *Voprosy istorii*, No. 4 (April 1962), p. 21.

hand, phenomena characteristic of the second stage are perceived now as well.[26]

Moreover, Soviet commentators declared that unlike its predecessors, the third stage had not developed in conjunction with a world war, but rather had taken shape out of "the sharp, qualitative changes in the distribution of the forces of socialism and capitalism."[27] Finally, Soviet spokesmen took the position: "to say that the transfer from one stage of the general crisis of capitalism to another is determined *without fail* by new revolutionary breaks in the imperialist chain . . . would signify seeing only one element in the development of the world revolutionary process—the falling away from capitalism of still more countries—and not to see the other, namely, the growth of the socialist system."[28] As a result, the new stage was not necessarily connected with new revolutionary breakthroughs, a posture that has provoked sharp questioning within the communist world.

To a considerable extent, the new stage was testimony to an optimistic appraisal by Moscow in 1961 of the prospects for revolutionary advance[29] in the near future.[30] Soviet interna-

[26] *Ibid.*, italics added.

[27] *Ibid.* Arzumanian, *Krizis mirovogo kapitalizma* . . . , p. 12, ascribes the shift to the "decisive changes in the distribution of power."

[28] Dragilev, "Ob osobennosti . . . ," p. 20, italics added. Arzumanian's rejoinder followed the path taken by Dragilev, but the former added somewhat defensively (*Krizis mirovogo kapitalizma* . . . , p. 12): "Besides, in conditions of the third stage a new break in the chain of imperialism was accomplished in Cuba. The world socialist system has grown into such a mighty force that successful revolution is possible now in any geographical region, [and] independently of the dimensions of a country."

[29] Richard Lowenthal, "The End of an Illusion," *Problems of Communism*, Vol. XII, No. 1 (January-February 1963), pp. 1-10.

[30] After 1961, however, the phrase came to acquire connotations more similar to the "relative stabilization of capitalism" that Stalin

tional relations observers appear to have concluded that the changed distribution of power, brought on primarily by the passing of American invulnerability (reinforced by the decolonization process and divisive tendencies in the Western camp), had brought on a change in the international system, especially in the relationship among the major actors, analogous in magnitude and scope to the kind of change usually associated with a major European or world war. Another, more important, reason seems to have animated the decision to introduce a new stage in capitalism's general crisis. The introduction of a new stage was apparently intended to bolster the case for the Soviet definition of the epoch as one whose "principal characteristic . . . was that the world socialist system is becoming the decisive factor in the development of society,"[31] rather than as "the epoch of imperialism, wars, and proletarian revolutions," the traditional Leninist definition the Chinese favor.[32] While leaving the basic myths of the past unchallenged and thus avoiding a clash with Lenin on his "home ground"—Khrushchev, by introducing a new stage, evidently was attempting to create a doctrinal basis for asserting that one must not "mechanically repeat now . . . what Vladimir Il'ich Lenin said many decades ago on imperialism,"[33] and for criti-

---

referred to in 1924 than to the "third period" of revolutionary advance that he declared in 1928 to be imminent. References to the "new, third stage" in 1963-64 did not stress its relation to revolutionary advance.

[31] E.g., the 1960 Eighty-one Party Statement, in Hudson, Lowenthal, and MacFarquhar, eds., *The Sino-Soviet Dispute*, p. 178, italics deleted.

[32] The Chinese were criticized ("Za torzhestvo tvorcheskogo Marksizma-Leninizma . . ." [For the Triumph of Creative Marxism-Leninism], *Kommunist*, No. 11 [July 1963], p. 19) for not "even mentioning the new stage of the general crisis of capitalism" in their June 14, 1963 letter.

[33] Khrushchev, *O vneshnei politike Sovetskogo Soiuza*, Vol. II, p. 62.

cizing "Communists, and especially Communists who are statesmen and political figures," who "rehash old truths from past centuries."[34] For Khrushchev, the modern epoch was post-imperialist, both in the sense that it was no longer the case that "imperialism to a significant degree determined the course and character of international relations,"[35] and in the sense that Lenin's analysis of imperialism could be transcended[36] in the name of creative Marxism-Leninism.

The concept of "the new, third stage of capitalism's general crisis" bears crucially on our understanding of the Soviet perception during the Khrushchev years of the hierarchical configuration of the then contemporary international system. The view of the contemporary system differed radically from the conspiratorial Bolshevik view and conformed instead generally with reality, or with Western notions of reality. Khrushchev and other Soviet commentators retained Stalin's scorn —contempt might not be too harsh a word—for the "squirrels" of international politics. Soviet observers continued to see the international system as hierarchically structured, largely on the basis of power differential: "Juridically all states are equal in their sovereignty. But from the point of view of economic potential, magnitude of territory and population and, what is especially important, from the viewpoint of the actual influence on the whole system of international relations, states are not, it goes without saying, equal."[37] At the same time,

For an excerpted English-language version see Hudson, Lowenthal, and MacFarquhar, eds., *Sino-Soviet Dispute*, p. 137.

[34] *Pravda*, January 7, 1963.

[35] "Za novye pobedy . . . ," p. 7.

[36] Robert C. Tucker makes the same point in connection with the "new content" of peaceful coexistence, in *The Soviet Political Mind*, p. 213.

[37] V. K. Sobakin, *Kollektivnaia bezopasnost'* . . . , p. 28.

while the continued hierarchical cast to the Soviet perception was reflective of attitudes compatible with "great power chauvinism," it was incompatible with the conspiracy thesis. In the Khrushchev period, hubris, not pathology, was the watchword of Soviet perspectives on the international system.

THE CENTRAL structural feature of contemporary international politics was that there was no longer one dominant power. That was the distinctively novel feature to which Soviet theorists referred when they adverted to the third stage of the general crisis of capitalism and connected it to the changed distribution of power.

Previous shifts in the distribution of power had resulted in changes within the international order, as one capitalist state after another was obliged to yield first place. As a result of World War II and its byproducts, it was England's turn to yield first place to the United States.[38] The United States' "positions of strength policy"[39] was in turn undermined as a result of a process beginning with the formation of the socialist camp and Soviet development of the atomic bomb and culminating in the announcement by the Soviet Union that it had successfully tested an intercontinental ballistic missile. As a result of these developments, the United States lost its geographic position of dominance. Its ability to avoid a crushing blow at its heartland if its decision-makers "unleashed" a war was eliminated; its capacity to choose the optimal moment for entry into a world war was destroyed. Now the United States would be involved in general war from the outset.[40]

[38] E.g., S. Viskov, "The Crisis of Imperialism's Foreign Policy," p. 21.

[39] For a description of the analytical and manipulative uses of this concept by Soviet spokesmen, see below, pp. 165-79.

[40] Materials on which this paragraph is drawn include: Arzumanian, *Krizis mirovogo kapitalizma* . . . ; Dragilev, "Ob osobennosti . . . ,"

The pattern of previous shifts did not, however, hold in this instance. Obviously no capitalist power could take the United States' place. "World development does not go in the direction of the transfer of leadership from one capitalist state to another, world development goes from capitalism to socialism and communism."[41] More significantly, for the present neither could any other state (for example, the Soviet Union).[42] The United States, having lost its hegemonic position, still clearly retained its ability to block the aspirations of any other actor. The implication was as obvious as it was bizarre to a person schooled in Leninism and having endured the educational experience of Stalinism domestically. In the present historical phase, no single power was dominant; the dominant power *category* had been eliminated.

For John H. Herz, with the advent of the atomic era, "the roof blew off the territorial state" because the atomic bomb, coupled with aerial means of delivery, destroyed the "specific element of statehood which characterized the units composing the modern state system in the classical period, . . . their . . . 'impermeability.' "[43] For Khrushchev the advent of the atomic era *blew the top off the international order.*

With the passing of the dominant-power category the international order was headed by, at most, eight great powers—the U.S., the U.S.S.R., Great Britain, France, West Germany, Communist China, India, and Indonesia. An examination of

---

V. D. Sokolovskii, *Voennaia strategiia.* See also Chapter v below, pp. 172-74 and the documentation cited there.

[41] Arzumanian, *Krizis mirovogo kapitalizma* . . . , p. 144.

[42] An article in *World Marxist Review*, Vol. v, No. 4 (April 1962), by Y. Y. Karyakin [Iu. Kariakin], "Allen Dulles Instead of Karl Marx" (p. 85), acknowledged that for the remainder of the twentieth century "it is quite clear that no single state will predominate in the world."

[43] *International Politics in the Atomic Age*, at pp. 104 and 96.

Soviet commentary indicates that these powers were not undifferentiated among themselves. In fact, the great powers could be separated into two distinct gradations.

The two gradations corresponded to separate conceptions of great-power status, one pre-atomic, the other atomic. These in turn were based on pre-atomic and atomic concepts of power. All eight great powers possessed either large population/sizable territory or a powerful economy; the United States and the Soviet Union, of course, had both. Any other power, regardless of the policies of its decision-makers, was apparently obliged to possess one or the other element to secure Soviet recognition of its great-power status. These pre-atomic factors reflected an assumption that quantity and mass —expressed in crude output, size, and population indices— were indicative of great power, and that such qualitative differences as these indices might obscure could more or less be discounted in the measurement of power. They also reflected an underlying premise that power-as-potential can be translated into power-in-being, into instrumentalities with which desired effects are achieved.[44]

The pre-atomic concept of great-power status, which differed in no appreciable manner from concepts generally associated with Stalin ("permanently operating factors") or Mao ("masses decide everything"), was carried over into the nuclear age. Khrushchev parted company with Mao (but not Stalin and Lenin), in that he and other Soviet observers claimed that economic development took precedence over population, while Mao apparently assumed the reverse. Where Khrushchev and his cohorts parted company with Mao, Stalin,

[44] Shulman, *Stalin's Foreign Policy Reappraised*, p. 270, emphasizes the Soviet disposition to assume that physical power can be translated into political power.

and Lenin was in relegating these elements of power (output, size, and population) to a distinctly secondary but *not* unimportant place. They have become subsidiary, in the age of nuclear weapons and missiles,[45] to atomic weapons and high-speed delivery systems.

The United States and the Soviet Union, "the two greatest powers in the world," "the two world giants," the states which possessed atomic and hydrogen weapons *and* high-speed delivery systems, took precedence. Elephants lacking "atomic teeth" were not in the same class with tigers—imperialist or modern revisionist—which did in fact possess these weapons. Lacking atomic capability, an actor retained its great-power status but had to defer to the atomic powers. In the words of a Spanish communist supporter of Moscow's ideological position,

> In the 20th century, the century of technological revolution, man discovered new means, including atomic energy, making for the powerful development of production.... Since atomic energy is not yet accessible to most countries, those who possess it *have a tremendous superiority*. A country possessing the secret of nuclear energy for military purposes could dictate its will to large and densely populated countries not possessing this secret..... Imperialism, armed with

[45] One of the more remarkable facets of Soviet commentary under Khrushchev (and in the three years since October 1964, as well) was the preoccupation precisely with *the age* of nuclear weapons and missiles. The technological determinism that it suggests is reminiscent of the later Engels. It is noteworthy that Soviet analysis during this time shared with Engels a belief that disarmament is possible (expressed in the latter's famous essay, "The Foreign Policy of Russian Czarism," written in 1890; for a translation of Engels' article see Karl Marx and Friedrich Engels, *The Russian Menace to Europe* [Glencoe, Ill.: The Free Press, 1952], pp. 25-55).

nuclear weapons, can be paralyzed in its action only by socialism, which is also armed with nuclear weapons.[46]

The two major atomic powers were also unique in that they were world powers[47] with a general interest in the allocation of values. The remaining great powers were able to make their influence felt only on a geographically limited scale and did not appear to take the "global picture" into consideration. This attitude was especially evident in Soviet polemics with the Chinese who, Soviet observers intimated, were blinded by their "special aims or interests," and were therefore unable to realize the *global* implications of a decision to grant China thermonuclear weapons. "It would be at the very least naive," Moscow declared, "to imagine it possible to pursue one policy in the West and another in the East, to wage a struggle against arming West Germany with nuclear weapons and against the spread of nuclear weapons in the world with one hand and with the other supply these weapons to China." "If the leaders of any country, great or small," it continued, "refuse to see the world situation as it is, if the point of departure of their policy is that the only important thing for them is what happens in their own house while what goes on in other parts of the world is unimportant, this type of thinking reeks of cramped provincialism and scholasticism. In life these views are simply dangerous because of their adventurism."[48]

[46] Santiago Carrillo, "Some International Problems of the Day," *World Marxist Review*, Vol. VI, No. 5 (May 1963), p. 8, italics added.

[47] E.g., Khrushchev's speech to the Supreme Soviet (in *Pravda*, December 12, 1962; trans. in *Current Digest*, Vol. XIV, No. 51 [January 16, 1963], pp. 3-8 and No. 52 [January 23, 1963], pp. 3-11).

[48] Cf., e.g., Government Statement, *Pravda*, September 21 and 22, 1963; trans. in *Current Digest*, Vol. XV, No. 38 (October 16, 1963); and especially *Pravda*, August 21, 1963 (trans. in *Current Digest*,

Thus the Chinese had a point in alleging that the "only country the leaders of the C.P.S.U. look up to is the United States."[49] The United States and the Soviet Union were in a category apart from the other great powers. In the Khrushchevian perspective the contemporary international order was headed by these two powers. A considerable gap in power separated them from other states, including the remaining great powers—Communist China, Great Britain, France, West Germany, India, and Indonesia—and was derived from qualitatively different capabilities.[50]

Of the remaining great powers, the inclusion of West Germany and Indonesia among the second-order great powers was the most open to question, but for different reasons. Soviet sources in the early 1960s asserted that West Germany, with Italy and Japan, had lost "its significance as a great power." Such assertions were not, however, reflective of Soviet estimates of West Germany's relative power position, since there were transparent policy-relevant reasons why Soviet statements were not likely to acknowledge that West Germany had rejoined the powers. More indicative were such depictions of the Federal Republic as a "state with a powerful 'conventional' army"; "a force . . . having a marked influence on its overseas partner"; one of the "four main capitalist powers"; "a state in the first rank of imperialist states."[51]

Vol. xv, No. 34) (September 18, 1963), p. 11, from which the quotation in the text above is drawn.

[49] "Peaceful Coexistence—Two Diametrically Opposed Policies," *Peking Review*, Vol. vi, No. 51 (December 20, 1963), p. 16.

[50] It was alleged, however, that the gap between the United States and the west European powers was narrowing. See below, pp. 150-51.

[51] The citations in the above paragraph are to be found, respectively, in A. A. Gromyko et al., *Diplomaticheskii slovar'*, Vol. 1, p. 257; A. Sovetov, "New Trends and the Realities," *International Affairs*, No. 8

The notion that Indonesia was a great power first appeared in Khrushchev's speech on his return to Moscow from a General Assembly appearance in 1960. In that speech he was careful to avoid any detailed explanation of why Indonesia should be included as one of the great powers; instead, he limited himself to asking rhetorically, "Why . . . should France be adjudged a great country and Indonesia not?"[52] Indonesia does have attributes (its population) which correspond to Soviet notions of the requisite elements of power. In considering Indonesia a great power, it appears that Soviet sources had evolved a supplemental and manipulative conception of great-power status: those *influential* countries that pursued anti-imperialist policies. Indonesia was a great power because it was a highly populated country pursuing foreign policies that coalesced objectively with the "world historical process." Japan, despite a large population and a high level of economic development, was not a great power because it was allied with American imperialism.[53] In contrast with the gap between the first and second-rank great powers, therefore, the line separating the least of the great powers of the second rank and the most powerful of the remaining independent powers was relatively amorphous, inasmuch as great powers merely had more of the same power elements which other independent actors possessed, or pursued different policies. In some ill-

(August 1963), p. 44; A. Galkin et al., "Tekushchie problemy mirovoi politiki: obzor" [Current Problems of World Politics: A Review], *Mirovaia ekonomika*, No. 7 (July 1959), p. 28; V. Gantman et al., "Tekushchie problemy mirovoi politiki" [Current Problems of World Politics], *Mirovaia ekonomika*, No. 1 (January 1963), p. 11.

[52] *Pravda*, October 27, 1960; trans. in *Current Digest*, Vol. xii, No. 42 (November 16, 1960).

[53] A distinction pointedly made to the Japanese in a Soviet aide mémoire; see *Pravda*, January 29, 1961.

defined manner, these quantitative differences constituted step-level differences.

The differences that separated states like Japan,[54] Italy, Canada, Australia, and Sweden, among the industrial states, from the second-rank great powers appeared founded on an intuitively based judgment that the former had a more circumscribed ambit of influence. Each of the near second-rank powers was itself capable of exacting a price for having its immediate interests impinged upon.[55] What separated *all* these states from the remaining independent states was that each of them would have been an actor in the international arena, although greatly more circumscribed in its ability to act, even if there were no Soviet Union to impede the United States in its "big stick" policy.

The remaining formally independent states were independent operationally only in the context of the third stage of the general crisis of capitalism. Now that socialism was becoming the decisive factor in world development,

> *international relations undergo structural change* [italics in original]. . . . The main tendency of international relations

[54] For the period 1950-55, however, the authors of Volume II of *International Relations Since World War II* chose to deal with "the policy of American imperialism in Japan" and the "new forms of military, economic, and political dependence of Japan on the U.S.A." (AN IMEMO, *Mezhdunarodnye otnosheniia* . . . , Vol. II, pp. 452, 462.) For a criticism of this approach see V. Trukhanovsky [Trukhanovskii], "From the Korean War to the Paris Agreements," *International Affairs*, No. 10 (October 1964), p. 101.

[55] Witness the remark of P. Rysakov, "Severo-Atlanticheskii blok i strany Severnoi Evropy" [The North-Atlantic Bloc and the Countries of Northern Europe], *Mirovaia ekonomika*, No. 3 (March 1962), p. 87: "Swedish neutrality, while also utilizing international recognition, depends mainly on the armed forces of Sweden itself and not on an international guarantee, as for instance does Swiss or Austrian neutrality."

> in the period when imperialism dominated was increasingly to place the destinies of the world in the hands of a small group of the biggest states. The relations between the "Great" Powers which competed for world markets and spheres of influence and for world supremacy were becoming the main content of international relations. Even formally independent but small and weak states had to orient themselves on some "Great" Power, because *their voice by itself* [italics added] carried no weight at all. Today an opposite tendency prevails: the number of states which shape world developments on an equal footing with the "great" states is steadily growing.[56]

"A few years ago, only two opposing camps, the socialist and the imperialist, were active in international relations. Today the countries of Asia, Africa, and Latin America that have freed or are freeing themselves from foreign aggression have also begun to play an active role in international affairs."[57] "In the international arena, a new force, *unknown previously in the history of international relations*, has appeared: a group of neutralist states."[58]

[56] S. Viskov, "The Crisis of Imperialism's Foreign Policy," p. 23.

[57] Khrushchev, Central Committee Report, in *Pravda*, October 18, 1961, trans. in *Current Digest*, Vol. XIII, No. 41 (November 8, 1961), p. 3. This passage, by explicitly differentiating between the two camps and the neutralist powers, constituted one of the least ambiguous indications that Khrushchev had abandoned the two-camp thesis.

[58] D. Aleksandrov and O. Nakropin, "Mirnoe sosushchestvovanie i sovremennost'" [Peaceful Coexistence and Modern Times], *Mirovaia ekonomika*, No. 12 (December 1961), p. 34, italics added. To the Western observer, depending perhaps on whether or not he finds "neutralism" a concept distinct from "neutrality," such assertations may seem quaintly naive or pathetically ill-informed misreadings of the diplomatic record. But in the context of a political system whose leaders and ideologues claimed to perpetuate the Leninist world-view,

As can be readily seen, however, such pronouncements affirming the autonomy of neutralist states did not lend themselves to a clear distinction between anti-imperialism as a policy and *independence* as a category. Was the substance of such assertions merely a reevaluation, given changed historical circumstances, of the question, "Who are our allies?". Was operational independence a laudatory category for those who were Soviet allies "objectively" or "subjectively?"[59] Was this only another example of the traditional Bolshevik obfuscation of agreement with control?

Affirmative answers reflecting an analysis that emphasized continuity with the past have much in their favor. There is no doubt that the description of the policies of nonsocialist countries as policies of independence or (even more of a tip-off) "real . . . independence"[60] generally referred to policies pursued by anti-imperialist or anti-American actors. Independence, in this sense, no more represents an analytical category, however crude, than does a definition of the national bourgeoisie (in the words of A. M. Rumiantsev, then editor-in-chief of *Problems of Peace and Socialism*) as a category which "can include all sections of the bourgeoisie, industrial and

---

such assertions are both comprehensible and remarkable—since in the traditional Marxist-Leninist view, it had always been assumed that there were no neutrals and only two camps.

[59] For an inventory of Soviet categorizations of Asian, African, and Latin American countries in terms of their foreign-policy orientations, see Thomas P. Thornton, "Communist Attitudes Toward Asia, Africa and Latin America," in Cyril E. Black and Thomas P. Thornton, eds., *Communism and Revolution: The Strategic Uses of Political Violence* (Princeton, N.J.: Princeton University Press, 1964), pp. 245-69.

[60] E.g., AN IMEMO, *Mezhdunarodnyi ezhegodnik: politika i ekonomika*, 1963, p. 31.

commercial. What counts is its attitude to imperialism."[61] Moreover, Soviet observers were very sensitive to the possibility that, as one specialist put it, "liberation . . . only begins with political independence . . . in many African countries, for example . . . and is often confined to the granting of a national anthem, flag, and a seat in the United Nations."[62]

Nevertheless, independence, to some Soviet international relations observers writing in Khrushchev's last years in office, did have a certain content which distinguished the formally independent states, regardless of their policies, from the null powers. It should be stressed, however, that this was a contentious matter among Soviet specialists—evidence that, by the time of Khrushchev's removal, the ideology, by defining the modes of analysis, persisted in encumbering thought—and one on which the last word apparently had not been heard by October 1964. In Soviet writings the issue was posed in a way that makes possible the abstraction for analytical purposes of the dominant pattern, the blurring of ally and independence, and permits us to determine what differences there were between colonies and dependent countries, to what extent the formally independent small states were separable from the null powers.

Ivanov, for one, argued that "*the overthrow of the political power of the colonialists (the colonial regime of administration) is . . . the first, . . . if decisive, step towards the complete liquidation of colonialism.*"[63] V. I. Pavlov maintained a similar position: "Given the arrangement of basic world forces—imperialism and socialism—now having taken shape, the po-

[61] "Building a United Anti-Imperialist Front," *World Marxist Review*, Vol. VI, No. 1 (January 1963), p. 83.

[62] K. Ivanov, "Present-day Colonialism and International Relations," p. 43.

[63] *Ibid.*, p. 39, italics in original.

litical and economic limitations on self-sufficiency connected with entrance into aggressive groupings does not entail, for all their seriousness, semi-colonial status. In addition, the dependent countries were part of the colonial system of imperialism, which, clearly, it is impossible to recreate in its prior capacity by one or another directive of foreign policy.[64]"

Evidently not all Soviet theorists came to this conclusion. Ivanov reported that "the similarity of social and economic features of the situation in the colonies and formally independent countries is so striking that it has made some scholars regard the two as a single group." This view, he asserted, is "still current . . . [among Soviet scholars] and has caused a great deal of confusion."[65] "Others," he continued, "have gone to the extent of denying that there is any difference between colonies and dependent countries and insist that the winning of formal political independence makes no difference to their real status. This latter view, in essence the Rosa Luxemburg view, has now been discarded by Soviet scholars. . . ."[66]

[64] V. I. Pavlov, review of A. M. Rumiantsev, ed., *Sovremennoe osvoboditel'noe dvizhenie i natsional'naia burzhuaziia*, in *Narody Azii i Afriki*, No. 5 (sent to press September 28, 1961), p. 221.

[65] K. Ivanov, "Present-day Colonialism and International Relations." He gave as an example *Polozhenie sel'skogo khoziaistva v koloniiakh i drugikh slaborazvitykh raionakh* [The Situation of Agriculture in the Colonies and Other Underdeveloped Regions] (Moscow: Izdatel'-stvo AN SSSR, 1958). He was evidently referring to AN IMEMO, *Polozhenie sel'skogo khoziaistva i krest'ianstva v koloniiakh i drugikh slaborazvitykh stranakh* [The Situation of Agriculture and the Peasantry in Colonial and Other Underdeveloped Countries] (Moscow: Izdatel'stvo AN SSSR, 1958). The publication date is important because such a position was more acceptable then.

For a general analysis of the dispute within the Soviet Union concerning the appraisal of the "Third World," to which the controversy reported by Ivanov directly relates, see Ra'anan, "Moscow and the Third World," passim.

[66] K. Ivanov, "Present-day Colonialism. . . ." Ivanov elaborated

Similarly, Pavlov reported that "among Soviet Orientologists, there exist divergent constructions of the concept 'dependent' . . . in contemporary conditions. Several researchers assume that states of the East, drawn into aggressive military blocs and foregoing thereby important facets of their sovereignty, should be considered dependent countries in the traditional understanding of this term."[67]

If we assume that Pavlov's and Ivanov's position reflected the dominant trend in Soviet thinking during Khrushchev's last years in office, then a major step from the encumbering grips of ideology had been taken. It might be inferred that Soviet observers had recognized that under conditions of

---

on the reference to Rosa Luxemburg in a way which provides insight into "the confusion" caused by the currency of a view which was merely "a camouflaged version" of "in essence, the Rosa Luxemburg view."

"Colonialist ideology spilled over and infected even a section of the West European working class, [they] saw no way out of the nightmare; they underestimated mature anti-imperialist movements and revolutions, which broke out here and there, and tried to hide behind a facade of Leftist phrases about the 'unfeasibility' of even the political emancipation of the oppressed nations and peoples under imperialism, which, they believed, would 'not allow' such emancipation (in exactly the same spirit as some present-day dogmatists declare real peace or disarmament unfeasible so long as any imperialist state remains in the world)."

[67] Pavlov, review of Rumiantsev, *Sovremennoe* . . . , p. 221. Cf. Pavlov's earlier remark, p. 219, with respect to the policy-relevance of this dialogue: "The study of the role of the national bourgeoisie of the countries of Asia, Africa, and Latin America . . . is one of the tasks of Marxist-Leninist science. The dogmatic nature [*dogmatichnost'*] of several of our prior concepts of the national bourgeoisie have limited for a certain time the full utilization of those opportunities which co-operation of the countries of socialism with the states of the East holds."

mutual deterrence, the formal political independence of a small state was potentially sufficient for it to act independently, although limited in degree by its economic dependence and military alliances.

In any case, the distinction between the colonies, dependencies, and protectorates, and the politically independent states had come to be considered at least *potentially* profound. With colonialism, but not "neo-colonialism," virtually at an end, the null-power gradation, it follows, was also virtually ruled out. Thus the hierarchical configuration of the international system was immensely more complex than the international system Marxist-Leninists expected. The two anti-podal gradations, the single dominant power and the null powers, had atrophied. Instead Soviet observers in the Khrushchev years separated the world order into two world atomic powers, a handful of developed and potential great powers, several major independents, a large number of small but independent actors whose degree of independence varied considerably, and finally, at the bottom, a few null actors.

The most salient discontinuity in the gradation of powers was the gap between the world atomic powers and the other great powers. The line separating the great but nonatomic powers of the second rank from the major independents was noticeable but unclear. The dividing line between the major independents and all other independent powers was highly nebulous. Finally, the distinction between small and null powers had become potentially significant.

The changed structural elements in the international hierarchy have important implications for the rigidity of the hierarchy. Soviet commentary during Khrushchev's tenure in power was not elaborate, but several observations about it are in order. Soviet analysis continued to expect the range of values over which a major power could command deference from a smaller power to be extensive. By the end of Khrushchev's term, however, the range was assumed to be *finite,* since a major power could not deprive a small power of its independence except at the risk of suffering severe deprivations itself. This was true at least for the small states not members of an imperialist alliance system.

The allocation of values and distribution of power were no longer synonymous. Given the absence of a dominant power and the distribution of power between the two world atomic powers, it was no longer the case that, in the absence of a situational calculus, values would be "distributed strictly proportionate to power."[68] Soviet commentary, in effect, recognized a condition wherein the maneuverability of the small powers was greatly enhanced. This was expressed in assertions that the major imperialist powers could no longer have their way with the small powers since the Soviet Union's nuclear shield deterred the Western powers from "exporting counter-revolution"; or in assertions that the imperialists were obliged to render aid to, say, India in order to prevent that country from taking a noncapitalist path. Soviet commentary also occasionally acknowledged that the small powers played the game both ways: some leaders in the underdeveloped world used the United States to get greater amounts of aid from the Soviet Union.[69]

[68] Cheprov and Iudin, "Nesostoiatel'nost' politiki . . . " p. 79.

[69] For a statement to this effect, see Mikhail Kremnyev [Kremnev], "The Non-Aligned Countries and World Politics," *World Marxist Review,* Vol. VI, No. 4 (April 1963), p. 31: "Some neutralist leaders, for example, are not adverse to playing up their 'independence' and 'no-bloc' policy of non-alignment, as a bargaining counter to wrest political advantages for their country, or an extra million dollars in credit." Kremnev presumably was among those least persuaded that

With respect to relations between the United States and its major European allies, Soviet analyses after the Twenty-second Party Congress, but prior to Khrushchev's removal,[70] strongly emphasized the narrowed range of values over which the United States could command deference from its west European allies.[71] At the same time, and of even greater importance as an indication of the lessened rigidity of Soviet conceptions of the hierarchical order, Soviet international relations specialists pointed to the increased capacity of the European powers to affect the range of American values. Thus West Germany, according to Sovetov, has undergone a "gradual but quite obvious transformation from a grateful debtor and obedient executor of the will of U.S. imperialism into a force that is having a marked influence on its overseas partner."[72] Even more significantly, Sovetov asserted that "from now on" the European powers have the capacity to involve the United States in nuclear war "without prior notice."[73] Hav-

---

Khrushchev's diligent cultivation of the Nassers of this world was likely to result in major political gains for Soviet policy.

[70] It is incorrect to assert, as Vernon V. Aspaturian has done, that "Khrushchev had a certain contempt for Britain and France as being little more than client states of the United States," or that Khrushchev "perceived the West as a single entity dominated by the U.S." ("Changing Soviet Perceptions of Realignments in the International Community," Paper No. 3 prepared for a conference sponsored by Columbia University on "The Soviet Union After Khrushchev: Implications for Arms Control," held on April 1-5, 1967, p. 120.)

[71] See especially the articles by A. Sovetov: "Contradictions in the Western Bloc," *International Affairs*, No. 6 (June 1963), pp. 3-8 and "New Trends and the Realities," *ibid.*, No. 8 (August 1963), pp. 42-48.

[72] *Ibid.*, p. 45.

[73] *Ibid.*, p. 44. In context, it appears that Sovetov was referring only to Britain and France—the states with nuclear capability. For catalytic war accusations directed at the Communist Chinese, see below, p. 152.

ing acknowledged this possibility for states which "to be sure . . . can [not] claim to rival the U.S.A. with any measure of success,"[74] little would seem to have been left, by the end of Khrushchev's tenure, of the Bolshevik expectation that power relationships are uni-directional, or of the traditional penchant for perceiving the international hierarchy as rigidly structured.

Equally significant as evidence of the erosion of traditional perspectives on the international order was the intensified concern after the Cuban missile crisis about the possibility of catalytic war (the initiation of general war by an actor not a world power). Prior to October 1962 Soviet commentary was appreciably more concerned with the dangers of escalation and accidental war than with catalytic war. From 1960 on, however, Soviet commentary had pointedly asserted that *no* power was invulnerable and that even countries which managed to stay out of a general war would suffer inordinate damage. After the Soviet-American confrontation in October 1962 there were increasing intimations that Soviet leaders suspected China of attempting to embroil the United States and the Soviet Union. Thus Khrushchev, in an attack on "people, who call themselves Marxist-Leninists," contended: "If one looks at matters objectively," he cannot but conclude that in the Cuban missile crisis "they actually behaved like people trying to provoke a conflict; they wanted to bring on a clash between the Soviet Union and the United States," a clash which would mean "causing a world thermonuclear war." "It would be interesting to see how they would conduct themselves in such a war . . . ," he continued, "Evidently they would prefer to sit it out."[75]

[74] Sovetov, "New Trends and the Realities," p. 44.

[75] *Pravda,* December 13, 1962, trans. in *Current Digest,* Vol. XIV, No. 52, p. 3.

There were few changes in the Soviet depiction of the international order in the three years after October 1964. Following the pattern observed during 1960-64, Soviet post-Khrushchevian commentary declined to challenge Lenin on his home ground by calling into question the basic myths of the past. Instead, international relations prior to the beginning of capitalism's general crisis continued to be described as a "struggle for place" among a "closed 'club' of great powers."[76] At the same time, those accounts which concerned themselves with defining the nature of the epoch[77] continued to maintain that in the mid-fifties, a new, third stage of capitalism's general crisis had begun, and to analyze it in a fashion characteristic of the Khrushchev years. A case in point was the theses of the Institute of World Economy and International Relations, issued—ironically, in the light of the role of the "third stage" in legitimating the historical transcendence of Lenin's *Imperialism*—on the occasion of the publication of *Imperial-*

[76] See, for instance, AN IMEMO, *Stroitel'stvo kommunizma . . .*, p. 10.

[77] The qualification may be an important one. The theses of the Institute of World Economy and International Relations, adopted to commemorate the 50th anniversary of the publication of Lenin's *Imperialism*, contain a hint that the "dogmatists" who did not accept the conclusion that a third stage in the general crisis had emerged in the mid-fifties were to be found at home as well as abroad: "The mistaken, dogmatic evaluation of the prospects of the development of capitalism is *used* by the leftist adventurist elements—pursuing their own nationalist, chauvinist goals—for the promotion of concepts to the effect that 'revolution flows from the barrel of a gun.'" It is conceivable, therefore, that the failure of the Party to mention the new, third stage in *its* theses celebrating 50 years of communist rule in Russia stems partly from internal opposition on the part of those most inclined to let Lenin *and* Stalin do their thinking for them. For the Party theses see *Pravda*, June 25, 1967.

ism, the Highest Stage of Capitalism. In its theses[78] the Institute reaffirmed the "conclusion" that "a new third stage of the general crisis of capitalism" had opened "with the middle of the fifties," notwithstanding the fact that no world war or major economic disaster had taken place, and attacked the policy implications of those "dogmatists" who argued otherwise. The view that "further development of the revolutionary process" will only occur as "a result of deep economic crisis and world war," it was argued, could only "lead to an incorrect orientation in revolutionary strategy and tactics, to the justification of passivity in the struggle for the political and economic interests of the toilers."

Against the doctrinal backdrop of the third stage of capitalism's general crisis, furthermore, Soviet commentary in 1964-67 continued the trend noted after the Twenty-second Congress toward muting the differences separating the major actors. While there was little reason to suspect that in the Soviet appraisal the United States and the Soviet Union were regarded as anything other than "the most powerful states militarily and economically in today's world,"[79] there were grounds for assuming that, in the Soviet view, the gap separating the two great powers of the first rank and the other major states was continuing to narrow. Tactical considerations doubtless played an important part in explaining why Brezhnev and Kosygin were noticeably less prone than their predecessor to use phrases which differentiated markedly between the United States and the U.S.S.R., on the one hand, and the remaining major actors, on the other. Avoiding such statements diminished the credibility of Chinese charges, end-

[78] "Uchenie V. I. Lenina ob imperializme i sovremennost'," pp. 4-5.

[79] I. Lemin, "Velikaia Oktiabr'skaia sotsialisticheskaia revoliutsiia i mirovaia politika," p. 13.

lessly reiterated, of the existence of an American-Soviet global condominium and facilitated the cultivation of Paris by ascribing to the Americans the view that France was a "middle power."[80] The evidence, nevertheless, precludes an exclusively manipulative explanation. Since the Twenty-second Congress Soviet observers have steadfastly maintained that the United States' relative power position within the capitalist camp has weakened; they have marshaled evidence that lends credence to this conclusion. Moreover, the point has been made in the Soviet press that under conditions of *détente*—where the elements unique to the power inventory of the superpowers are less relevant politically—the gap between the great powers narrows.[81]

The corollary assumption, that economic resources have increased in political significance under conditions of lessened expectations of general war, appears to be one reason that post-Khrushchevian commentary has further upgraded Japan in its scheme of things. The third volume of *International Relations Since World War II*, for instance, depicts 1956-64 as years of "tempestuous growth in the Japanese economy, as a result of which Japan has assumed a place among the leading industrially developed imperialist states." As a consequence, "Japanese imperialism, . . . gradually increasing its influence in international affairs, has become a dangerous competitor of the United States, England, and other capitalist countries."[82] Lemin similarly in mid-1967 characterized

[80] Y. Nikolayev [Nikolaev], "Soviet-French Relations—an Important Factor of World Politics," *International Affairs*, No. 12 (December 1966), p. 11.

[81] *Ibid.*, p. 10.

[82] AN IMEMO, *Mezhdunarodnye otnosheniia . . .* , Vol. III, p. 479. Cf. D. V. Petrov, *Vneshniaia politika Iaponii posle vtoroi mirovoi voiny* [Japan's Foreign Policy Since World War II] (Moscow: Izdatel'stvo "Mezhdunarodnye otnosheniia," 1965).

Japan as one of the "new 'power centers' of international affairs."[83] The upgrading of Japan, by rendering still more amorphous the line separating the lesser ranked great powers and the major independent states, lent further credence to my prior observation that, in the Soviet calculus, the hierarchical gradations of states are seen as becoming decreasingly differentiated in power terms and that the international order is becoming less rigid.

With respect to the lesser states, too, Soviet commentary continued to extricate itself from the Leninist-Stalinist mold. In 1965 the Institute of World Economy and International Relations sponsored a major conference devoted to considering the major consequences of the emergence of a world in which there were no null powers, a world of metropoles without colonies. In addition, the major post-Khrushchevian doctrinal statement, *The Construction of Communism and the World Revolutionary Process*, gave further indication that political independence, in the dominant Soviet view, was potentially sufficient for independent action by declaring:

> It is characteristic of the world capitalist system now that along with imperialist states there are liberated national-independent states which come out against imperialism, and liberated countries where pro-imperialist regimes govern. One of the fundamental trends of world social development now is the liberation of formerly enslaved countries. The prospect of full independence is opened for states which have thrown off colonial rule but have still not secured full state sovereignty. Therefore the position of dependent countries and semi-colonies in contemporary conditions is de-

[83] Lemin, "Velikaia Oktiabr'skaia . . . , "p. 15.

> fined not as a transitional form of state *dependence* but as a transitional form of state *independence*.[84]

It would seem, therefore, that such changes in Soviet perspective to be detected since Khrushchev's ouster are largely accounted for by the ability of Soviet observers to react to changes in the international order. Khrushchevian and post-Khrushchevian Soviet perspectives on the hierarchical configuration of the present international system have conformed generally with reality or accepted Western notions thereof. An analysis of Soviet perspectives on the international order fails, therefore, to indicate that ideology has proved a hindrance to the Soviet appraisal of the present international system. Instead, it suggests that ideological "erosion" may be something of a misnomer. Erosion connotes a gradual process of encroachment whereby issues of least political significance are the first to be removed from the ideological realm. With respect to the Soviet appraisal of the contemporary international order, however, it was precisely in the analysis of the present, the realm of greatest policy relevance, that ideology least intruded on Soviet perspectives. It is to Khrushchev's credit that during his tenure in power the doctrinal innovation of the third stage of capitalism's general crisis was developed, which encouraged the separation of the policy-relevant world of modern international politics from the encumbrances of Lenin's *Imperialism* and the Leninist-Stalinist propensity to regard the international system as structured in rigidly hierarchical terms.

[84] AN IMEMO, *Stroitel'stvo kommunizma . . .* , p. 234.

Chapter Five: The Distribution of Power

AS a concept "balance of power" has been used in Western international relations commentary by ivory-tower and participant observers alike, to characterize the distribution of power at a given juncture, to refer to international systems as a whole, and to refer to the policies of actors. Regardless of whether the user has situation, system, or policy in mind, the phrase "balance of power" is subject to a plethora of meanings. In its three most common connotations it refers to any distribution of power, an equilibrium of power, or—conversely—to preponderance of power, that is, to disequilibrium.[1] The multiple uses of the phrase frequently cause analytical obfuscation. Nevertheless, an analyst reveals attentiveness to central features of international politics when he uses the phrase "balance of power." Indeed, when the many ways in which the concept has been employed are sorted out, one has a goodly supply of valuable devices for categorizing international systems. Establishing which meanings of balance of power are to be applied in describing a situation, system, or policy is not an unreasonable device for differentiating

[1] A fourth connotation restricts the "balance of power" in meaning to a system in which all, or almost all, states pursue a policy of opposing any state which threatens to dominate the world (or Europe, when it was the known world). In other writings, by contrast, "balance of power" takes on characteristics of a historical or natural law—testimony, no doubt, to the pervasive notion that it is at least partially an automatic process. It has been used to mean power politics generally, and even has been equated with either war or peace. For extensive analysis and commentary see Ernst B. Haas, "The Balance of Power: Prescription, Concept, or Propaganda," *World Politics*, Vol. v, No. 4 (July 1953), pp. 442-77; also Inis L. Claude, Jr., *Power and International Relations* (New York: Random House, 1962), pp. 11-93.

among international systems or comparing international relations perspectives over time or across cultures.

Questions such as the following indicate the importance of concepts subsumed under the rubric, balance of power. What inferences can an observer draw from the distribution of power? Is a particular power configuration characterized by a balance (equilibrium) of power, or does one side have the balance of power in its favor? Are the policies of states characterized by all-around striving for hegemony, or are some states (if so, which ones?) content to achieve a position in which no other state may successfully strive for hegemony? To what extent does the balance of power operate automatically? For a balance of power system to function, must states pursue a balance of power policy? Will the system function even if they do not?

Although the Russian language lacks a phrase with the richness of the English "balance of power"—though one notes with regret the appearance in recent years of the ambiguous *balans sil*[2]—the Russian equivalents of its various meanings play a prominent part in Soviet commentary and analysis. Distribution of power (generally rendered *sootnoshenie sil*

[2] There must be something insidious about "balance of power." One prominent Soviet historian, in a book analyzing "the foreign policy of England at the first stage of capitalism's general crisis" (V. G. Trukhanovskii, *Vneshniaia politika Anglii na pervom etape obshchego krizisa kapitalizma 1918-1939gg.*), in referring to Britain's policy of maintaining a balance of power, used a curious admixture of Russian and Western terminology, *balans sil* (p. 13). A Soviet reviewer, V. Popov, stated: "the author emphasizes the main principle of English foreign policy was and remains the principle of the balance of power"—only Popov describes the English principle as one of *ravnovesie sil* [equilibrium]. Just to confuse matters even more, Popov added: "this principle, writes Trukhanovskii, had as its goal first of all and mainly the establishment of English control in Europe." *Mirovaia ekonomika*, No. 1 (January 1963), p. 154.

[literally, correlation of forces of power] or less frequently, *rasstanovka sil* [the disposition of forces] or *gruppirovka sil* [the grouping of forces]), power politics (*politika sily*), equilibrium (*ravnovesie*), and preponderance of power (*pereves sil*) are common phrases in Soviet discourse.[3]

This chapter traces the changing Soviet description in the last years of Khrushchev's tenure of the global distribution of power and discusses the changes in the characterization and appraisal of the distribution of power in the three years after he went into involuntary retirement. Chapter 7 will analyze the Soviet evaluation of the direction and speed of the international system, against a backdrop of the balance of power as system and policy.

One element the traditional Marxist-Leninist analysis of political relationships shares with Western international relations thinking is its preoccupation with the balance of power in the sense of distribution of power. In fact, the intensity of the Soviet preoccupation with distribution of power has caused Raymond Garthoff to call it the "central concept for regarding political phenomena."[4] In this respect, the Marxist-Leninists have been more royalist than the king, more realist than

[3] For an inventory of Russian terms used in rendering the English "balance of power," see Raymond Garthoff, "The Concept of the Balance of Power in Soviet Policy Making," *World Politics*, Vol. IV, No. 1 (October 1951), pp. 85-111.

Unlike *pereves sil*, *ravnovesie* is not unambiguous; it connotes stability as well as equality. When Stalin, at the Fourteenth Party Congress in 1925, explained that "the current streak of 'peaceful coexistence'" had resulted from "a certain temporary *ravnovesie sil*," he was presumably not asserting the claim, enthralled by revolutionary hubris as he may have been, that the Soviet Union equalled the other countries of the world. The balance was one not of power but of existence; the Soviet Union had temporarily to tolerate the continued existence of the capitalist world and vice-versa.

[4] Garthoff, "Concept of the Balance of Power," passim.

the anthropomorphic realists. The distribution of power between the main protagonists constitutes the core element in the description of a given international situation.

In the Soviet view, those protagonists are and have been traditionally the forces of socialism and imperialism. The confrontation represents to the Soviets what Arnold Wolfers has felicitously termed the "relationship of major tension," and what Soviet observers label the "basic contradiction of the contemporary world." For Soviet analysis, "the basic contradiction" constitutes an expression in doctrinal terms of a world-power, dominant-system perspective on world politics. In the Soviet appraisal the main contradiction between socialism and imperialism shapes the nature of all other contradictions, and the intensity of the contradicton largely determines the global expectations of violence. For Khrushchev and his successors the assumption that there is *a* main contradiction symbolizes the centrality of Soviet-American relations in avoiding a third world war. And this centrality underlies the thinking that led Soviet observers, in a striking departure from the Leninist theory of war, virtually to exclude the possibility of intra-imperialist war. The Chinese, by contrast, have taken the position that the "fundamental contradictions in the contemporary world" are the "contradiction between the socialist camp and the imperialist camp; the contradiction between the proletariat and the bourgeoisie in the capitalist countries; the contradiction between the oppressed nations and imperialist [nations]; and the contradictions among imperialist countries and among monopoly capitalist groups." "Nobody," they declare, "can obliterate any of these fundamental contradictions or subjectively substitute one for the rest."[5]

[5] "A Proposal Concerning the General Line of the International Communist Movement," *Peking Review*, No. 25 (June 21, 1963), p. 7.

Paradoxically, however, in the mid-sixties the movement of Soviet-American relations away from "the pole of power," along with the narrowing of the gap between the first-order great powers and the other major actors, has to a certain extent vitiated the overriding role of the main contradiction in the Soviet calculus. As a result, for instance, Soviet observers from 1962-63 on began to show greater concern for the possibility of catalytic war, which by its very nature indicates that Soviet analysts were obliged to look beyond the Soviet-American relationship. It is at least possible, therefore, that under conditions of lessened expectations of violence Soviet formulations regarding contradictions might move closer to the Chinese appraisal by deemphasizing the significance attached to the contradiction between socialism and imperialism. There has been as yet no evidence that such a development was in the offing, although there have been hints in the Soviet specialized international relations press that there may be domestic, as well as foreign, dogmatists pressing for a reformulation of the doctrine pertaining to contradictions. At the present, the authoritative position continues to be that the main contradiction is between socialism and imperialism.

SCARCELY an article or book devoted to international relations was published, or a foreign policy speech delivered, during the period covered by this study in which there was no reference to the distribution of power among the major protagonists and the implications which should be drawn from correctly appraising that distribution. For this reason, the Soviet appraisals revealed, on the whole, an effort to convey in an internally consistent manner perceived shifts in the distribution of power. The propaganda function of the distribution of power played a role subsidiary to its descriptive purpose.

In spite of the frequency and centrality of Soviet formulations about the distribution of power, translating and decoding them is an ambitious task. One reason for this is the fact that while Soviet analysis of the global distribution of power focused on the main contradiction, the terms of reference were not constant, a ploy which renders the task of comparison exceedingly difficult. For example, how should one compare formulations asserting that the preponderance of power is on the side of peace; on the side of peace, democracy, and socialism; and on the side of socialism—unless one ascribes, as seems implausible in many instances, these variations to mere rhetoric? As a result, while it is rather easy to designate the chief terms of reference which Soviet international relations spokesmen employed in the years between the Twentieth Party Congress and October 1967 to characterize the balance of power as situation, it is more difficult to amplify the content of these terms of reference.

One can summarize the development of Soviet thinking about the power configuration as having come full circle: from one definition of the balance of power as situation, as distribution of power, to another, *preponderance of power*, to still another—*equilibrium*, and finally back to *sootnoshenie sil.* One may assign fairly specific time-spans during which each definition prevailed as the central organizing concept in describing the present distribution of power. Prior to 1959 "distribution of power" (usually *sootnoshenie sil,* occasionally *rasstanovka sil*) was used exclusively. Beginning with 1959 and continuing until late 1961, although formulations involving the generic phrase, distribution of power, prevailed quantitatively, formulations containing *pereves sil* (a favorable balance of power, or preponderance of power) came to the fore. Then, after late 1961, the focal term of reference in Soviet description became *ravnovesie sil* (equilibrium).[6] Finally, since October 1964 there has been a return to the more ambiguous and nondescriptive distribution of power. But careful textual analysis is necessary before one can demonstrate to what extent these terms have the same connotations in Soviet writings that they do in Western description.

To give content to the Soviet perception under Khrushchev of the distribution of power, and to trace the responsiveness of Soviet observers to changes in the distribution of power, particular attention will be given the Soviet response to two developments in the post-Twentieth Party Congress period—the beginning of the missile age in 1957 and the subsequent American response in the early 1960s to changes in the distribution of power. The first may be regarded as constituting or revealing a shift in the distribution of power favorable to the Soviet Union and the socialist camp, the second an unfavorable shift. It was within the context of these two developments that Soviet writers during Khrushchev's tenure in power made the greatest effort to articulate their appraisal of the global distribution of power. In addition, such evidence of a reappraisal of the distribution of power as has appeared since Khrushchev's ouster will be discussed both for its bearing on current Soviet perspectives and for its relevance to an appraisal of what Soviet observers considered the consequences of the changing Khrushchevian characterization.

[6] In light of Stalin's use of *ravnovesie sil* in 1925, perhaps "resurgence" is more precise. However, just as peaceful coexistence had a "new content," so did *ravnovesie sil*; it was no longer temporary and had connotations much closer to the Western notions of balance and equilibrium than to stability.

The Distribution of Power

When in 1957 the Soviet Union announced the testing of an intercontinental ballistic missile and successfully placed in orbit the first earth satellite, Soviet international relations spokesmen quickly took advantage of the impact these events had on the international situation, particularly on the global distribution of power. While the observations frequently were manipulative, especially with reference to the changed strategic value of such specific aspects of power as foreign bases, an analysis of the Soviet appraisal of the global distribution of power, per se, shows that Soviet characterization was expressed carefully. As a result, this would seem to preclude an argument that Soviet claims in 1957-58 about the changed distribution of power were entirely propagandistic. (If, however, such was the case, it is fittingly ironic that both Chinese and American elites took Soviet assertions seriously, with the consequence that the Chinese advocated, and the Americans pursued, policies that were detrimental to Soviet ambitions.) This is not to deny, however, that Khrushchev was attempting to secure political gains by boasting of the impact of sputniks on the distribution of power—which he clearly was.[7]

The salient feature of Soviet analysis at the time was the use, as the basic term of reference, of the distribution of power, and not equilibrium[8] or preponderance of power. Soviet commentary was conspicuously silent about the actual distribu-

[7] Arnold Horelick and Myron Rush, *Strategic Power and Soviet Foreign Policy* (Chicago: The University of Chicago Press, 1966).

[8] In fact, the concept of equilibrium was subjected to severe criticism. Witness M. Marinin's attack on the Yugoslavs, "Nekotorye osobennosti nyneshnego etapa mezhdunarodnykh otnoshenii" [Some Unique Features of the Contemporary Stage of International Relations], *Mirovaia ekonomika*, No. 6 (June 1958), pp. 3-14.

tion of power, and focused almost entirely on the changed distribution of power. The customary formulation asserted that there had been a shift "in favor of socialism." The evaluation by Leonid Il'ichev, a major spokesman on doctrinal matters throughout the Khrushchev years, of "the impact of the sputniks on the world situation, on relations between Socialist and capitalist countries, on foreign policy and international relations," exemplifies the significance ascribed by Soviet observers. "It is hardly necessary," Il'ichev declared, "to prove at length that their launching has enhanced the moral and political influence and the role of the Soviet Union in present-day international relations. . . . But it is not just a matter of an increase in the weight and prestige of one country. *It is a question of a change in the balance of forces [sootnoshenie sil] between Socialism and capitalism, of the strengthening of the former and the weakening of the latter.*"[9] Quite obviously, in the Soviet analysis the advent of the missile age involved more than a mere change in the distribution of power. Instead it was alleged that an especially significant alteration—bordering on the qualitative—in the distribution of power had taken place. As one editorial declared, the developments in 1957 had revealed "the radical changes which had taken place" in the distribution of power.[10] Others spoke of the "serious change in the distribution of power"[11]; the present "real" (but unspecified) distribution of power which could give the imperialists pause;[12] and the "new" (again unspecified)

[9] L. Ilyichov [Il'ichev], "The Sputniks and International Relations," *International Affairs*, No. 3 (March 1958), p. 11, italics in original.

[10] "Osnovnaia zadacha sovremennosti," p. 5; M. Rubinshtein, "Nauka i mezhdunarodnye otnosheniia" [Science and International Relations], *Mirovaia ekonomika*, No. 6 (June 1958), p. 43.

[11] Marinin, "Nekotorye osobennosti . . . ," p. 14.

[12] Colonel A. Kononenko, " 'Lokal'nye voiny' v politike i strategii SShA" ['Local Wars' in U.S. Policy and Strategy], *Mirovaia ekonomika*, No. 10 (October 1958), p. 25.

distribution of power.[13] Soviet formulations conveyed an impression that striking changes had been perceived in the distribution of power. Soviet observers obviously were aware that the Soviet Union and the socialist camp had achieved a major gain in their relative positions of power.

What these formulations failed to convey was the Soviet perception of the actual distribution of power between the two camps. One is drawn to the view that the failure to make explicit the distribution of power was not accidental. Perhaps a reason for this was some ambivalence in Moscow about the political significance of the sputniks. Indeed, M. Baturin may have had the Soviet dialogue in mind when he noted that, "Not all may have yet grasped the influence which man-made earth satellites will exert in world relations. Western commentators—*and not they alone*—seem to ignore the fact that the importance of Soviet scientific and technological advances is not confined to the purely scientific sphere. . . . *They are also of major social significance*."[14] In particular, it was not clear whether the distribution of power had already changed or was now changing. Marinin,[15] polemicizing with the Yugoslavs, declared in a lead editorial: "It was impossible to be oriented correctly in the complex labyrinth of international affairs if one did not realize that the distribution of power had changed radically in favor of socialism." Others depicted the distribution of power as "changing ever more in favor of socialism,"[16] while yet another major spokesman—

[13] B. Artemov, "O sovetsko-amerikanskikh otnosheniiakh" [On Soviet-American Relations], *Mirovaia ekonomika*, No. 11 (November 1958), p. 23.

[14] "Peace and the Status Quo," *International Affairs*, No. 1 (January 1958), p. 71, italics supplied for the words "and not they alone."

[15] Marinin, "Nekotorye osobennosti . . ." p. 4.

[16] "Osnovnaia zadacha sovremennosti" [The Fundamental Task of Modern Times], *Mirovaia ekonomika*, No. 1 (January 1958), p. 5.

Korionov—spoke of the distribution of power "tipping still further"[17] in favor of the socialist camp. A second reason for the failure to make explicit the distribution of power was that Soviet commentators were agreed that the socialist camp was still in an inferior position vis-à-vis the West. The focus on shifting relative power positions indicates the formulation may be construed to mean that within the framework of a continued balance of power on the side of capitalism, the gap had been narrowed.[18]

To justify an assumption that the claims of a dramatic shift in the distribution of power were testimony to continued Soviet perception of socialism's inferior position[19] requires that several statements be accounted for, statements which do not seem to gibe with expectations based on this assumption.[20] For instance, consider the following from an editorial in *International Affairs*:

[17] V. Korionov, "The Crisis of the 'Positions of Strength' Policy," *International Affairs*, No. 3 (March 1958), p. 34.

[18] If we consider Soviet descriptions of intra-capitalist relations, for instance, we note that on several occasions in recent years Soviet polemicists observed that the distribution of power had changed in favor of Germany. In this instance, since we know that in the Soviet view Germany was not the greatest capitalist power and had no prospects of becoming so in the foreseeable future, we also know the formulation referred only to a narrowing of the gap. Moreover, one has a suspicion that if the Soviet ruling group thought the distribution of power favored the socialist camp (as opposed to having changed in favor of the socialist camp), it would have advanced this claim.

[19] For a statement that prior to the emergence of socialism from the confines of a single country (or strictly speaking, as Soviet books sometimes now acknowledge, at a time when "only the young Soviet state and revolutionary Mongolia were opposed" to imperialism), "the preponderance [*pereves sil*] of power was on the side of the old world," see A. A. Gromyko, ed., *Mirnoe sosushchestovanie—Leninskii kurs*, p. 3.

[20] As readers of Donald S. Zagoria's *The Sino-Soviet Conflict, 1956-61* will realize, the citations in the following pages oblige us to modify sev-

> The world socialist system has now become the decisive factor in averting war and in the struggle for peaceful co-existence. Shoulder to shoulder with the Soviet Union, the peoples of China, Poland, Czechoslovakia and other European and Asian People's Democracies have joined forces in the united socialist camp, *whose strength is now greater* than that of imperialism. The strength of the socialist camp prevents war not only between the capitalist and socialist countries but also between the capitalist countries themselves.[21]

Similarly, what are we to make of Khrushchev's (presumably) studied ambiguity in contending, at almost the same time, that while "the U.S. ruling circles have always thought they were stronger than we were," "we, however, have another opinion on this score,"[22] or his calling into question

---

eral subsidiary observations he has made in connection with Soviet calculations of the distribution of power. The validity of his central point, however, is reconfirmed—namely, that no Soviet observer has ever claimed that Soviet possession of ICBMs gave the camp *overwhelming* superiority over the West, or that a Soviet first strike could effectively preclude an American second strike.

[21] "An Imperative Demand," *International Affairs*, No. 1 (January 1958), p. 3, italics added. The assertion that war between capitalist countries is prevented was exceptional. In the sixties Soviet commentary usually employed the polemically safer formulation, that the possibility of war "cannot be excluded." (See, e.g., Khrushchev, "Za novye pobedy . . . ," p. 17.) However, A. Galkin in 1961 did assert that the "fear of socialism . . . prevents these contradictions from growing over into armed conflicts." "Some Aspects of the Problem of Peace and War," *International Affairs*, No. 11 (November 1961), p. 30.

[22] N. S. Khrushchev, *K pobede v mirnom sorevnovanii s kapitalizmom* [For Victory in Peaceful Competition with Capitalism] (Moscow: Gospolitizdat, 1959), p. 24.

the doctrine of capitalist encirclement because it was "no longer certain who encircles whom"[23]?

Equally important, we must account for the considerable evidence that at least some Soviet analysts believed a historical shift had been brought on by the new missile age.[24] In fact, Soviet specialized international relations journals treated the effects on the international system of the changes in the distribution of power in a way which seemed an adumbration of the "third stage of capitalism's general crisis," and which since 1960-61 has become authoritative doctrine. Thus, while Il'ichev wondered: "if the launching of the sputniks is not only a scientific but also a social phenomenon, . . . do they not mark the dawn of a new era in international relations, and will they not lead to a radical reappraisal of many ossified conceptions of both military and diplomatic strategy?"[25]—he also asserted the now familiar view that "the position of those who support co-existence between countries with different social systems has become more stable than ever before. *The world has entered a new stage of co-existence.*"[26] At least

[23] *Ibid.*, p. 154.

[24] Zagoria, *The Sino-Soviet Conflict*, contends that "Soviet spokesmen [have not] indicated [that] the fall of 1957 marked a 'turning point' in the balance of forces" (p. 161).

[25] Il'ichev, *The Sputniks . . .*, p. 7.

[26] *Ibid.*, italics in original. On the other hand, see the attack, in the context of renewed polemics with Yugoslavia, by N. Nazarov ("Ideinye korni revizionizma v voprosakh mezhdunarodnykh otnoshenii" [Ideological Roots of Revisionism in Questions of International Relations], *Mirovaia ekonomika*, No. 7 [July 1958], p. 29) on "American revisionists" for speaking "of a supposedly 'new era' of peaceful coexistence which supposedly has already arrived." This may have been part of a desperate effort to suggest differences where there were none, rather than an attack on Il'ichev. The C.P.S.U. in 1958 found itself torn be-

one Soviet spokesman did indicate specifically that in 1957 a turning point in the world situation was in the process of being initiated. In an article entitled, significantly, "Several Unique Attributes of International Relations in the Present Stage," M. Marinin declared that "from whatever side we approach an evaluation of the present stage of international affairs, its special significance stands out first and foremost. Undoubtedly, it must become [*dolzhen stat'*] a turning point in the development of international relations."[27]

Several observers related the new historical period specifically to the distribution of power.[28] In reference to "the distribution of power in the world arena . . . [which] has changed radically in favor of socialism, to the detriment of capitalism," Marinin observed: "this is not a temporary phenomenon but a fact of world-historical significance which expresses deep changes in the course of world development."[29] M. Rubinshtein said that "the creation of intercontinental

---

tween the Chinese and Yugoslav ideological positions. As the polemics intensified, several of the formulations resorted to became more defensible. Thus the claim that Soviet deterrence *prevented* war between capitalist states was usually avoided.

[27] Marinin, "Nekotorye osobennosti . . . ," p. 3. On p. 5 Marinin spoke of the "turning-point nature" of the contemporary period of international relations. See also the statement of Dmitriev, *Pentagon . . .* , p. 171, characterizing the events in the fall of 1957 as having evoked "a *decisive change* in the distribution of power in favor of the Soviet Union, in favor of the world socialist system," and his remark (on p. 172) that they "changed radically the military-political geography of our planet and also the nature of contemporary war." Italics added.

[28] Zagoria, while acknowledging that "the Russians did speak . . . of a 'new era' . . . in international relations," had contended "they did not relate this 'new era' to a change in the balance of forces between the Communist and Western powers." *The Sino-Soviet Conflict*, p. 161.

[29] Marinin, "Nekotorye osobennosti . . . ," p. 4.

rockets, with the aid of which the Soviet sputniks were launched, are leading to a strategic revolution, which is also a revolution in international relations. The appearance of the sputniks put an end to the dogma of technical superiority of the U.S. It signifies a radical change in the distribution of power."[30] Another Soviet commentator declared: "the launching of earth satellites by the Soviet Union with the aid of intercontinental ballistic rockets began a new *period* in the history of international relations. The illusion of inaccessibility of any territory is fully and totally dispelled. If before some country could wage war on alien territory in conditions of relative personal security, then today it has become clear to all that such calculations are absurd."[31]

What, then, can be said about the Soviet appraisal of the distribution of power at this juncture? All things considered, there remains the compelling conclusion that Soviet commentators considered the socialist camp to be in an inferior position vis-à-vis the West. What *had* happened in the Soviet view was that the United States had lost its privileged position of strategic invulnerability. Now the U.S., like the other great powers, probably could not gain from a world war and certainly would suffer greatly were one to break out. The importance of this point cannot be stressed too strongly. It may seem curious that Soviet observers should place so much emphasis on it, especially when the Soviet Union was the only World War II successor state. But from their vantage point

[30] Rubinshtein, "Nauka . . . ," p. 43. See also Dmitriev, *Pentagon . . .*, p. 277.

[31] Artemov, "O sovetsko-amerikanskikh . . . ," p. 22, italics added. General Talensky [Talenskii], "Military Strategy and Foreign Policy," *International Affairs*, No. 3 (March 1958), p. 27, said: "The main thing about the ICBM is that it makes it possible to strike *any* part of the world." Italics added.

it has merit, since the United States emerged from World War II unscathed, prosperous, and unquestionably the world's mightiest power.

For the first time the United States was finding itself confronted by an actor of the same qualitative order. In the *future,* but only in the future, "the United States will . . . be only one Great Power competing with another Power just as great. The days of U.S. military superiority . . . were short-lived and are gone with the wind."[32] This was the most distinctive feature of contemporary international relations in the Soviet perspective. It was now the case that no power could resort to the ultimate means of coercion without expecting and experiencing severe deprivation.

This evaluation does not mean that in the Soviet view the Soviet Union or the socialist camp was equal to or stronger than the United States and the West—except in one curious sense. Soviet commentators implied that the socialist camp could deal a blow to the European capitalist countries and to the United States that would be as unacceptable and intolerable to those countries as a blow to the Soviet Union would be. Soviet statements in 1957-58 seemingly do not reveal conclusively whether Soviet observers expected the Soviet Union and the socialist camp to emerge worse off than the capitalist world; but it is clear that by 1957-58 the Soviet view was that the *heartlands* of *all* states would suffer, including the Soviet Union and the United States.

As a result, the West was deterred.[33] The claim that the

[32] Korionov, "The Crisis . . . ," p. 33.

[33] One tell-tale indication of Soviet confidence in the deterrent capability of the U.S.S.R. was the disappearance of hints concerning pre-emption. "The idea of pre-emption was brought up and fairly clearly defined in the spring of 1955 and seemed to be more or less officially

socialist camp's "strength is now greater" is thus more accurately interpreted as a poorly formulated assertion of deterrence and confidence in the diminished likelihood of war—as well as, perhaps, a means of intimidating the West. The "forces of peace"—more accurately, the *chances* of peace—were now greater than imperialism and the forces of war. Gen. Talenskii expressed it far more precisely in 1960 when he asserted, "the defensive might of the socialist camp clearly exceeds the military possibilities of the aggressive blocs of capitalist states"[34]: the United States' capacity to coerce was not as great as the Soviet Union's ability to punish attempts at coercion.[35]

What the Russians did not assert—and here they diverged sharply from their Chinese comrades in perception and policy prescription—was that the U.S.S.R. was now in a position to coerce with relative impunity. The contrast, for instance, be-

---

adopted at that time. . . . But there were few other references in various sources in the next year or two, and it seemed to drop out from late 1957 until late 1961." Raymond Garthoff in Robert D. Crane, ed., *Soviet Nuclear Strategy* (Washington, D.C.: The Center for Strategic Studies, Georgetown University, 1963), p. 35.

[34] Talenskii, "Neoproverzhimyi vyvod istorii" [The Indisputable Conclusion of History], *Kommunist*, No. 7 (May 1960), p. 39, italics added.

[35] Pursuing this line of reasoning, a Soviet observer, given the stated postulate that imperialism was the only source of war, might describe the camp of socialism and peace as having a preponderance of power even if the socialist camp were *strategically* only equal to or inferior to the West. For a detailed elaboration of this train of thought see N. M. Nikol'skii, *Osnovnoi vopros sovremennosti* [The Basic Question of our Times] (Moscow: Izdatel'stvo "Mezhdunarodnye Otnosheniia," 1964), who, borrowing from Klaus Knorr's *The War Potential of Nations*, introduces to Soviet literature the concept of "peace potential" or deterrent capability; see especially p. 269.

tween Khrushchev's admission—"Of course, we [the Soviet Union], too, will suffer great losses"[36]—and the Chinese statement that "the United States, for the first time in history . . . [is in] a position *where neither escape nor striking back is possible*,"[37] could scarcely be more clearcut. (Presumably these divergent formulations had been debated at the November 1957 conference of ruling parties.) Nor were Soviet international relations commentators as optimistic as the Chinese about the range of issues concerning which the Soviet Union could utilize successfully and credibly the threat to initiate central war in order to secure political gains—which is not to say that the Soviet Union abstained from rocket-rattling.[38] In summary, Soviet observers did not claim that the socialist camp had military strategic superiority (it was not until 1960 that such a claim was advanced), and hesitated even to assert military equality; rather they were content to *deny* American superiority.

In Soviet thinking, the military power ratio is only a part of the over-all distribution of power. "The distribution of power," Khrushchev explained in an interview in January 1958, "is a broad question; it includes political, economic,

[36] Khrushchev, *Pravda*, November 19, 1957.

[37] *Shih-chieh chih-shih* [World Culture], December 20, 1957, cited in Zagoria, *Sino-Soviet Conflict*, pp. 162-63, italics Zagoria's.

[38] According to Talenskii, the Soviet government hoped to make use of the *"greater advantages in defensive power . . . for renewed efforts for peace, for ending the arms race, banning nuclear weapons and their tests, establishing atom-free zones, reducing armed forces and their withdrawal from foreign territories, and easing the international tension in other ways."* ("Military Strategy and Foreign Policy," *International Affairs*, No. 3 [March 1958], p. 26, italics in original.) The ICBMs, in brief, would be used to lower tension *and* to secure U.S. withdrawal from Europe.

and military factors."[39] "As regards the economic factor," the most Khrushchev would claim was that

> the Soviet Union and other socialist countries, as no one can any longer deny, have achieved great successes in the development of their economy and rapidly are changing the distribution of power in their favor. Under conditions of peaceful economic competition, we have no doubts whatsoever that the task set by V. I. Lenin, of overtaking and surpassing the most developed capitalist countries . . . economically, will be successfully resolved by the Soviet people. We may say that *we have already outlined the plans for the practical resolution of this task*.[40]

Economically the socialist camp was clearly in a position of inferiority to the West. Therefore, since Moscow also did not believe the socialist camp was militarily stronger than the West, if *only* deterrence obtained and not first-strike counterforce, the socialist camp was still in an inferior position in the over-all distribution of power. This being the case, we may reassert that the Soviet formulation depicting a shift in the distribution of power in favor of socialism was carefully ex-

[39] Khrushchev, *K pobede* . . . , p. 15. The rank-order probably reveals Khrushchev's voluntaristic bias toward the importance of politics. (By "political" in this context, Khrushchev was referring to the policy choices of states.)

"The Soviet Union and other socialist countries steadfastly pursue a policy of peace, come out for peaceful coexistence with various social structures. . . . The U.S.S.R. supports the just national-liberation struggle of the peoples. . . . Such a peace-loving and humane policy . . . cannot but evoke sympathy toward the Soviet Union, cannot but *increase its weight and influence* in international affairs."

Ibid., italics added.

[40] *Ibid.,* italics added.

pressed so as to acknowledge tacitly that the distribution of power, in the Soviet view, still favored the capitalist camp.

This view diverged markedly from the Chinese appraisal. The Chinese[41] argued that the camp was superior even before 1957; the ICBMs, according to the Chinese, had only revealed "*the superiority of the anti-imperialist forces in even more concentrated form.*"[42] An explanation for these divergent appraisals points to the interaction of policy disposition and perception and draws attention to fundamental assumptions concerning the nature of power in international politics. Soviet and Chinese commentators rank differently the various elements in the power mix of an actor. As we have seen in other contexts, the Russians generally have assigned more weight to economic might as a measure of political power than have the Chinese. This tendency under Khrushchev echoed Stalin's appraisal, despite the fact that it served as a foil for Mao's charges of "economism" against Khrushchev.[43] The Chinese attached greater importance to "the masses" as a factor of political power. The Chinese and Russians also seem to have different definitions of power. In international politics, Soviet analysis during the Khrushchev regime was disinclined to treat political power and the resort to violence as synonymous. In 1957-58 there was as yet no overt evidence,[44] as there was to be in the early sixties, that many of the more modernist Soviet observers regarded as outdated Clausewitz's and Lenin's dictum that war is the continuation of politics by

[41] See Zagoria's astute observations, pp. 160-68.

[42] *Jen-min jih-pao*, November 27, 1957, cited in Zagoria, *Sino-Soviet Conflict*, p. 165, italics Zagoria's.

[43] The rejoinder of AN IMEMO, *Stroitel'stvo kommunizma . . .*, to Chinese charges of "economism" was, "There is 'economism' and economism" (p. 129).

[44] For a discussion of the Clausewitz controversy, see below, pp. 222-23.

other means. Neither would any Soviet observer, then or now, accept Mao's view that "political power grows out of the barrel of a gun," or assert, as Mao has, that "War is the continuation of politics; in this sense war is politics and war itself is a political action." Indeed, several articles written in 1958 attacked views similar to the above statements. In one article two Soviet military historians attacked the "bourgeois *conception*"—thus in all probability indicating that the criticism was directed at nonbourgeois figures—that "war merges with politics and therefore war is politics and politics is war."[45] Il'ichev declared that "arms are not the only instrument of national policy, a fact which, to a degree, is being understood in the West."[46]

In Soviet opinion, the maximum political effectiveness of the ICBM could be attained through its combined use as a symbol of the superiority of socialism over capitalism and as a military instrument.[47] As a symbol, the sputniks conveyed the impression that socialism was the wave of the future, and therefore that peaceful atomic power and earth satellites were "*the standard-bearers of socialist civilization*," as symbolic of socialism as "the steam engine and electric generator" had been "*of 19th century capitalist civilization*."[48] For Western decision-makers, therefore, a "realistic policy"[49] would involve ad-

[45] M. Mil'shtein and A. Slobodenko, "Problema sootnosheniia politiki i voiny v imperialisticheskoi ideologii" [The Relation of War and Politics in Imperialist Ideology], *Mirovaia ekonomika*, No. 9 (September 1958), p. 63.

[46] Il'ichev, "The Sputniks . . . ," p. 12.

[47] Note the criticism of "Western observers" who "confine the importance of sputniks to the purely military sphere," in M. Baturin, "Peace and the Status Quo," p. 71.

[48] *Ibid.*, italics in original.

[49] It was at this juncture—1958-59—that Soviet commentators, includ-

justing to this prospect. Derivatively, of course, this adjustment by the West would result in tangible gains for the Soviet Union (e.g., Berlin). Militarily the greatest effectiveness of the ICBM would lie in preventing the imperialists from interfering with the progress of national liberation movements and the advance of communist control in the underdeveloped countries. The Soviet appraisal of the ICBMs seems to have been somewhat more oriented to a Lasswellian concept of power, as the capacity to rearrange values, than the Chinese position, and less disposed to *equate* power with coercion. Soviet expectations about power, in a sense, were more manipulation-inclined and less control-oriented.

Preponderance

During 1959-61, following the first appraisal of the implications of the missile age for the distribution of power between the camps, Soviet description of that distribution increasingly revealed confidence in the strength of the socialist camp. There were many reasons for optimism. Salient episodes in the cold war, along with a steady closing of the economic gap between the camps, Soviet space successes, and, until 1958-59, the seemingly successful reintegration of the camp after 1956 (especially when measured against a stagnant American economy, a not altogether successful satellite program, and perennial crises in NATO), combined to create high expecta-

---

ing Khrushchev, began asserting that the United States must now deal with the Soviet Union from "positions of reason" and abandon its "positions of strength" policy. For an assertion that the *men* of reason "are in the majority even among the most deadly enemies of Communism," see, *inter alia*, Khrushchev's 1960 Bucharest speech, English translation in Hudson, Lowenthal, and MacFarquhar, eds., *The Sino-Soviet Dispute*, p. 133.

tions in Soviet minds that socialism was the wave of the near future.[50]

The changes in formulation may be briefly summarized in terms of *pereves sil,* favorable balance; they were revealed in the greater disposition by Soviet commentators to assert Soviet preeminence in a broadening range of categories. The imagery used to describe the shift went directly from that of an international order in which the West still predominated to one in which the emerging reality was the predominance of the socialist camp. This shift was highly indicative of the persistence in the Soviet Union of expectations of a rigidly hierarchical international order. The switchover position, in other words, normatively and descriptively, still was considered an essentially transient phenomenon in which the old order would give way to the new.[51]

The first hint of socialist camp preponderance as the new reality was given by Khrushchev in his concluding remarks at the Twenty-first Party Congress: "If we take the countries which are in the world socialist system and the countries which are waging a valiant struggle against imperialism and colonialism for freedom and national independence, the preponderance of forces [*pereves sil*] is now on the side of the

[50] For a competent survey of the developments giving Soviet communists cause for optimism, see Richard Lowenthal, "The End of an Illusion," *Problems of Communism*, Vol. XII, No. 1 (January-February 1963), pp. 1-10.

[51] In light of what follows, Donald Zagoria's contention that "the Russians did not—and still do not—assert that the overall strength of the Bloc exceeds that of the West," *The Sino-Soviet Conflict*, pp. 158-59, needs to be amended. The Russians never asserted that the camp possessed an *overwhelming* superiority. Moscow is not disposed to take the risks the Chinese advocate until it possesses such qualitative superiority, at least militarily.

peace-loving countries and not on the side of the imperialist states."[52]

In 1960 assertions of superiority became more specific and less contingent. It was claimed in the aftermath of the U-2 incident that "the distribution of power between the two systems is steadily changing. For several years now these changes have obtained for socialism a preponderance of power over capitalism in the scales of the planet."[53] Statements appeared claiming the preponderance of military power for the socialist camp.[54] Finally, the Statement of the Eighty-one Parties gave definitive vent to the formulation that "*the superiority of the forces of socialism over those of imperialism, of the forces of peace over those of war, is becoming ever more marked in the world arena.*"[55]

A new international order was forming, in which the rules of the international game would be determined by the socialist camp, and the power pyramid would be capped by the Soviet Union. "In contemporary conditions, the pre-conditions

[52] Leo Gruliow ed., *Current Soviet Policies III* (New York: Columbia University Press, 1960), p. 201.

[53] V. Gantman et al., "Tekushchie problemy mirovoi politiki" [Current Problems of World Politics], *Mirovaia ekonomika*, No. 7 (July 1960), p. 32.

[54] Most notably, Khrushchev's January 14, 1960 speech to the Supreme Soviet (*Pravda*, January 15, 1960), and his assertion in March 1960 that "the Soviet Union is now the world's strongest military power" (*Izvestiia*, March 2, 1960). See also I. Kon, "Problemy mezhdunarodnykh otnoshenii v sovremennoi burzhuaznoi sotsiologii" [Problems of International Relations in Contemporary Bourgeois Sociology], *Mirovaia ekonomika*, No. 2 (February 1960), p. 67: "Not only ideologically but military-strategically as well, the preponderance has turned out to be on the side of socialism."

[55] Hudson, Lowenthal, and MacFarquhar, eds., *Sino-Soviet Dispute*, p. 178, italics in original.

are created so that socialism is in a position to determine, in growing measure, the character, methods, and trends of international relations."[56] The most important element underlying this vision was a belief that Soviet deterrent capability had synthesized a new unity of theory and practice. The atom bomb had separated war and revolution for the first time. In this period—1959 to 1961—Soviet observers from Khrushchev down seemed confident that peace and worldwide accession to power by Leninist parties of a "new type" were compatible.

At the same time, and in several ways, peace took priority over accession to power. To the Soviet way of thinking, peace—the absence of violence between states—was a necessary and desirable prerequisite to revolution. (The Chinese, on the other hand, continued to see revolution as prerequisite to peace.) Also, securing peace was a more immediate task. Finally, peace was that which the socialist camp could now secure, given its present strength, which explains why the Chinese and Russians[57] have each accused the other of *underestimating* the distribution of power: the Chinese were referring to the capacity to effect revolutions, the Russians to the capacity to achieve peace. Thus the "denominator" in the Soviet equation referred to the preponderant position of "the

[56] Khrushchev, "Za novye pobedy . . . ," p. 7.

[57] For an early example of an overt Soviet attack on "some dogmatists who recognize verbally" that a "sharp turning-point in the distribution of power" had occurred but who do not draw the proper conclusions, see M. Marinin, "Chelovechestvo mozhet i dol'zhno zhit' bez voin" [Mankind Can and Must Live Without Wars], *Mirovaia ekonomika*, No. 8 (August 1960), p. 5. Interestingly, in view of Khrushchev's reference in 1962 to imperialism's "atomic teeth," Marinin added, "of course, this does not signify that imperialism has already lost its teeth" (*ibid.*).

peace-loving countries,"[58] of "peace, democracy, and socialism,"[59] while the Chinese adverted to the "anti-imperialist forces," or "socialism and all the oppressed peoples and nations of the world."[60]

In the Soviet conception major revolutionary gains were deferred to the future—but to the near future; how major and how near may perhaps be best gauged from Academician S. Strumilin's disquieting article, "The World Twenty Years From Now."[61] In that article, Strumilin declared: "We do not know how many of these countries will fully enter the commonwealth of socialist countries in the next ten to twenty years." However,

> we can expect with certainty that their gravitation toward this camp will increase with each year, rather than diminish. . . . The growth in the population of the socialist camp attributable to the addition of new members just since 1945,

[58] E.g., Khrushchev's concluding remarks at the Twenty-first Party Congress, cited in Gruliow, ed., *Current Soviet Policies III*, p. 201.

[59] E.g., Cheprov and Iudin, "Nesostoiatel'nost' politiki voennykh blokov," p. 80.

[60] These particular phrases are taken from the *Jen-min jih-pao* editorial of November 24, 1957 (cited in Zagoria, *Sino-Soviet Conflict*, p. 165) and "A Proposal Concerning the General Line of the International Communist Movement," *Peking Review*, Vol. VI, No. 25 (June 21, 1963), p. 7.

The Chinese have referred on occasion to "peace forces"—as they did in the editorial "Full Steam Ahead," in the January 1, 1958 *Jin-min jih-pao* (Zagoria, *Sino-Soviet Conflict*, p. 170). But, as the editorial's title suggests, the context clearly indicates immediate revolutionary advances were being advocated.

[61] Strumilin, "Mir cherez 20 let" [The World 20 Years From Now], *Kommunist*, No. 13 (September 1961), pp. 25-36, at p. 27. For an English translation see *Current Digest*, Vol. XIII, No. 38 (October 18, 1961), pp. 3-7.

> after the world war, reached not less than 830,000,000 persons by 1960. . . . We can expect that in the future this irreversible process of the socialist camp's expansion will proceed according to approximately the same rate and volume.
>
> But out of prudence, let us even assume that not more than 30% of the populations of the neutral countries and not more than 10% of those of the imperialist camp take the socialist road during the next twenty years, and that in the first decade—up to 1970—the percentages are only half of these.

To secure peace, a *pereves sil* might suffice. But a new revolutionary stage required the achievement of an overwhelming or decisive preponderance of power. That would come, it was said at the Twenty-first Party Congress, only when the socialist camp had achieved "superiority . . . over the world capitalist system in material production, the decisive sphere of human activity."[62] As a result of the fulfilling of the tasks of the seven-year plan, it was claimed, "the countries of the world socialist system will produce more than half of the total world industrial output."[63] Then there would have been created a "real possibility of excluding world war from the life of society even before the complete triumph of socialism, even with capitalism existing in part of the world."[64] In 1965, moreover, according to a lead article in *Mirovaia ekonomika*, "the entrance of the Soviet Union and the whole socialist camp into the decisive period of peaceful economic competition with capitalism will signify . . . the beginning of

[62] "Control Figures of the Development of the U.S.S.R. National Economy in 1959-65," cited in Gruliow, ed., *Current Soviet Policies III*, p. 25.

[63] *Ibid.*

[64] Khrushchev's Report to the Congress, *ibid.*, p. 58.

a qualitatively new stage in the development of the liberation movement of the working class."[65] Until that time, however, "the Party's principal [task in international relations] in the forthcoming seven year period . . . [was] to gain the maximum amount of time in the peaceful economic competition of socialism with capitalism."[66]

Equilibrium

The Strumilin article was to be the apogee of Soviet optimism. The American reaction to a potential missile gap, the Sino-Soviet crisis, the overextension of Soviet commitments, several specific failures at home and abroad, and more generally the sobering effects of experiencing the responsibilities and frustrations[67] which (as Americans have known for two

[65] N. Kolesov, "Semiletnii plan i mezhdunarodnoe rabochee dvizhenie" [The Seven-year Plan and the International Labor Movement], *Mirovaia ekonomika*, No. 5 (May 1959), p. 3. I am not aware of this particularly blunt and optimistic phraseology having been used at the Twenty-first Congress. Neither the "Control Figures . . ." nor Khrushchev's "Report to the Congress . . . " nor his "Concluding Remarks" contain the assertion.

[66] "Resolution of Twenty-first Congress . . . ," in Gruliow, ed., *Current Soviet Policies III*, pp. 209-10.

[67] On the responsibilities and burdens of power note the admonition directed to Mao by the *Pravda*, January 7, 1963 editorial:

"Communists, and especially Communists who are statesmen and political figures, cannot act like irresponsible hacks. After all, holding power as they do, they are responsible for the destinies of peoples and states, and, what is more, for the destiny of the world socialist system. They are obliged to approach assessment of the inescapable consequences of a modern thermonuclear war reasonably and with the highest sense of responsibility, and not rehash old truths from past centuries or hurl empty, bombastic phrases."

English translation in *Current Digest*, Vol. xv, No. 1 (January 30, 1963), p. 6.

For another statement emphasizing the negative aspects of power, also compare the following: "It has fallen to the *lot* of the Soviet people

decades) accompany world-power status—all combined to effect an appreciable diminishing of Soviet claims concerning the socialist camp's global power status.

Of all these developments, America's reaction in the early sixties to the prospect of a missile gap was the focal point of Soviet commentary. The Soviet concentration concerned three facets of the American reaction: the tremendous increase in United States strategic might and limited-war capability; the American reaction at the level of strategic doctrine (most notably, Maxwell Taylor's ideas about flexible response); and the reappraisal by official Washington and those whom Soviet observers purport to regard as its authoritative spokesmen—specifically Walter Lippmann—of the global distribution of power and the movement of the international system. The American reaction was thus seen as constituting a chal-

---

to bear the main burden of the struggle against imperialism. It is not an easy thing to bear such a burden, and the Soviet people have had to go without many things." (V. G. Korionov, "Proletarian Internationalism—Our Victorious Weapon," *International Affairs*, No. 8 [August 1963], p. 17, italics added.) This latter observation expanded on Khrushchev's statement at the Twenty-second Party Congress, that "*the great mission of being the pioneers of communist construction . . . has fallen to the lot of the Soviet people. . . .*" *Pravda*, October 18, 1961; English translation in *Current Digest*, Vol. XIII, No. 40 (November 1, 1961), p. 5, italics in original.

Quite obviously, both these statements were intended to bolster Soviet claims to deference from other communist states and nonruling parties. Nevertheless, the tone contrasts strikingly with that expressed by Lenin at the First All-Russian Congress of Soviets. There, it will be recalled, Tsereteli (the Menshevik Minister of Posts) declared, "at the present moment there is no political party which would say: 'Give the power into our hands, we will take your place.' There is no such party in Russia," whereupon the official record reports "Lenin from his seat: 'There is [such a party].' " As cited in E. H. Carr, *The Bolshevik Revolution, 1917-1923* (London: Macmillan and Co., Ltd., 1950), Vol. I, p. 90.

lenge both to the strictly military-strategic distribution of power, as well as to the evaluation of the over-all distribution of power.

The United States "intensification of the arms race" in the first months of the Kennedy administration appears to have exacerbated the ongoing dialogue within the Soviet ruling group concerning the adequacy of the Soviet deterrent. That debate, which has been analyzed elsewhere,[68] need not concern us here, except for its relation to Khrushchev's and the international relations specialists' view of the distribution of power. The important thing in this context is that in October 1961, for the first time since 1957, a major Soviet figure—Marshal Rodion Malinovskii—intimated that under certain conditions the Soviet Union might preempt. "The methods of breaking up the opponent's aggressive plans by dealing him a crushing blow *in good time* [italics added]," Malinovskii declared, "will be of *decisive significance* [italics in original]."[69] This, coupled with other intimations[70] from the Soviet press in the period October 1961 (i.e., after Deputy Secretary of Defense Roswell Gilpatric's speech) to March 1962, suggested grave misgivings on the part of some Soviet observers lest the defining characteristics of imperialist international relations be restored. The McNamara doctrine, some Soviet commentators appear to have reasoned, raised the threat that the United States might reassume its position of relative

[68] See especially Wolfe, *Soviet Strategy at the Crossroads.*

[69] *Pravda,* October 25, 1961.

[70] Note in particular the warning (the timing of which was presumably not accidental) by A. Galkin, "Some Aspects of the Problem of Peace and War," *International Affairs,* No. 11 (November 1961), p. 33, that "a disturbance in the balance tempts *the reckless elements of the imperialist camp to use the temporarily favourable situation to destroy those whom they consider their enemies*" (italics added).

strategic invulnerability and thus restore the rigidly hierarchical cast to the international order, as well as restore the rules of the international political game that had been characteristic of the period when "imperialism determined the main course and content of international events."

Khrushchev, by contrast, at the Twenty-second Party Congress continued to take the inward-oriented, rather quiescent posture implicit in his Twenty-first Congress statements, that "material production" was "the decisive sphere of human activity" and that when the countries of the socialist camp "produce more than half of the total world industrial output" there would have been created a "real possibility of excluding world war from the life of society even before the complete triumph of socialism." "When the Soviet Union," he declared, "becomes the first industrial power, when the socialist system has been transformed completely into the decisive factor in world developments—and when the forces of world peace have multiplied still further, the scales will be tipped permanently in favor of the forces of peace and the barometer of the international climate will point to 'clear, the danger of world war is gone forever.' "[71]

By March 1962, however, after the Soviet military had taken certain steps—nuclear weapons tests, the development of the "global rocket," the redeploying of launch sites—which apparently increased the credibility of the Soviet deterrent, the protagonists in the intra-Soviet dialogue appear to have been in agreement that the threat of a return to predeterrent, pre-1957, pre-"post-imperialist" international relations had abated. They were similarly agreed that the Soviet Union possessed

[71] Khrushchev's Report on the New Party Program, *Pravda*, October 18, 1961, trans. in *Current Digest*, Vol. XIII, No. 48 (November 29, 1961), p. 8.

minimally adequate deterrence[72] against direct attack on the Soviet Union or other socialist countries *contiguous* to it.[73] Thus it became possible for "Commentator" to bury the myth of American invulnerability for the second time in four years (the first burial, as we have seen, having taken place after the development of the ICBM):

> The Soviet armed forces have powerful nuclear weapons of the newest design. *If anyone had doubts about this,* they lost them after the Soviet nuclear tests at the end of last year. The creation by Soviet scientists and engineers of the global rocket, invulnerable to anti-missile systems and carrying a multimegaton nuclear warhead, *has conclusively buried the*

[72] But only *minimally* adequate; a plausible case has been made by Arnold L. Horelick, "The Cuban Missile Crisis: An Analysis of Soviet Calculations and Behavior," *World Politics,* Vol. xvi, No. 3 (April, 1964), pp. 363-89, that it was precisely at this time that the decision was taken to implant missiles in Cuba in order to redress the strategic balance. It may also be the case that, as Khrushchev argued on a number of occasions (his most definitive exposition being his December 12, 1962 speech to the Supreme Soviet), the Soviet Union emplaced the IRBM's in Cuba to deter the United States from attacking Cuba. *Pravda,* December 13, 1962, trans. in *Current Digest,* Vol. xiv, No. 52 (January 23, 1963), pp. 3-6.

[73] See General Talenskii's observation in an article entitled "The 'Absolute Weapon' and the Problems of Security," *International Affairs,* No. 4 (April 1962), p. 25:

"In view of the advantages of a surprise attack, both sides will undoubtedly take advance measures so as to minimize the danger of such an attack and be able to retaliate with a knock-out blow. In present-day conditions there is every possibility for this.

"The modern level of nuclear saturation, it is important to realize, is so high that it is no longer possible to destroy all means of retaliation even through a surprise attack based on highly accurate intelligence data concerning the location of nuclear-rocket facilities. There will always be enough of them left to strike a crushing retaliatory blow."

> *myth of the invulnerability of the United States of America.* If it was once possible to determine the approximate areas where Soviet rocket installations were deployed, . . . now these calculations are useless. The launching sites for global rockets can be situated literally at any point on the vast Soviet territory, and rockets can come in on target from any direction.[74]

Both Khrushchev and Malinovskii took comfort in the successful development of the "global rocket," which Khrushchev enthusiastically announced in his electoral campaign speech of March 16, 1962:

> The time when the U.S.A. could consider itself invulnerable in a war, fenced off from the theaters of military operations on other continents by the vast expanses of the oceans, is far in the past. In present-day conditions, it is just as vulnerable as all the other countries in the world.
>
> The situation now is changing still more. Our scientists and engineers have created a new intercontinental rocket, which they call global; this rocket is invulnerable to anti-missile weapons.[75]

Malinovskii avoided suggesting a preemptive strategy. He omitted the phrase, "in time," from the formulation he had used at the Twenty-second Party Congress; he referred now to "breaking up the opponent's aggressive plans by dealing him a crushing blow."[76] Noting the "tempestuous" rate of

[74] *Pravda*, March 31, 1962, italics added.

[75] *Pravda*, March 17, 1962, abridged trans. in *Current Digest*, Vol. XIV, No. 13 (April 25, 1962), p. 6.

[76] R. Malinovskii, "Programma KPSS i voprosy ukrepleniia vooruzhennykh sil SSSR" [The CPSU Program and Questions of Strengthening the Armed Forces of the U.S.S.R.], *Kommunist*, No. 7 (May 1962), p. 15.

The editors of the RAND translation of Sokolovskii's *Voennaia stra-*

technological developments Malinovskii described the global rockets almost as enthusiastically as Khrushchev had. They were, he also declared, "invulnerable to modern anti-missile defense."[77]

This consensus over the minimally tenable Soviet deterrent was expressed in a description of the distribution of military power, which was a step backwards from previous Soviet estimates. Rather than assert claims of a military *pereves sil,* Soviet commentators in mid-1962 fairly consistently described the military position of the two camps as being in equilibrium. In some instances, the Malinovskii formula of January 1962[78] was employed—but in contexts showing greater confidence in the second-strike capability of the Soviet Union.[79] Other

---

tegiia noted the omission. (See RAND, *Soviet Military Strategy*, p. 166.) Wolfe, in *Soviet Strategy at the Crossroads*, p. 67, points out that the phrase, "in time," is contained in both the 1962 and 1963 editions of Sokolovskii.

[77] Malinovskii, "Programma KPSS . . . ," p. 2.

[78] Malinovskii at that time had said that President Kennedy's recognition that "our forces were equal" was "a more or less correct admission." Malinovskii did add, "I *think* that the socialist camp is now stronger than [the United States and its NATO allies]. But let us go so far as to grant the forces are equal," and then contradictorily, "I will state with all my authority as the U.S.S.R. Minister of Defense . . . that we are now the stronger and of course we are not standing still." *Pravda*, January 24, 1962, trans. in *Current Digest*, Vol. XIV, No. 4 (February 21, 1962), p. 19, italics added.

[79] For one such article, see V. Korionov, "Lippman protiv Lippmana" [Lippmann vs. Lippmann], *Kommunist*, No. 9 (June 1962), p. 122: "In past years imperialist politicians have needed to learn to speak, for them, decidedly unusual words: the equality of the forces of socialism and capitalism militarily." How the use of the phrase "favorable balance of power" can become blurred into the concepts of equilibrium and confidence in deterrence, even in Russian, is illustrated by Korionov's subsequent statement: "The world socialist system, as emphasized in the Report of the Central Committee of the CPSU to the Twenty-second Congress, has become a reliable shield. . . . And the fact that the preponderance of forces is on the side of the socialist

commentators were content to imply equality by denying American claims to military superiority.[80]

Evidently this did not mean, however, that the U.S.S.R. was militarily equal, in its own eyes, to the U.S., except in the sense that each side would consider intolerable the consequences to itself of a thermonuclear exchange. For it was at this stage that Soviet authorities permitted, tolerated, or encouraged Marshal Sokolovskii and his colleagues to publish an awesome picture of American military might.[81] Similarly, wide dissemination was given to statements declaring that never before had imperialism been so strong. Gen. Nikolai Talenskii perhaps let the cat out of the bag when in the April 1962 issue of *International Affairs* he remarked that "*there was a time when the military might of a state, if superior to that of its probable enemy or bloc enemies, guaranteed a certain degree of security*,"[82] but that such a situation no longer held true.

As long as the United States had pursued what Soviet writers somewhat inexactly termed a massive retaliation policy (more accurately, the "new, new look"[83]), the Soviet Union's "new look" strategy—a doctrine most systematically enunciated by Khrushchev in his January 14, 1960 speech—served it ade-

---

commonwealth of peoples is a great happiness for all mankind" (*ibid.*).

The first edition of Sokolovskii asserts, "Thus, under today's conditions, when there is a 'balance'. . . ." The second edition (1963), p. 80, adds "in the West's estimation."

[80] M. Marinin, "Leninizm i segodniashnii mir" [Leninism and Today's World], *Mirovaia ekonomika*, No. 4 (April 1962), p. 16 and Khrushchev, in *Pravda*, July 11, 1962, trans. in *Current Digest*, Vol. XIV, No. 28 (August 8, 1964), pp. 3-10.

[81] Sokolovskii (1962 edn.), *op.cit.*, pp. 88-90.

[82] Talenskii, "The Absolute Weapon . . . ," p. 27, italics added.

[83] Ably described in Samuel P. Huntington, *The Common Defense* (New York: Columbia University Press, 1961), pp. 88-112.

quately. However, when in 1961 the United States adjusted to the changed distribution of power, and the Taylor ideas about flexible response were adopted, Russia's essentially passive deterrence posture[84] placed it in the strategic bind from which the United States had just managed to extricate itself. How could the Soviet Union effectively deter the "export of counter-revolution" from nonsocialist countries or prevent the overthrow of socialist regimes in areas not adjacent to itself—much less create a strategic environment in which something still designated "world revolution" would be accelerated? In these circumstances what alternative did the Soviet Union have besides "humiliation or holocaust"? Soviet commentary suggests that the challenge of the American reaction to the Soviet Union stemmed in no small measure from the American adjustment of strategy, as opposed to the adjustment of force structure. At the same time, once the Soviet Union had apparently also adjusted its force structure —an adjustment presumably easier for the Soviet Union, with its long ground-force tradition—an American strategy of flexible response was preferable in the Soviet view because that policy was less fraught with the possibility of uncontrolled escalation.[85]

[84] One tantalizing unexplained mystery of recent Soviet foreign policy is whether choice, necessity, or both, caused the U.S.S.R. to pursue such a policy. If we knew the answer, we could speak about long-range Soviet behavior changes (or lack thereof) much more cogently. For speculation see the introduction to a new edition of Herbert Dinerstein's *War and the Soviet Union* (New York: Frederick A. Praeger, 1963) and Alexander Dallin et al., *The Soviet Union, Arms Control and Disarmament* (New York: the School of International Affairs, Columbia University, 1964), especially pp. 96ff.

[85] The relation, asserted in Soviet writings, of the adoption by the United States of the flexible response doctrine to the changed distribu-

However, the American reaction, militarily, both in its strategic and structural dimensions and the threat it posed to the military-strategic distribution of power, and Soviet descriptions thereof were merely one facet of the American response. In addition, Washington in the early 1960s reappraised the *over-all* distribution of power, and from such stock-taking arrived at an optimistic picture of the United States' power position and of the direction of the international system.

Moscow placed great significance on the American response to Soviet claims concerning the over-all distribution of power at this level, the level of estimates and expectations. And well it should have, for the American estimation of the situation directly repudiated one major assumption on which Khrushchev's effort[86] to reunify theory and practice had been

---

tion of military power is well documented. For a discussion at length see Sokolovskii, 1962 edn., pp. 69-77, 1963 edn., pp. 75-87.

See *ibid.*, 1963 edn., p. 84, for a statement:

> "the decision as to which objectives should be the ones nuclear strikes are launched against—against strategic weapons or cities—depends to a considerable degree on the weapons system on hand and on its quantity. If the weapon is so inaccurate that it cannot be used to destroy small-dimension targets such as ballistic missile launching pads or airports, and its numbers are insufficient, it can be used only against large objectives, for example, cities."

Finally, the second edition of Sokolovskii and the articles associated with its reissuance indicate clearly a decreased estimate of the danger of escalation apparently associated with changes in weapons systems and strategies. Witness the November 2, 1963 *Krasnaia zvezda* [Red Star] article by four authors (I. Zav'ialov, V. Kolechitskii, V. Larionov, and M. Cherednichenko) of *Voennaia strategiia,* who misquote themselves as having said any armed conflict between the nuclear powers "can grow" into nuclear war; they had actually said "inevitably grow." On the latter point see Thomas W. Wolfe, "Shifts in Soviet Strategic Thought," *Foreign Affairs*, Vol. XLII, No. 3 (April 1964), pp. 475-86.

[86] On Khrushchev's effort, see below, pp. 251-58.

based: that realism, *as Soviet spokesmen used the term in 1959-61* (an awareness that communism was the wave of the future and a consequent willingness to acquiesce relatively quietly in its arrival),[87] was becoming the dominant trend in American ruling circles. The Kennedy administration set out as a matter of policy to dispel the assumption. The reappraisal by Western observers, official and otherwise, of the global distribution of power provoked a profound reaction in Soviet commentary, reflecting the extent to which Moscow, as the Soviet Union became increasingly permeable, felt constrained to rebut rather than ignore Western arguments. Soon after Khrushchev's intercontinental rockets speech, several articles appeared in the general party organs and in the specialized press, which seemed at first glance designed to deprecate Western optimism. The articles were obviously intended to undercut the political impact of an analysis claiming that the distribution of power had changed in the West's favor. A passage from a 1962 review of current international politics illustrates the tenor of these observations. Informing its readership that Walter Lippmann had asserted that the distribution of power had in the past year become more favorable to the West, the authors declared: "Neither Lippmann nor any other ideologues of the imperialist bourgeoisie can, it goes without saying, support their optimism even to the slightest extent by persuasive arguments."[88]

[87] See below, pp. 221-22; also Brzezinski, *Ideology and Power*, pp. 105 and 171.

[88] E. Alekseev et al., "Tekushchie problemy mirovoi politiki" [Current Problems of World Politics], *Mirovaia ekonomika*, No. 7 (July 1962), p. 7. For other articles attempting to explain why "at this time" such a reappraisal should have taken place, see M. Marinin, "Leninism . . . ," pp. 16-17; V. Korionov, "Lippmann protiv Lippmana"; A. Galkin, "Vneshniaia politika umiraiushchego imperializma" [The Foreign

Closer examination reveals that in the process of criticizing Western reappraisals Soviet analysts were actually diminishing their claims, although circumspectly, concerning the overall distribution of power, just as they had modified their description of the strategic distribution of power. Soviet international relations commentators attempted to accomplish the trick of communicating selectively to disparate audiences through a single medium by skillfully using several ploys typically resorted to in Soviet dialogue. Thus the manner in which Soviet writers joined issue with Western observers not only provides a fairly precise appraisal of the impact of the American reaction on the Soviet depiction of the distribution of power between the two major powers, but illustrates some general principles in the decoding of Soviet symbolic notation.

Direct alterations in formulation provided the clearest indication that Soviet observers recognized an adverse shift had taken place. One such change that occurred in the aftermath of the Cuban crisis[89] was retaining *pereves* as the term characterizing the relationship of forces, while at the same time altering the numerator and denominator. Moscow now described the global distribution of power as characterized by a preponderance of power in favor of the forces of *peace*—not peace and socialism—over the forces of *war*—not war and imperialism. The contrast provided by the first edition

---

Policy of Moribund Imperialism], *Mirovaia ekonomika*, No. 6 (June 1962), pp. 6-10; V. Gantman et al., "Tekushchie problemy mirovoi politiki" [Current Problems of World Politics], *Mirovaia ekonomika*, No. 1 (January 1962), pp. 5-7; and N. Inozemtsev, "Edinstvo zapada?" [Western Unity?], *Mirovaia ekonomika*, No. 3 (March 1963), pp. 63-65.

[89] Although Soviet commentary reflected concern over the Western reappraisal as early as spring 1962, outright alteration in formulation does not seem to have occurred prior to the Cuban confrontation.

(1962) and the second edition (1963) of Sokolovskii, *Military Strategy*, illustrates the difference:

> . . . the CPSU proceeds from the premise that growing forces exist in the world which are capable of preserving and strengthening peace, and that there are indications of a growing preponderance of the forces of socialism and peace over those of imperialism and war. [1962]
>
> . . . the CPSU proceeds from the premise that growing forces exist in the world which are capable of preserving and strenthening peace. Confirmation of this is the fact that the ideas and policies of peaceful coexistence are shared by a larger number of people and that it wins newer and newer victories with each day. . . . The Soviet Union cannot rely on the 'good will' of the imperialists, but relies, first of all, on the might of the socialist camp and on the continually growing preponderance of the forces of peace over the forces of reaction and war. [1963][90]

The change of numerator and denominator had the effect of diminishing Soviet claims concerning the relative power of the socialist camp.[91] By separating socialism and peace and

[90] Sokolovskii, *Voenniaia strategiia*, 1962 edn., p. 3, 1963 edn., pp. 7-8. See, too, V. Gantman et al., "Mirovaia politika v nachale 1963 goda" [World Politics at the Outset of 1963], *Kommunist*, No. 2 (January 1963), p. 94, who speak of ". . . a clear preponderance in favor of peace." In polemics with the Chinese, Soviet spokesmen asserted their belief that the "*forces of peace and progress* in our times are mightier than the *forces of reaction and war* and they can hold their own." *Pravda*, July 15, 1963, italics added.

[91] As Khrushchev said in his December 12 speech, "If you go left, you come out on the right." (*Pravda*, December 13, 1962, trans. in *Current Digest*, Vol. XIV, No. 52 [January 23, 1963], p. 3.) This, I take it, comes as near to recognizing the legitimacy of the international

implicitly recognizing that some participants on *both* sides were not in the peace camp, the formulation represented a clear repudiation of the Manichean world-view.

In addition, after Cuba, stress was placed on the ontological rather than existential nature of Soviet claims to possess a preponderance of power. Whereas in early 1962 a Khrushchev spokesman—Korionov—could still express gratitude that the "preponderance of power [was] on the side of the socialist commonwealth of peoples,"[92] a year later the focus was more distinctly future-oriented. The emphasis was on the nature of the *growing* preponderance of power. In 1963 a lead article could appear whose author, I. Lemin, was content to assert: "the preponderance of the forces of socialism and peace over the forces of imperialism and war is an all-sided material preponderance which is no longer far away [and] an already present political and moral preponderance."[93]

One further innovation in describing the distribution of power should be noted. The focus shifted from a description of the socialist camp's *gains* to an emphasis on imperialism's *losses*. Soviet foreign policy commentators described the distribution of power as "now shaping not in favor of imperialism but against it,"[94] "far from being to the advantage of capitalism,"[95] and asserted that "imperialism had long ago lost

---

order as any Soviet "Marxist-Leninist" has ever gone; the center reflects consensus while each global "political party" has its extremist "lunatic fringe."

[92] Korionov, "Lippmann," p. 123.

[93] Lemin, "Leninskii printsip mirnogo sosushchestvovaniia i sovremennost' " [The Leninist Principle of Peaceful Coexistence and Modern Times], *Mirovaia ekonomika*, No. 4 (April 1963), p. 8.

[94] "The Only True Road," *International Affairs*, No. 1 (January 1962), p. 10.

[95] Sh. Sanakoyev [Sanakoev], "Our Idea of a World Without Arms," *International Affairs*, No. 7 (July 1962), p. 49.

its former priority."[96] These cumbersome expressions had ambiguity as their main attribute. They neither claimed nor denied a preponderance of power for the forces of socialism; they did not even explicitly convey the impression that the socialist camp's position had improved. The expression merely asserted a weakening of imperialism's power, with the implications to be drawn left to the reader.

If we adopt the generally tenable hypothesis that in instances of this kind the formulation will reflect the *most* that Soviet commentators felt they could confidently assert, it seems to imply a reduction in Soviet claims stemming from a growing awareness that (in game-theoretical rather than Marxist-Leninist jargon) international politics is not a two-person, zero-sum game, as well as a growing disenchantment with the underdeveloped countries. The awkward, negatively expressed formulations suggested a realization that a capitalist loss of power was not translated directly into a *commensurate* gain in power for the socialist camp—and this presupposes more than two persons in the global power-equation "game."

Less direct, but in some respects more revealing, evidence of diminishing Soviet claims about the socialist camp's relative power position may be extracted from the lines of argumentation Soviet observers employed and avoided. The supporting evidence mustered, for instance, ostensibly to refute Western contentions, seemed in large measure to concede their validity. In strategic commentary, Soviet analysts had taken comfort in claiming that "since the United States does not possess high-yield thermonuclear warheads of several tens of megatons, such as those possessed by the U.S.S.R., we consider our superiority in nuclear weapons over the Western bloc to be indisputable," but, as the RAND editors of Soko-

[96] Marinin, "Leninizm . . . ," p. 16.

lovskii's *Military Strategy* note, they failed conspicuously to mention "the question of superiority in numbers of missiles."[97] In much the same way, Marinin pointed to "the level and range of the development of science, the education and political consciousness of the broad masses of the population, the cadres, their ideological armament," as elements which could "not be 'abstracted' from a scientific evaluation of military-economic potential," and asserted that "in these areas socialism has significantly outstripped capitalism."[98]

The implication seems inescapable, that given the traditional Soviet thinking about the constituent elements of power, Marinin was grasping at straws. One other element, conspicuous by its omission, which Soviet observers had previously thought highly significant, should be noted. Particularly in a context which refers to the "political consciousness of the broad masses," as a favorably asymmetrical element in the global distribution of power, it is striking, but not surprising, that the *organizational* unity of the socialist camp was passed over. Marxist-Leninists have always clung to a belief in the superior political capability of a political organization which institutionalized Lenin's "party of a new type." Even in their darkest hour the organizational weapon seemed the element to justify a belief in the ultimate turning of the tide. In 1962, however, the Soviet press was describing the organizational strength of the capitalist camp in glowing terms,[99] while Soviet leaders could see the socialist camp dis-

[97] RAND, *Soviet Military Strategy*, p. 297n.

[98] Marinin, "Leninizm . . . ," p. 16.

[99] Two major books reflecting divergent perspectives in other respects (*Military Strategy* and *International Relations Since World War II*) both reflected Soviet awe at the organizational strength of the capitalist camp. (Sokolovskii, 1962 edn., p. 68; AN IMEMO, *Mezhdunarodnye otnosheniia . . .*, Vol. 1, p. xxiv.) The 1963 edition of Soko-

integrating around them. The conspicuous omission noted here probably reflected a growing discomfiture on the part of the Soviet leadership concerning the relative viability of the two systems.[100]

There were indications, moreover, that Soviet international relations commentators, in their efforts to rebut Western assertions contending an altered distribution of power, were engaged in a considerable reexamination of the nature of power as it pertained to the global *sootnoshenie sil*. Such a reappraisal was consonant with the Soviet emphasis on the novelty of what I have termed post-imperialist international relations. It also corresponded to the felt need to formulate the distribution of power in ideology-reinforcing terms, in the context of a polemic in which the antagonist held most of the cards (as well as guns and butter). The antagonist looked especially unlike a paper tiger or even a colossus with feet of clay when the data of the global situation was filtered through traditional Soviet perspectives. A reckoning of the distribution of power, which postulated the constituent elements of power to be military might, economic capacity, and organizational cohesiveness, was not likely in this instance to engender revolutionary optimism. One tack taken by Soviet observers involved attempting to discredit Western arguments by suggesting they were founded on class-bound, outdated notions of power.[101] Thus it was charged that Western observers,

---

lovskii, in response to dissension between the United States and France, showed less persuasion of the ability of the United States to organize the camp (1963 edn. p. 74).

[100] Inozemtsev, "Edinstvo zapada?" p. 65, specifically adverts to, but fails to come to grips with, the relation of the Sino-Soviet split to the global distribution.

[101] Marinin, "Leninizm . . . ," p. 16. For related statements see Inozemstev, "Edinstvo zapada?" p. 65 and V. Gantman et al., "Mirovaia politika . . . ," p. 6.

"generalizing from their own experience of the struggle for ruling position in the confines of the capitalist system, . . . mechanically transfer these criteria from their sphere to the competition of two opposed socio-economic systems. . . ." Given previous Soviet notions about the constituent elements of power, it was more than a little ironic to encounter Marinin attacking the "ideologues and strategists of imperialism [for ignoring] the many-faceted essence of the [problem] of the distribution of power."[102] It was certainly not only these observers who "in referring to the distribution of power . . . quite often have in mind the direct power distribution [*silovoe sootnoshenie*], that is, the distribution of military and economic potential."[103] Once again, this line of argumentation seems more to accept than to rebut Western contentions that there had been an adverse shift in the distribution of power.

Soviet observers, moreover, showed a growing awareness that power potential, measured by traditional indices and the political capacity to achieve desired effects, were not necessarily synonymous, that in fact under certain conditions military power potential might even be counterproductive:

> Never before has the military potential of imperialism been so great or its military organization so comprehensive. It looks as though this apparent 'might' has turned the heads of the leading men in bourgeois military science and their employers. They are still afraid to admit even to themselves that the possibilities of utilizing this military strength are being steadily reduced and that it is less and less an effective weapon of imperialism's foreign policy of expansion.[104]

[102] Marinin, "Leninizm . . . ," p. 16.

[103] *Ibid.*

[104] V. Pechorkin, "Crisis of Imperialism's Military Doctrine," *International Affairs*, No. 7 (July 1962), p. 33. Pechorkin, it should be noted,

Nevertheless, the immediate polemical purposes of the Soviet statements do not detract from the impression that the global situation had prompted an effort to grapple with the nature of power. Under circumstances where, in John H. Herz's phrase, "power can destroy power from center to center,"[105] Soviet observers appear to have concluded that their previously held notions about power were no longer applicable. There was evidence of an awareness of the *relational* aspect of power not characteristic of the strong traditional Soviet disposition to view political power as asymmetrical and unidirectional. (In a sense, the "new, third stage of capitalism's general crisis" expresses doctrinally the assumption that between the world powers unidirectional power relations are not possible.[106]) There was also evidenced in the polemic with Western analysts a somewhat greater emphasis on the *situational* aspects of power. "The competition of the two social systems," one spokesman remarked, "does not take place in a hermetically sealed flask but in the wide world which is undergoing the greatest revolutionary changes in the history of mankind. Naturally, therefore, in defining the distribution of power between capitalism and socialism, it is impossible not to bear in mind the decisive laws of our epoch."[107]

Similarly, it is revealing that in their articulation of Western views Soviet observers actually restructured the dialogue

---

was concerned that doctrinal innovation (like Maxwell Taylor's) when translated into force-structure changes would increase the effectiveness of Western military might in *limited* war contexts. *Ibid.*, pp. 33-35.

[105] Herz, *International Politics in the Atomic Age*, p. 108. In Soviet military-strategic jargon, the equivalent to Herz's phrase would be the repudiation of the traditional distinction between front and rear. That distinction has long since been repudiated.

[106] See Chapter 4 above, passim.

[107] Marinin, "Leninizm . . . ," pp. 16-17.

in a way which implied that an adverse shift in the distribution of power had occurred. Soviet writers attacked the argument that a radical shift in the distribution of power[108] had occurred. In other words, notwithstanding Soviet statements differentiating the military-strategic and over-all distribution of power, Soviet observers in their treatment of the challenge to their appraisal of the over-all distribution of power argued, in more abstract and ideologically phrased terminology, precisely that which they had contended about the military-strategic distribution of power. Predeterrence imperialist international relations, in which one or more actors could avoid having severe sanctions inflicted on its homeland, were gone forever, and the strategic element had proved crucial in this regard.[109]

The implication seems to be that there was a downward revision—history had taken a zig-zag—but that the downward revision had a distinct limit. Just as in the heady days of 1958-60, when Soviet claims were carefully hedged, in 1962-64 Soviet authors perceived the changes in the distribution of power between capitalism and socialism, between the United States and the Soviet Union, within a context of changes between world systems and world powers. In 1960 Soviet observers continued to acknowledge the United States' world power status; in 1962-64 they insisted the Soviet Union had not been deprived of that status.

In response to the American trifold reaction—the increase in military power, the reappraisal of strategic doctrine, and the rethinking of the over-all distribution of power and of the

[108] E. Alekseev et al., "Tekushchie problemy mirovoi politiki" [Current Problems of World Politics], *Mirovaia ekonomika*, No. 7 (July 1962), p. 7; Gantman et al., "Mirovaia politika . . . ," p. 6.

[109] In this regard, see especially Inozemstsev, "Edinstvo . . . ," p. 64.

movement of the international system—to the threat of a missile gap, and shocked by a series of other developments at home, within and without the camp, the Soviet leadership under Khrushchev reverted to an appreciably more restrained description of the distribution of power. The 1960-61 formulation, expressed in terms of *pereves*, suggested the imminent arrival of the emerging reality. The description in 1964, expressed in terms of a *ravnovesie sil*, suggested both a diminution in estimates of the existential reality and in the imminence of the ontological reality. By 1964 the emerging and existential realities were separated by a considerable gap; *ravnovesie*, with its connotations of stability and equilibrium, suitably expressed the expectations of the Soviet leadership. The Soviet elite integrated the temporary reversal in the world historical process by, once again, elongating temporarily its time perspective.

FROM THE vantage point of three years' distance, which separates this writing from Khrushchev's ouster in October 1964, however, it is evident that even *ravnovesie*, in the eyes of many among the Soviet ruling group, was an excessively bold formulation, and there had been considerable discontent about the more enthusiastic formulations in fashion during the early sixties.[110] As a result, after 1965 these claims were shelved.[111] Instead, Khrushchev's successors have returned to the use of

[110] Even at the Twenty-second Congress, it was clear that there was opposition to Khrushchev's most optimistic formulations. See above, Chapter III, note 32.

[111] AN IMEMO, *Stroitel'stvo kommunizma* . . . , p. 379, to press December 10, 1965, uses *pereves sil.* Marinin, in "Sotsialisticheskii internatsionalizm i politika voinstvuiushchego imperializma" [Socialist Internationalism and Militant Imperialism], *Mirovaia ekonomika,* No. 6 (June 1966), p. 17, attacks Khrushchev for relying on "the automatic action of a preponderance in the distribution of power."

formulations depicting the global distribution of power—*sootnoshenie sil.* The formulations have varied in content. For instance, Suslov in 1965 made the cautious claim that the distribution of power in the world arena was "generally favorable to socialism,"[112] while Brezhnev[113] at the Twenty-third Congress denied that "the growing aggressiveness of imperialism" was by any means an indication "of any change in the distribution of power in the world in its favor." (A hint of the modesty of Brezhnev's contention is contained in an article by D. Meln'ikov, in which he asserts that imperialism can no longer "change the distribution of power in its favor, become anew the dominant factor of world development, liquidate the great social and political gains of the toilers."[114]) Similarly, the formula employed in the resolutions adopted at the Twenty-third Congress attest that "the distribution of power in the world continues to change in favor of socialism, the worker and national-liberation movement."[115] Common to these and other formulas since September 1965 was their avoidance of the use of *pereves*, preponderance, or *ravnovesie*, equilibrium—both of which conveyed a specificity Soviet spokesmen presumably wished to avoid.

Khrushchev's more enthusiastic claims about the distribution of power, his successors appear to have concluded, were part and parcel of his approach to international relations,

[112] *Pravda*, June 5, 1965, trans. in *Current Digest*, Vol. XVII, No. 22 (June 23, 1965), p. 5.

[113] *XXIII s"ezd Kommunisticheskoi Partii Sovetskogo Soiuza: Stenograficheskii otchet* [The Twenty-third Congress of the Communist Party of the Soviet Union: Stenographic Record] (Moscow: Politizdat, 1966), Vol. I, p. 19.

[114] D. Meln'ikov, "Novaia epokha v mezhdunarodnykh otnosheniiakh" [A New Epoch in International Relations], *Mirovaia ekonomika*, No. 11 (November 1965), p. 5.

[115] *XXIII s"ezd . . .*, Vol. II, p. 303.

which, after his ouster, they chose to designate as a "voluntarist and unrealistic approach to the phenomena and events of international life," fraught "with grave consequences," and capable of giving rise either to smug overconfidence or to weakness in the face of the military threat from imperialism."[116] The direct bearing of these charges on Khrushchev's view of the global distribution of power was made manifest in the attacks which appeared in *Mirovaia ekonomika* in 1965-66 on the "automatic" and "passive" implications of Khrushchev formulations. "The enhancement of the might [of socialism] in and of itself and the change in the distribution of economic forces in the world arena in favor of socialism," one editorial observed, "does not decide automatically in which direction—peace or war—international events will develop."[117] Another *Mirovaia ekonomika* editorial, this time in 1966, warned that "there is nothing further from the genuine interests and the tasks of furthering socialism than to rely on the automatic action of a preponderance in the distribution of power."[118] Khrushchev, by his successors' reckoning, had claimed too much and utilized those claims to justify inaction.

At the same time, Soviet commentary in 1964-67 about the distribution of power was strikingly similar in several respects to that in evidence in the last years of Khrushchev's tenure in office. The Soviet commentators remained generally the same; in particular, "M. Marinin" (presumably Ia. S. Khavinson) continued to serve as the major Soviet contributor to the dialogue on the global distribution of power. In his 1966 article

[116] *Pravda*, August 8, 1965, trans. in *Current Digest*, Vol. XVII, No. 32 (September 1, 1965), p. 3.

[117] Mel'nikov, "Novaia epokha . . . ," p. 12.

[118] Marinin, "Sotsialisticheskii internationalizm . . . ," p. 17.

on the distribution of power, the most elaborate Soviet statement on the subject since October 1964, moreover, his discussion, as it had in 1962, took the form of a rejoinder to Walter Lippmann's observation that the distribution of power had become more favorable to the West. Like his earlier article, Marinin's 1966 article was just as important for what it omitted. With respect to the "problem of the distribution of military potential," for example, he cited Malinovskii's Twenty-third Party Congress statement—which had by implication virtually acknowledged Soviet strategic inferiority—that "our Armed Forces . . . are not created for attack but for the defense of the borders of our country, for providing the security of our people and of countries friendly to us." In addition, he pointed to "the first-class rockets which are in many respects novel in principle," and to the fact that "a blue defense belt"—an anti-missile complex—had been "completed." These claims, plus the "characteristic fact" that "the U.S. Secretary of the Navy, Nitze," had been "obliged very recently to recognize" the magnitude of the Soviet submarine fleet permitted Marinin to declare that Lippmann's claim of U. S. military preeminence had been "for a long time overthrown by the distribution of real war potential between the United States and the Soviet Union." No mention, however, was made of missile numbers; nor did Marinin claim more than to have rebutted Lippmann's position. Similarly, while Marinin had much to say about Lippmann's misapprehension of the prospects of Western unity, his rejoinder to Lippmann's contention that the Sino-Soviet conflict benefited the West was conspicuously defensive in tone. "That imperialism counts on the strengthening of differences within the world communist movement is beyond doubt. However, the process of international consolidation taking place in the socialist countries, the uniting of the *majority* of them on the basis of proletarian internationalism—this is an objective factor rendering the most direct influence on the problem of the distribution of power."[119]

In addition to replicating the pattern of conspicuous omission found in Soviet commentary in the early sixties, Marinin's article and other post-Khrushchevian commentary continued to reveal an appreciation of the situational nature of power relations, an appreciation again apparently prompted in part by an awareness of the distasteful conclusions the traditional Soviet calculus might produce. To appraise correctly "the distribution and disposition of class and political power in the world arena," one article stated, necessitates an awareness that "in the contemporary epoch, the very concept 'power' has changed its content. A primitive understanding of power as only . . . the number of cannons and dreadnoughts or hydrogen bombs and rockets will not withstand scrutiny."[120] Or, in Marinin's words, "Inasmuch as the struggle of the two systems takes place in a world in the process of revolutionary change, it is natural that one of the necessary conditions" in the appraisal of the distribution of power "is the calculation of which of the two systems this process is directed against."[121]

Post-Khrushchevian commentary on the distribution of power, furthermore, revealed an even greater separation between the existential and ontological reality than had been in evidence under Khrushchev. In the statements of Soviet observers in 1962-63 there was a recognition that history had zig-zagged. In 1966 the danger inherent in assuming that the changed distribution of power "makes impossible any kind of zig-zag

[119] *Ibid.*, p. 13, italics added.

[120] Mel'nikov, "Novaia epokha . . . ," p. 9.

[121] Marinin, "Sotsialisticheskii internationalizm . . . ," p. 13.

in isolated zones, in isolated stages of the world historical process,"[122] was being stressed.

As a result, Soviet revolutionary time-perspectives were explicitly elongated. In the debate among the Bolsheviks over the signing at Brest-Litovsk, Stalin had scored a debater's point against Trotsky by charging him with calculating revolutionary imminence in weeks while Lenin and Stalin more realistically were thinking in months. Similarly, socialism in one country had implied a revolutionary perspective running into decades. Even Khrushchev had talked of the full-scale building of communism, and in 1960-61 apparently held high expectations for major revolutionary advance in the sixties and seventies. By 1966 his successors were consoling themselves that "Marxist-Leninists" had no "grounds for 'regretting' the tempo of the development of the revolutionary processes in the world" by pointing to the time required to displace feudalism with capitalism: "The replacement of feudalism by capitalism occupied an epoch which embraced several centuries. With that, as it is well known, the zone of its dissemination was not so enormous, since capitalism left whole continents untouched. *In comparison with this replacement* [of feudalism by capitalism], the replacement of capitalism by socialism is taking place at a significantly more rapid tempo, spreading simultaneously over an immeasurably larger zone."[123]

[122] *Ibid.*, p. 17.
[123] *Ibid.*, p. 16, italics added.

Chapter Six: United States Foreign Policy from the Soviet Perspective

IF ONE were to assume that Bolshevik perspectives and Soviet perspectives in the years after the Twentieth C.P.S.U. Congress were essentially identical, there would be scarcely any reason to examine the evolution of Soviet perspectives on the motivations and behavior of the major imperialist power, the United States. A modest familiarity with Leninism would suffice to anticipate Soviet perspectives on United States foreign policy. One would expect Soviet observers to argue that the bourgeoisie made the key political decisions, that the state was little more than a front organization for Wall Street, an instrumentality of the ruling class. Because the United States is the leading imperialist power, one would "know" that, to the Soviets, these bourgeois "ruling circles," animated by considerations of power and/or profit, were seeking to dominate the world and destroy socialism. One would not need to be told that the United States was the main enemy, the main antagonist in the global *kto-kogo* [who-whom].

One can, in fact, cite much about American motives in the period examined which does little more than repeat the traditional Marxist-Leninist utterances about their capitalist enemies. Prior to 1960 evidence of any major reappraisal of American foreign policy was almost totally absent from the specialized press. The 1960 Moscow statement of the eighty-one communist parties similarly contained numerous references in the traditional vein to an undifferentiated and hostile American imperialism.

Nevertheless, to equate Soviet and Bolshevik perspectives on American goals and behavior would misread the record of Soviet commentary in the latter years of Khrushchev's tenure in power and, to a lesser extent, that of the three years since his ouster as well. It would, furthermore, ignore a major dimension of the Khrushchevian reappraisal of communist doctrine pertaining to international relations, one with significant bearing on the changing Soviet-American relationship, and central to the charges by the radical wing of "the world communist movement"—that Moscow had not only obliterated the distinction between friend and foe, but had, in fact, completely reversed the calculus. This chapter summarizes the most important components of the evolution of Soviet perspectives on American foreign policy during Khrushchev's term of office, and compares and contrasts, where possible, Khrushchevian and post-Khrushchevian perspectives on American foreign policy.

It should be emphasized at the outset that all the caveats entered by the present author in the introductory chapter with respect to the difficulties in deciphering Soviet symbolic notation are especially relevant to such an intensely political matter as American foreign policy. Highly manipulative considerations all too often underlay both the utterances of major political figures and the commentary of second-level specialists. As a result, statements about American motives, as well as, to a lesser degree, American capabilities and even the American decision-making process, were used to register approbation or disapprobation of particular moves and short-run policies of the United States. The highly sensitive nature of American-Soviet relations evidently intimidated many Soviet scholars, who, especially prior to 1963, were reluctant to analyze postwar U.S. foreign policy and were all too prepared to limit their remarks to repeating the formulations of Khrushchev or of Party documents. As V. K. Furaev, a Soviet historian, has said: "The closer we approach the present, the less profound the scientific research and the narrower the evidentiary base" of Soviet analysis of Soviet-American relations. "In place of serious analysis, he observed, several authors in the recent past" have engaged in "the simple reiteration and commentating on one or another speeches or pronouncements."[1]

It is possible, however, to speak with some assurance about the main trends in the evolution of Soviet perspectives during the Khrushchev years.[2] This evolution, it should be stressed, lent greater plausibility to Khrushchev's *détente* policy, and was part of his unsuccessful effort to resynthesize the unity of theory and practice in the atomic age.[3] This evolution embraced a reconsideration of the decision-making process in American foreign policy, a growing specificity and realism in the characterization of American capabilities, and an increasingly benevolent attitude toward American motives. Taken together, the result was a Soviet image of U.S. foreign policy behavior in the atomic age that was considerably at variance with conventional Bolshevik notions about the main enemy.

[1] V. K. Furaev, "O sostoianii i perspektivakh izucheniia istorii otnoshenii mezhdu SSSR i SShA v Sovetskoi istoriograficheskoi nauke" [Concerning the Prospects for the Study of the History of Relations Between the U.S.S.R. and the U.S.A. in Soviet Historiography], unpublished conference paper presented on March 23, 1965 in Moscow. Professor Furaev graciously provided me with a copy of his paper. A brief summary may be found in "Aktual'nye problemy istorii sovremennykh mezhdunarodnykh otnoshenii" [Topical Problems of the History of Contemporary International Relations], *Novaia i noveishaia istoriia*, No. 4 (July 1965), pp. 164-65.

[2] See also Nathan Leites, "The Kremlin's Horizon," RAND Memorandum RM-3506-ISA (March 1963) and Alexander Dallin, "Russia and China View the United States," *The Annals*, Vol. 349 (September 1963), pp. 154-62.

[3] See below, pp. 251-58.

A major aspect of the Soviet reappraisal is the relation between America's economy and its political system. The conspiracy strand in Soviet analysis—which had assumed that the political process in Washington was but a microcosm of intra-capitalist controversy—was muted somewhat, although it was still possible to find articles in the early 1960s that purported to identify particular cabinet members with particular monopolist regional groupings. During this time, the more innovative Soviet political economists attacked writers such as A. I. Sheerson and I. Kuz'minov who in the mid-fifties had, following Stalin's formulation, used subordination" [*podchinenie*] to characterize the relationship of the bourgeois state vis-à-vis the capitalists.[4] Rather than assert that the state was a mere instrumentality of the ruling class, Soviet economists began to ascribe an autonomy to the government hitherto undetected in Soviet commentary, and to show some awareness of the change in the relationship of the "bourgeois" state to the capitalist economy which two world wars, a semi-mobilized cold war, Keynesianism, and other factors had engendered. The new autonomy of the state was increasingly emphasized after Kennedy succeeded Eisenhower. It was concluded that a shift of phases in the American system had occurred; capitalism—American capitalism in particular—had actually evolved from monopoly capitalism into state-monopoly capitalism.[5] It became fashionable in Soviet commentary to characterize the relationship between the American econ-

[4] S. A. Dalin, *Voenno-gosudarstvennyi monopolisticheskii kapitalizm v SShA* [Military-State Monopoly Capitalism in the U.S.A.] (Moscow: Izdatel'stvo Nauk, 1961), p. 328.

[5] Precisely when the United States moved from monopoly capitalism to state-monopoly capitalism remains a subject of controversy among Soviet scholars. The point is that in the early sixties many Soviet economists began to write as though the phase change had engendered a change in the relative weight of the state in policy determination.

omy and polity as one of the interdependence [*srashchivanie*] rather than subordination.

Soviet commentators in the early 1960s pointed to an additional phenomenon which, they argued, had the effect of enhancing the self-sufficiency of the state in foreign policy making: the greatly increased role of international relations[6] in the world historical process and in the internal politics of bourgeois—and socialist[7]—states. In particular, Soviet commentators, including Khrushchev, argued that the institution of the American presidency had been strengthened and that, as a result, it was possible to speak of the White House acting independently of Wall Street.

The shift of focus from Wall Street to the White House was accompanied by a corresponding stress on the Pentagon as a force operating relatively independently of both monopoly capital and the White House and exercising pressure on the White House. "The Pentagon is not only a military tool of imperialist policy but a body which has a growing role to play in shaping this policy, specially in the foreign field."[8] The resulting image of American foreign policy in the Khrush-

[6] This point is particularly emphasized in AN IMEMO, *Mezhdunarodnye otnosheniia* . . . , Vol. 1, p. vi.

[7] In an essay published in 1963, describing the ongoing debate over the merits of personal diplomacy, one Soviet commentator, A. A. Galkin, asserted that "internal political questions are beginning to yield first place to the vitally important problems of foreign policy." V. Z. Lebedev, ed., *O sovremennoi Sovetskoi diplomatii* [Concerning Contemporary Soviet Diplomacy] (Moscow: Izdatel'stvo IMO, 1963), p. 145.

[8] The above passage happens to have appeared in an article sent to press a week after Khrushchev's removal. (P. Vladimirsky [Vladimirskii], "The Pentagon's Diplomacy," *International Affairs*, No. 11 [November 1964], p. 40.) It is likely that it was representative of the statements in the Soviet press prior to Khrushchev's ouster. For similar attitudes see especially V. Gantman et al., "Mirovaia politika . . . ," p. 6 and Dmitriev, *Pentagon i vneshniaia politika SShA*.

chevian perspective bore a marked similarity to C. Wright Mills' power elite model, in that the decisions were seen as a product of the interaction of economic, military, and political orders, with the American president playing an especially significant role. The Chinese were on solid doctrinal grounds when they asked "the leaders of the C.P.U.S.A." in 1963 whether they "still" accepted "the Marxist-Leninist theory of the state and admit that the U.S. state is the tool of monopoly capital for class rule?" and wondered "how can there be a President independent of monopoly capital, how can there be a Pentagon independent of the White House, and how can there be two opposing centres in Washington?"[9]

Soviet commentary in 1963-64 began to go "beyond the power elite." During the last years of Khrushchev's tenure, enthusiasm for the military-industrial complex argument and conspiracy thesis seemed to dissipate. Soviet spokesmen, including Khrushchev and the specialists, periodically professed to detect some enthusiasm for disarmament within major segments of the American business community. Indeed, the propensity to differentiate (the watchword of the last years of the Khrushchev years) was very much in evidence in several Soviet descriptions of the groups within the American ruling group and the policies advocated by various representatives of monopoly capital. The statement of N. N. Inozemtsev on his return from the United States, cited by Vernon Aspaturian, nicely illustrates the trend toward complexity among more modernist specialists on American politics. The specialists had gone beyond Khrushchev's crude dichotomy of realists and maniacs in attempting to circumvent the limits of class analysis. "It is common knowledge," Inozemtsev remarked,

[9] "A Comment on the Statement of the Communist Party of the U.S.A.," *Peking Review*, Vol. VI, Nos. 10-11 (March 15, 1963), p. 59.

> that in the conditions of capitalist reality monopoly capital is the center of political reaction. However, the monopolistic bourgeoisie of the U.S.A. is by no means unified or homogeneous; by no means all of its representatives support the 'madmen' or the 'war party'. . . . There are deep contradictions between the group of influential monopoly associations directly engaged in war production and all the other industrial and banking corporations, some of them very large but still deprived of access to the 'pie' of government military orders.[10]

Equally important, the more innovative Soviet analysts—especially in the Institute of World Economy and International Relations—began in the last two years of Khrushchev's tenure in office to include elements *outside* the bourgeoisie as being in on American foreign policy decision-making. Lobbying, it was explicitly recognized, was carried on by groups other than "Big Business." Thus in one Soviet enumeration, to which reference was made above, "trade unions, churches, and other organizations including the AFL-CIO, the National Farmers' Union, the American Medical Association" were identified as having "their own lobbies."[11]

In short, in the last years of Khrushchev's power, Soviet perspectives on the American decision-making process evolved toward something that embraced the elements usually in-

[10] *Pravda*, December 25, 1963, as cited by Aspaturian in Barry Farrell, ed., *Approaches to Comparative and International Politics*, p. 258. See, too, Gantman et al., "Mirovaia politika . . . ," p. 6; V. Pechorkin, "About 'Acceptable War,'" *International Affairs*, No. 3 (March 1963), pp. 20-25; and V. V. Kortunov, "Ideological Struggle in Conditions of the Peaceful Co-existence of the Two Systems," *International Affairs*, No. 8 (August 1963), p. 7.

[11] G. Yevgenyev [Evgenev], "Lobbying in the U.S.A.," *International Affairs*, No. 6 (June 1963), pp. 93-94.

cluded by Western commentators on American foreign policy.

Determining the Khrushchevian outlook on American capabilities is an appreciably more difficult task than that involved in taking note of the changed Soviet calculus of the American foreign policy process. For one thing, the distinction between motives and capabilities is highly tenuous. Generally Soviet statements about American or "imperialist" capabilities did not refer to capabilities in the abstract, but instead were a rough cost-calculus entailing assumptions about the motives and rationality of American decision-makers. Thus Khrushchev's assertion in 1959, that imperialism was no longer capable of destroying communist rule in the Soviet Union by force, constituted a calculus that Western decision-makers would be unwilling to pay the cost of achieving an intended effect, such as the reestablishment of noncommunist rule in the Soviet Union, rather than an assertion that in the strictest sense such capability no longer existed. Similarly Soviet commentators during the Khrushchev years, in their polemics with the Chinese about the nature of American imperialism, tended to pose a dispute over motives in terms of capability. To give credence to the Soviet contention that socialism was "turning into the decisive factor in world development" (and hence that the rules of the international game were no longer solely determined by imperialism and that through disarmament general war could be eliminated even while imperialism existed), Soviet spokesmen confined themselves to claiming that while the nature of imperialism had not changed, its capabilities had. This position was considerably less dangerous tactically than its alternative, which was to state that in the atomic age the priorities[12] of United States decision-makers had changed—this, by implication, denied the imperialist essence of American foreign policy.

[12] But see below, pp. 221-22.

Nevertheless, it is possible to describe the broad outlines of the Soviet appraisal of American capabilities under Khrushchev, by studying primarily the Soviet reappraisal of the global distribution of power.[13] There were two dominant themes, seemingly contradictory at first glance, but which were, in fact, reconcilable. The first was a qualitative decline in the relative power of the United States, noted by Soviet observers, which served, among other things, to justify optimism for revolution. The Soviets identified three developments external to the United States that had resulted in a weakening of the U.S.'s global position. The first and, most important, theme for the Soviet observers was the Soviet development in the late 1950s of an intercontinental ballistic missile. The second theme was the emergence at the end of the 1950s and in the early 1960s of the Afro-Asian bloc of independent states. These two developments were thought to have provided impetus to the third theme—the reemergence of Europe and the resulting weakening of the United States' position within the imperialist camp.

At the same time, Soviet observers cautioned that the United States was "still strong," and thus urged a minimum risk policy. At no time, not even during the optimistic years 1957-61, did Khrushchev or Soviet international relations specialists ever deny world-power status to the U.S. Rather the thrust of Soviet writings was that American leaders were faced with adjusting to a world in which it was necessary to treat another power more or less as an equal,[14] a world in which the United States was merely *one* of "the world's giants," merely *one* of the "two greatest powers in the world."[15] Similarly, during

[13] See above, Chapter V.

[14] For subtle speculation on the *degree* of equality from a psychoanalytical viewpoint, see Leites, "The Kremlin's Horizon."

[15] The citations are from Gantman et al., "*Mirovaia politika* . . . ," p. 6 and Gromyko's speech in the Supreme Soviet, *Pravda*, December 14, 1962.

these years, Soviet claims about strategic capabilities were at their most extreme,[16] but nowhere in Soviet commentary, in contrast with Chinese writings, was the suggestion to be found that the U.S. lacked the capacity to deliver a punishing second strike on the Soviet Union.

After 1961, during Khrushchev's last years in power, Soviet statements about American capabilities became less grudging and appreciably more specific, especially concerning American strategic capabilities. The most detailed, published account of American military might was contained in Marshal V. D. Sokolovskii's *Voennaia strategiia.*[17] Drawing ostensibly on the figures of the London Institute for Strategic Studies, it gave an elaborate breakdown of the number, type, and range of the missiles and airplanes the United States had at its disposal in 1962-63—which for Soviet experts aware of Soviet missile strength at that time, must have been sobering—as well as the planned operational missile capability of the United States in 1966.

Moreover, in the early 1960s it became more evident that underlying much of the Soviet analysis of American foreign policy was the assumption that the United States would retain its world-power status throughout the rest of this century. Most of the Soviet commentary seems to have assumed that (a) revolution per se in the U.S was not on the horizon; (b) the chances of general war were slight; (c) another great depression or other economic or social catastrophe of such magnitude as to affect appreciably the international position of the United States was improbable;[18] and (d) that the

[16] For an account see Horelick and Rush, *Strategic Power and Soviet Foreign Policy.*

[17] Sokolovskii, 1963 edn., pp. 131-40.

[18] See especially S. M. Men'shikov, *Ekonomicheskaia politika pravitel'stva Kennedi* [The Economic Policy of the Kennedy Government] (Moscow: Izdatel'stvo "Mysl'," 1964).

growth rate projections for the United States by American economists, while high, were not exorbitant.[19] Small wonder, then, that the Chinese argued that while Khrushchev was in power "the only country the leaders of the CPSU [looked] up to was the United States."[20]

Soviet commentary during these years revealed an acute awareness of the United States' existing capabilities, as well as a projection of the international system for the policy-relevant future, in which the U.S. would be a major force. It also generally[21] manifested a noticeably more benign appraisal of the motives of the decision-makers acting in the United States' name than that conveyed by traditional Soviet formulations.

While Soviet observers had largely confined themselves to references about the change in American capabilities, Khrushchev and the international relations journals began in the early sixties to make cautious reference to a "major reappraisal of values"[22] taking place in the United States, a phraseology which hinted at a change in the nature of imperialism. From 1959 on, Khrushchev generally adopted the position that

[19] *Ibid.*, passim.

[20] "Peaceful Coexistence—Two Diametrically Opposed Policies," *Peking Review*, Vol. vi, No. 51 (December 20, 1963), p. 16.

[21] For a striking example of an article completely at variance with the mode of Soviet commentary in these years, see L. Zubok, "V. I. Lenin ob Amerikanskom imperializme i rabochem dvizhenii SShA" [V. I. Lenin on American Imperialism and the U.S.A. Workers' Movement], *Novaia i noveishaia istoriia*, No. 2 (sent to press March 1, 1963), pp. 50-64. This article is belligerently anti-American in tone and makes no mention of Khrushchev. It may therefore be further ammunition for those who argue that Khrushchev suffered an eclipse in the aftermath of the Cuban missile crisis, an argument developed, for instance, in Carl A. Linden, *Khrushchev and the Soviet Leadership, 1957-1964* (Baltimore: The Johns Hopkins Press, 1966).

[22] N. S. Khrushchev, *Kommunizm—mir i schast'e narodov* [Communism—Peace and Happiness of the Peoples] (Moscow: Gospolitizdat, 1962), Vol. 1, p. 304.

"reasonable men" or "realists" were in the majority in the American ruling group. "People of sound mind," Khrushchev said at Bucharest in 1960, ". . . are in the majority even among the most deadly enemies of communism—they cannot but be aware of the fatal consequences of another war."[23] As Khrushchev appeared to have become increasingly attracted by the prospect of a genuine Soviet-American *détente*, the concept "reasonable men" underwent an evolution. Initially, in 1959-60, "reasonableness" or "realism" referred to the propensity which Khrushchev professed to detect, on the part of the majority within American ruling circles to adjust to the realities of the changed global distribution of power and to acquiesce in the onward progression of the world historical process.[24]

In Khrushchev's opinion, the dominant forces in the American ruling group were so concerned with the preservation of their physical selves that they would willingly pursue a policy abnegating major American values. Gradually, the notion of realism was transformed. Especially after the Cuban missile crisis it came increasingly to refer to those who recognized a common stake in the avoidance of nuclear war and who consequently were disinclined to resort to war as an instrument of policy.

Some Soviet observers, especially those associated with the Institute of World Economy and International Relations, declared that the Clausewitz dictum had become irrelevant in the atomic age, not only to the foreign policy behavior of peace-loving socialist countries but also to the imperialist powers.[25] Indeed, one Soviet ideologue went so far, just prior to

[23] For an English-language version see Hudson, Lowenthal, and MacFarquhar, eds., *The Sino-Soviet Conflict*, p. 133.

[24] Brzezinski, *Ideology and Power*, p. 105.

[25] Gantman et al., "Tekushchie problemy . . . ," p. 9.

the signing of the test-ban agreement, as to argue that there was a growing "influence" of those "in the American ruling group" "who understand that in our age war and the arms race no longer can serve as an instrument of policy."[26]

Finally, "realism" became so broad that it included persons like Gen. Maxwell Taylor, who, as the pseudonymous "General A. Nevsky" recognized, was not "a man of peace but . . . [who] saw the need for a strategy which would better serve the imperialist aims of the USA,"[27] and members of the Morgan financial dynasty.[28] The realists among American decision-makers, in other words, were those intelligently pursuing American interests under conditions of mutual deterrence.[29] Realism had come to mean a commitment to the milieu goal of system maintenance.[30]

[26] I. Lemin, "Leninskii printsip mirnogo sosushchestvovaniia i sovremennost'" [Leninist Principle of Peaceful Coexistence and Today], *Mirovaia ekonomika*, No. 4 (April 1963), p. 9, italics added.

[27] Gen. A. Nevsky, "Modern Armaments and Problems of Strategy," *World Marxist Review*, Vol. VI, No. 3 (March 1963), pp. 31-32.

[28] Iu. Iudin, "Monopolii SShA i politika Vashingtona" [U.S. Monopolies and the Policy of Washington], *Mirovaia ekonomika*, No. 8 (August 1963), p. 47.

[29] In one sense, this latter perspective was consonant with the Chinese view, since the Chinese contend that "if the representatives of U.S. monopoly capital are 'sensible' at all, they are 'sensible' only in safeguarding the fundamental interests of their own class, in oppressing the American people at home and plundering other peoples abroad, and in executing their policies of aggression and war." ("Confessions Concerning the Line of Soviet-U.S. Collaboration Pursued By The New Leaders Of The C.P.S.U.," *Peking Review*, Vol. IX, No. 8 [February 18, 1966], p. 8). The difference, of course, was that for Soviet commentators, such "sensibleness" was desirable, whereas it was not for the Chinese.

[30] The concept of milieu goals has been developed by Arnold Wolfers, *Discord and Collaboration*, and refined by Inis L. Claude, Jr. in "National Interests and the Global Environment: a Review," *The Journal of Conflict Resolution*, Vol. VIII, No. 3 (September 1964), pp. 292-93.

Implicit in the latter assessment, which was as revealing of the Khrushchevian reappraisal of *Soviet* goals as of Soviet perspectives on American motives, was a belief that the successful pursuit of American interests by Americans was compatible with improving Soviet-American relations. Khrushchev even went so far in 1962 as to state in an interview with Gardner Cowles: "Nowhere do our interests clash directly, either on territorial or economic questions."[31] The gains, therefore, of the one country were not necessarily the losses of the other. This assessment also suggested that the contention that American ruling circles aspired to world domination—an assertion less frequently made in these years than in prior years or the period since 1965—had little importance for Khrushchev. American policy-makers might or might not aspire to world domination; as long as men of reason within the American ruling group determined American foreign policy, such an aspiration was irrelevant to American foreign policy behavior in the nuclear age.

Underlying all the notions of "reasonableness" was a rather strange image of the main enemy. Indeed, it is open to question whether the United States was the main enemy to Khrushchev toward the end of his rule. The traditional Bolshevik perspective had located the major capitalist power—in the postwar period, the United States—at the enmity pole of an enmity/amity continuum. The history of Soviet foreign policy had revolved around determining which of the intermediary groups, classes, and states separating the Soviet Union and the major capitalist power Moscow should align with and for how long. Right-oriented communists advocated, and rightist phases in Soviet foreign policy had pursued, an "inclusionist"

[31] N. S. Khrushchev, *Predotvratit' voinu, otstoiat' mir* [Prevent War, Preserve Peace] (Moscow: Gospolitizdat, 1963), p. 44.

strategy, while the leftist-orientation was typified by an exclusivist orientation: "He who is not with us is against us." Khrushchev, however, abandoned the Manichean perspective embraced by all Bolsheviks, left or right. Instead, the Khrushchevian imagery became more akin to that of a minority leader in a two-party national system. To Khrushchev, the Everett Dirksen of the world communist movement, the men of reason in the United States constituted the leading forces in the ruling opposition party, to be sure, and as such were the major adversary. Unlike the radicals of both systems ("If you go left, you come out right," Khrushchev declared),[32] however, the men of reason in the American "party" were people with whom "struggle *and* cooperation"[33] were necessary, desirable, and possible. Because they used power responsibly, they represented a lesser threat to Soviet values then either the Goldwaters or the Maos.

THE MONTHS immediately following October 1964 witnessed the appearance of a number of specialized works on American foreign policy, as well as on international relations generally. These works demonstrated virtual continuity with the trends in the evolution of Soviet perspectives in the last years of Khrushchev's tenure.[34] Of these, a "*kollektivnyi trud*" by sev-

[32] *Pravda*, December 13, 1962.

[33] It was the dialectical unity of struggle and cooperation which represented the "new content" of peaceful coexistence. For an analysis see Robert C. Tucker, *The Soviet Political Mind*, pp. 201-22.

[34] Among them were AN IMEMO, *Dvizhushchie sily* . . . ; I. M. Ivanova, *Mirnoe sosushchestvovanie i krizis vneshnepoliticheskoi ideologii imperializma SShA* [Peaceful Coexistence and the Crisis of the Foreign Policy Ideology of U.S. Imperialism] (Moscow: Izdatel'stvo "Mezhdunarodnye otnosheniia," 1965); AN IMEMO, *Stroitel'stvo kommunizma* . . . ; AN IMEMO, *Mezhdunarodnye otnosheniia* . . . , Vol. III.

eral specialists in the Institute of World Economy and International Relations, entitled *The Motive Forces of U.S. Foreign Policy* [*Dvizhushchie sily vneshnei politiki SShA*], was the most important, in that it, in fairly systematic fashion, brought together in one place most of the innovative trends in Soviet commentary on American foreign policy. *Motive Forces* appears in part to have been intended to prepare Soviet audiences for a major rapprochement with the United States.[35] That books such as *Motive Forces* were similar to other works on the United States in the years immediately prior to Khrushchev's ouster was scarcely surprising, since they were conceived and largely written[36] before his removal. What warrants emphasis is that they *were* published, and that in certain respects they were even closer to typical Western perspectives on American foreign policy than the modernist trend in Soviet commentary had been under Khrushchev.

With respect to American foreign policy decision-making, several themes were noted in Soviet accounts of this time. Soviet specialists continued to place great stress on the importance of the state apparatus in U.S. decision-making.[37] The same two explanations were advanced: the increased signifi-

[35] *Dvizhushchie sily . . .* , pp. 509-10.

[36] V. N. Baryshnikov's competent dissertation, *'Taivanskii vopros' v Kitaisko-Amerikanskikh otnosheniiakh* [The 'Taiwan Question' and Chinese-American Relations] (unpublished dissertation, AN SSSR, Institut Ekonomiki Mirovoi Sotsialisticheskoi Sistemy [Otdel Istorii]), was completed during 1964 and then revised to account for Khrushchev's removal by the simple expedient of covering Khrushchev's name with such phrases as "the Soviet government," etc.—occasionally failing even to change the ending of the verb.

[37] See especially *Stroitel'stvo kommunizma . . .* , p. 389, and *Dvizhushchie sily . . .* , p. 21.

cance of foreign policy matters "in public affairs,"[38] and the change in the relationship between the state and the economy within the United States. On the latter point, the authors of *Motive Forces* specifically attacked Stalin for having used "subordination" to describe the position of the bourgeois state vis-à-vis the capitalists, and informed their readers that "the founders of Marxism-Leninism" had "always emphasized . . . that the government is not only a shop assistant but also a stock holder." "One must not," they cautioned, "underestimate the relative self-sufficiency and the active role of the state [and] its unfailing tendency to transform itself from a servant into a master." In fact, "the bourgeois state," they declared, "sometimes even acts against the will of the majority of the ruling class."[39] Similarly, Soviet writings in the months after Khrushchev's removal (both before and after the November 1964 American election) took pains to emphasize the unique role of the American president "in the carrying out of foreign policy, in particular on questions of war and peace."[40] Also, Soviet commentators in this period stressed that the "contradictions and conflicts in the United States ruling circles about disarmament, the cold war, East-West trade [had] become a permanent factor of the internal political life of the U.S."[41] Soviet specialists on American foreign policy continued to show attention to forces outside the bourgeoisie that in-

[38] *Ibid.*

[39] *Ibid.*, pp. 20-21. In an article which repeats the substance of the introductory chapter of *Dvizhushchie sily* . . . , I. Lemin put it even more strongly by omitting "of the majority," i.e., it "sometimes even acts against the will of the ruling class." I. Lemin, "Vneshniaia politika SShA: dvizhushchie sily i tendentsii" [U.S. Foreign Policy: Motive Forces and Trends], *Mirovaia ekonomika*, No. 6 (June 1965), p. 26.

[40] *Ibid.*; *Stroitel'stvo kommunizma* . . . , p. 389.

[41] *Dvizhushchie sily* . . . , p. 22.

fluenced foreign policy, and for the first time, some specialists began to ascribe major significance to the influence of public opinion on American foreign policy-making.[42]

In gross terms the Soviet appraisal of American capabilities also underwent no appreciable changes in the immediate post-Khrushchev months. Books as widely divergent in authorship, character, and intended audience as *Marxism-Leninism on War and the Army*,[43] *Motive Forces, The Construction of Communism and the World Revolutionary Process*, and volume three of *International Relations Since World War II* analyzed the capabilities of the United States essentially from the same perspective on the nature of power as had been the fashion under Khrushchev—that economic (including scientific)[44] and military capacity and potential are the essential components of the United States' power internationally, and that in these terms the United States continued to outpace all countries other than the Soviet Union. Furthermore, there were indications that Soviet specialists on the American economy—"dogmatists" notwithstanding—continued to regard a major U.S. depression as improbable, that they were impressed by the use of Keynesian techniques by the Kennedy and Johnson administrations, and that they considered the minimum growth rate projections to the year 2000, contained in the book *Resources in America's Future*[45] (which was deemed

[42] E. I. Popova, *SShA: bor'ba po voprosam vneshnei politiki, 1919-1922gg.* [The USA: The Foreign Policy Struggle, 1919-1922] (Moscow: Izdatel'stvo "Mezhdunarodnye otnosheniia," 1966).

[43] *Marksizm-Leninizm o voine i armii* (Moscow: Voenizdat, 1965).

[44] Indeed, there seems to have been a definite upgrading of science as a variable making for political power internationally. See, for instance, *Marksizm-Leninizm . . .*, p. 265.

[45] Hans H. Landsberg, Leonard Fischman, and Joseph L. Fisher, *Resources in America's Future* (Baltimore: The Johns Hopkins Press, 1963).

sufficiently significant to warrant translation), not out of line. Again, with regard to strategic capabilities, there was nothing to suggest that Soviet observers in any way either questioned that the United States had the capacity to render a damaging second strike on the Soviet Union, or thought that any other bourgeois state could ever approximate significant strategic capability.[46]

It was equally evident that on at least one important matter relating to the Soviet appraisal of American capabilities in the first months after the October 1964 coup, there was no consensus in Moscow. The question at issue was whether under any foreseeable circumstances a Soviet "victory" might result from a thermonuclear exchange with the United States. The prevalent—but not unanimous, especially among the military[47] —view in Khrushchev's last years in power was that prospects were close to nil of ever denying the United States the capacity to cause the Soviet survivors of a thermonuclear exchange to "envy the dead." Khrushchev's removal, coupled with the American initiation of the bombing of North Vietnam in February 1965, appears to have created conditions in which those differing with the prevalent view during Khrushchev's tenure in office attempted to reassert their position. From the modest amount of evidence available, it is possible to infer that during the first year after Khrushchev this effort was not successful. In March 1965 G. Gerasimov, one of the few Soviet civilian commentators knowledgeable about strategic matters, published an article[48] in which he polemicized against the view that, through the creation of an anti-ballistic missile system, it might be possible to achieve "victory" in a thermo-

[46] *Mezhdunarodnye otnosheniia . . .*, Vol. III, p. 251.

[47] Wolfe, *Soviet Strategy at the Crossroads*, especially pp. 70-71.

[48] G. Gerasimov, "The First-Strike Theory," *International Affairs*, No. 3 (March 1965), pp. 39-45.

nuclear exchange. Such would require "a discovery, bordering on a miracle," to achieve the "means for the 100 per cent interception of nuclear missiles," and nothing less would be adequate. "The means of defence," he declared, "lag behind the means of attack. Today there is no absolute defence against a missile salvo. It is possible to expect to intercept and destroy part of the missiles, but to intercept and destroy all of the missiles is technically impossible. . . ." That he was attacking persons in the Soviet Union and not just "American ultras" who believe "in the inevitability of war" was made clear when he observed, "Even if the anti-missile defence intercepts nine out of ten missiles, the tenth will cause colossal damage justifying the loss of the first nine." There may well be "American ultras" who believe in the evitability of war; given the enormous asymmetry in 1965 between the number of American and Soviet missiles (which was offset somewhat by the size of the payload of Soviet missiles), however, the country hoping to ward off 9 out of 10 missiles could only be the Soviet Union. Further evidence of ongoing controversy as to whether victory might result from a thermonuclear exchange appeared in May 1965, when Gen. Talenskii warned that there could be "no more dangerous illusion" than to believe that thermonuclear war could be an instrument for achieving political goals.[49]

Perhaps the most startling assertions about American foreign policy to appear in the period immediately after Khrushchev pertained to American motives and behavior. Madame Popova's study,[50] for instance, seemed to be encouraging Soviet neo-isolationists[51] to believe that liberal neo-isolationism was a ma-

[49] Talensky, "The Late War: Some Reflections," *International Affairs*, No. 5 (May 1965), p. 15.

[50] Popova, *SShA: bor'ba po . . .* , pp. 346-51.

[51] Alexander Dallin, "Communist Diversity: Problems for Moscow

jor force in the United States, a thought encouraged by President Johnson in his 1965 State of the Union address and disconfirmed by the February 1965 bombing of North Vietnam.[52] Once again, however, it was the Institute of World Economy and International Relations' *Motive Forces* that served as the prime example.[53] The typical Khrushchevian characterization of the three most recent American presidents—Eisenhower, Kennedy, and Johnson—as reasonable and prudent men, disinclined to risk-taking and aware of the realities of the nuclear age, was advanced. The United States, the authors of *Motive Forces* argued, was less and less prone to use force at any level as an instrument of foreign policy. Instead, the United States was placing greater reliance on economic and other nonviolent forms of influence, thus keeping the East-West conflict below the violence threshold and creating conditions favorable for a major American-Soviet rapprochement. Beyond this, for the first time in Soviet commentary, the authors of *Motive Forces* redefined, albeit hesitantly and contradictorily, the alleged American drive for world dominance. Rather than construe "world domination" literally, they hinted, the United States should be seen as seeking merely to retain its position of leadership in the capitalist world. The authors, in addition, stated that a "community of national interests"[54] exists between the United States and the Soviet Union, and declared—in a book sent to press a month after the United

and Washington," in *Polycentrism: Growing Dissidence in the Communist Bloc* (Pullman, Wash.: Washington State University Press, 1967).

[52] See in this regard Bernard S. Morris, "Soviet Policy Toward the West," in Adam Bromke and Philip E. Uren, eds., *The Communist States and the West* (New York: Praeger, 1967), p. 22.

[53] *Dvizhushchie sily . . .* , especially pp. 3-55 and 494-510.

[54] *Ibid.*, p. 507.

States began to bomb North Vietnam—that "at the present time there exist no territorial [or] economic disputes and conflicts between [the United States and the Soviet Union], their national interests do not collide either globally or anywhere regionally."[55]

The works conceived during the Khrushchev era that went to press during 1965 constitute the high mark of Soviet perspectives on American foreign policy. From approximately September 1965 on, the modernist tide ebbed. Primarily, it would seem, this was a result of the Vietnam war. On all scores there was evidence, especially in *International Affairs* and the central newspapers, of a resurgence of more traditionalist modes of analyzing American foreign policy. A book was published in 1966 which, while its authors disassociated themselves from the Stalinist "subordination," nevertheless attacked the modernist formulation of "interdependence" and the emphasis on the autonomy of the state and its relations with the economy.[56] Articles appeared explaining why big business had picked Johnson over Goldwater, and intimating that Johnson's election campaign had been little more than a deception.[57] Many public utterances in 1965-66 were replete with references to (undifferentiated) imperialists, and statements appeared stressing the essential homogeneity of views within the American ruling group.[58] Even publications of the

[55] *Ibid.*

[56] *Voprosy gosudarstvennogo kapitalizma v imperialisticheskikh i razvivaiushchikhsia stranakh na sovremennom etape* [Questions of State Capitalism in Imperialist and Developing Countries at the Contemporary Stage] (Moscow: Izdatel'stvo Moskovskogo universiteta, 1966).

[57] See, in particular, the articles by "A. Sovetov": "The Aggressive Policy of U.S. Imperialism," *International Affairs*, No. 9 (September 1965), p. 67 and "The Soviet Union and Present International Relations," *International Affairs*, No. 1 (January 1966), pp. 3-9.

[58] Sovetov, "The Aggressive Policy. . . ." "It is important to bear in

Institute of World Economy and International Relations hinted that the "two tendencies" in American foreign policy were not as clearly defined as previously claimed, and warned that events had demonstrated that it was wrong to assume that the forces of reason in bourgeois states would "automatically" be in the majority.[59]

Similarly, after September 1965 there appeared to have been a definite strengthening of those in Moscow, primarily in the military, least prone to accept strategic parity—much less inferiority—vis-à-vis the United States. Thus, in September 1965 one Col. E. Rybkin, writing in *Kommunist vooruzhennykh sil,* attacked Talenskii by name and declared: "victory in war depends not simply on the nature of the weapons but on the distribution of power between the belligerent countries. Depending on [the latter], one can achieve a quick victory over the aggressor that will prevent further destruction and calamities."[60] An even more orthodox stance was adopted in July 1966 by a Col. I. Grudinin. Writing in *Red Star*, Grudinin also attacked Talenskii by name and characterized the views of Talenskii and others "who deny any possibility of victory in world nuclear-rocket conflict" as "mistaken and even harmful."[61]

---

mind that, although there was a contest between the two tendencies in U.S. foreign policy, there was, in the final analysis, no fundamental difference between them." See, too, Marinin, "Sotsialisticheskii internatsionalizm . . . ," p. 8.

[59] *Mezhdunarodnye otnosheniia* . . . , Vol. III, p. 61. Perhaps significantly, this volume went to press September 16, 1965.

[60] For an English-language version see Roman Kolkowicz, "The Red 'Hawks' on the Rationality of Nuclear War," p. 46.

[61] *Krasnaia zvezda,* July 21, 1966. If Rybkin is a "hawk," then Grudinin is a pterodactyl, for he attacked even Rybkin for taking into account somewhat the impact of modern technology on the nature of war.

The American intervention in Vietnam also brought out another divergence in perspective relating to American capabilities. It, too, had important policy-relevant consequences, since it bore greatly on Moscow's proclivity to risk a confrontation with the United States. In this instance, there was little doubt that the divergence of perspectives extended to the ruling group—as the Supreme Soviet election speeches in June 1966 made clear. In interpreting the events in Vietnam, Kosygin (along with Brezhnev and Podgornyi) adopted a stance consonant with the low-risk, Khrushchevian posture of emphasizing United States military might. "It would be incorrect," Kosygin stressed, "in conditions of the strengthening of the danger of aggression to minimize the possibilities and potential of the United States; we do not belong in the number of those who are inclined to draw such conclusions from the contemporary situation."[62] Evidently, G. I. Voronov, by contrast, *was* among those who drew such a conclusion (and thus was presumably more inclined to risk-taking than Kosygin), for he declared apropos of Vietnam that "the growing aggressiveness of imperialism is by no means a sign of its strength."[63] So, too, apparently, was A. N. Shelepin: "The events and facts of recent years," he asserted, "show that the American imperialists are conducting themselves increasingly irrationally . . . first of all because their positions have been shaken."[64]

The most strident and vigorous resurgence[65] of traditional-

[62] *Pravda*, June 9, 1966. For Brezhnev's and Podgornyi's statements see, respectively, *Pravda*, June 11, 1966 and June 10, 1966.

[63] *Pravda*, June 4, 1966.

[64] *Pravda*, June 3, 1966.

[65] A particularly vivid illustration of the return to the old phrases is contained in I. Ivashin, "The October Revolution and International Relations," *International Affairs*, No. 11 (November 1966), pp. 48-52.

ist characterizations of American foreign policy related to American motives and behavior. A bevy of articles and brochures appeared condemning the United States' world-gendarme role, and asserting that the U.S. had by no means abandoned its goal of world domination. The influential spokesman or (or spokesmen) using the nom de plume "A. Sovetov" went so far as to declare: "Even [the United States'] membership in the anti-Hitler coalition in the Second" World War was "determined by its drive for world domination."[66] Soviet commentators professed to see U.S. moves in Vietnam, the Dominican Republic, and elsewhere as part of a "single link." The United States was bracketed with West Germany as countries, unlike "many capitalist countries," wishing to continue the cold war.[67] In view of the foregoing, especially the attacks on American goals, it was not surprising that the

[66] "The Aggressive Policy . . . ," p. 63.

[67] A. Yermonski [Ermonskii] and O. Nakropin, "General Line of Soviet Foreign Policy," *International Affairs*, No. 9 (September 1966), p. 77. The authors hedged their attack by noting: "Although aggressive sentiments are now obviously dominant in Washington, it is well known that other, sounder tendencies exist in the U.S. capital. The strengthening of these tendencies will meet with due understanding on the part of the Soviet Union." Similar statements have appeared in more authoritative statements as recently as April 23, 1967. For instance, A. P. Kirilenko, in a speech commemorating the Ninety-seventh anniversary of Lenin's birth, emphasized that

"the Government of the Soviet Union has more than once declared we are prepared to work together with all capitalist countries on the basis of the principles of peaceful coexistence in the task of strengthening peace, in the development of mutually beneficial economic relations. This would apply equally to the U.S. if the government of that country would take the path of observing the norms of international law and would cease its involvement in the internal affairs of other countries and peoples."

Pravda, April 23, 1967.

Twenty-third C.P.S.U. Congress, in its resolutions, rejected the Khrushchev thesis and that of such books as *Dvizhushchie sily,* which had provided much of the rationale for deemphasizing American hostility: i.e., that under conditions of mutual deterrence the United States was moving away from its earlier reliance on the instruments of violence.[68]

Thus, in 1966-67 it appeared that the trend in Soviet commentary of the latter years of Khrushchev's tenure in power had been reversed. What was not readily apparent was the extent to which the reappearance of traditional characterizations represented a tactical, and transitory, response to the American bombing of North Vietnam. A manipulative explanation, as the Chinese purport to believe, has much to be said for it. Books like *Motive Forces,* they declared in 1966, express views which "are the very ones the new leaders of the C.P.S.U. would make themselves"[69] in circumstances more conducive to expressing a benevolent view of American foreign policy. Certainly the Soviet ruling group's reluctance to express charitable views of American motives when the United States was waging war against a socialist country is readily understandable. Whatever else the members of the Politburo are, they are not masochists. To give vent to favorable views about American foreign policy at such a time would only ex-

[68] It appears that members of the Institute of World Economy and International Relations were reluctant to abandon their position on this issue. A lead article in *Mirovaia ekonomika* a month before the Twenty-third C.P.S.U. Congress continued to affirm the view that "the possibilities of using [prior] methods have significantly contracted (although they have not fully disappeared) as a result of the sharp changes in the political situation and political climate in the world." N. Kolikov, "Osnovnye sily sovremennogo revoliutsionnogo protsessa" [Fundamental Forces of the Contemporary Revolutionary Process], *Mirovaia ekonomika,* No. 3 (March 1966), p. 6.

[69] "Confessions . . . ," p. 8.

pose them further to such vitriolic attacks from the pro-Chinese elements in the world communist movement as the following: "Today, every man, woman or child killed by U.S. imperialist bombs, bullets and poison gas—in Vietnam, the Dominican Republic or anywhere else—is a victim not only of U.S neo-fascism but also of those who preach the traitorous doctrine of 'peaceful coexistence' with imperialism, the 'reasonableness' of U.S. imperialist leaders, and the 'changed nature' of imperialism."[70] Moreover, the dominant figures in the Soviet ruling group have taken sufficient pains to make clear that the war in Vietnam is the primary obstacle to improved Soviet-American relations as to suggest that the duration in symbolic regression may be conterminous with the duration.[71]

There are, however, several important difficulties with such an interpretation. It assumes a control over the communications channels that oversimplifies Soviet reality and fails to consider the impact of external events on Soviet internal politics. (It is also possible that, in any event, a temporary conservative turn in policy would have followed Khrushchev's removal simply because the key Soviet power bases to which a person attempting to consolidate his power would appeal

[70] The passage is taken from an article entitled "Victory over Fascism —Stalin's Leadership," which appeared in the *Malayan Monitor* published in London and reproduced in *Global Digest*, Vol. II, No. II (August 1965), p. 49. Although Chinese and pro-Chinese Communists usually quote Soviet statements accurately, this author knows of no instance in Soviet commentary where, in so many words, the "changed nature" of imperialism has been asserted.

[71] Lemin, in a lead editorial in the June 1967 issue of *Mirovaia ekonomika* ascribed the Vietnam War to the "most reactionary circles of American imperialism," not to American imperialism, thus leaving the door open to accommodation with "realistic forces" in the American ruling group. I. Lemin, "Velikaia Oktiabr'skaia sotsialisticheskaia revoliutsiia i mirovaia politika," p. 14.

would be attracted by conservative symbols.) For the Vietnam war greatly facilitated the public expression of traditional Leninist-Stalinist characterizations by those for whom these characterizations retained a distinctly greater operational significance than for a Kosygin—at least in the sense that these symbols corresponded to the intensity of animosity felt toward the United States. Persons who fit this description appear to be drawn largely from three groups. They included military men (e.g., the now deceased Marshal Malinovskii, who termed the United States "worse than Hitler") with a stake in continued heavy military spending; old ideologues who during the past decade had been shunted into positions of relatively low status and little influence (like Ivashin and Deborin), and persons whose career patterns suggested a favorable disposition to domestic reactionary policies (like Shelepin, who also found the Hitler analogy attractive). For them, the war in Vietnam was not an isolated event, but evidence that the United States confronted Soviet interests in revolution in every corner of the globe.[72]

[72] It may be of some significance that Shelepin's December 10, 1966 speech was reported quite differently by *Izvestiia* and *Krasnaia zvezda.* The *Izvestiia* version, by omitting the italicized words in the following passage, seems to suggest the primary reason for the aggravated international situation is the war in Vietnam; whereas the *Krasnaia zvezda* version relates the worsening international situation to a more generalized confrontation of imperialist and revolutionary forces:

"As a result of the intensification of the aggressive schemes of the imperialists, a serious aggravation [of the world situation] has taken place. *World reaction, headed by the main force of war and aggression —American imperialism—now here, now there kindles the hotbeds of conflicts. The imperialists in a number of regions are striving to restore by force the colonial order, to stifle the national liberation movement of the peoples.* The U.S.A. has been waging for several years now a plundering, colonial war against the peoples of Vietnam."

Moreover, a manipulative explanation gives a misleading homogeneity to Soviet perspectives about American foreign policy, perspectives which, to reiterate, are strongly conditioned by priority calculations about *Soviet* policies. The record in 1966-67 indicates that the return to old symbols had proceeded at differential rates—a phenomenon most plausibly explained as indicating a reluctance by some to abandon previous positions—with some persons persistently holding modernist notions about several issues. On certain issues—the selection of the most suitable formula for categorizing the relation between the American economy and polity, for one—there was plainly no consensus, no "line," in Moscow.[73] It was likely, too, that with regard to the homogeneity of the American ruling group, the divergent formulations were partly products of divergent appraisals among the specialists, and, probably, the ruling group as well. Similarly, the continuing dialogue over the Clausewitz dictum (now no longer explicitly rejected) pointed to divergent appraisals of American motives and capabilities—and to divergent Soviet policy prescriptions.

An explanation emphasizing the manipulative character of the reappearance of old symbols, furthermore, probably fails to take into account the extent to which for all Soviet observers American foreign policy in 1965-67 cast doubt on new hypotheses and rekindled old fears. Even if the resurgence was a function largely of the perturbations in Soviet-American relations, it seems unlikely that at any time in the near

[73] Contrast Lemin, "Velikaia Oktiabr'skaia . . . ," p. 8; the statement by Ia. A. Pevzner at the International Conference of Marxists on the occasion of the Fiftieth anniversary of the publication of Lenin's *Imperialism* ("Mezhdunarodnaia konferentsiia Marksistov," *Mirovaia ekonomika*, No. 7 [July 1967] p. 72); *Voprosy gosudarstvennogo kapitalizma . . .* ; and the critique of that book by E. Lebedeva in a review in *Mirovaia ekonomika*, No. 7 (July 1967), pp. 155-57.

future Soviet perspectives on American foreign policy will be as favorably disposed to the United States as was the fashion in 1963-65. Out of the clash of the "two tendencies" in Soviet perspectives on the United States—represented by the *mode* of Soviet commentary in 1963-65, on the one hand, and 1965-67, on the other—there will probably emerge a new perspective on American foreign policy. In that perspective, there would be a continued place for the more differentiated and sophisticated analysis of the impact of internal political processes on American foreign policy exemplified by the work of the specialists in the Institute of World Economy and International Relations, but which would, however, be characterized, generally, by a more jaundiced view of American foreign policy goals and behavior than was the mode in 1963-65. There were already some indications of this new realism. Soviet observers —partly as a result of projection—seemed increasingly attracted by rather cynical, national-interest explanations of the behavior of states (including the United States), in which transnational class ties played an insignificant role. Examples of this new cynicism were already apparent in the specialized international relations literature in 1965-66. Thus in N. N. Iakovlev's[74] study of Franklin Roosevelt, Roosevelt is much less the "progressive" figure he has usually been made out to be in recent Soviet historiography and much more the conservative realist calculatingly preparing the nation for war. Similarly, in Barishnykov's analysis of the United States, China, and the Taiwan question, he speculates about a time when—Taiwan having lost its military significance—the United States will abandon the Chinese Nationalists in order to secure a

[74] N. N. Iakovlev, *Franklin Ruzvel't: chelovek i politik* (Moscow: Izdatel'stvo "Mezhdunarodnye otnosheniia," 1965).

rapprochement with Communist China.[75] Moreover, by 1967 evidence of such thinking began to be found in the central press as well. In February 1967 *Red Star* purported to detect a "Red China lobby" in the United States, and to note "open talk" in Washington that "the ruling circles of the United States [were] interested in the retention of power by Mao Tse-tung."[76]

This new trend, if such in fact it turns out to be, may provide a more stable basis for a durable American-Soviet relationship throughout the remainder of the century than either the traditionalists *kto-kogo* perspective *or* the dominant trend in Soviet commentary in the last years of Khrushchev's tenure. Khrushchev, perhaps to discredit the traditionalist perspective, did to a certain extent "prettify American imperialism;" as perceived by key elites within the two countries, the interests of the United States and the Soviet Union do and will clash. The new realism may facilitate an American-Soviet relationship in which peaceful coexistence, in precisely the Khrushchevian formulation, is possible: namely, a mixed-adversary relationship involving struggle and cooperation. What it will not facilitate is the reunification of theory and practice *within the framework of the atomic age.* In order to retain the inevitability of revolution under atomic age conditions, under post-imperialism, if there were no policy alternatives to bring reality into conformity with theory, Khrushchev had to prettify imperialism.

[75] Baryshnikov, 'Taivanskii vopros'. . . .

[76] *Krasnaia zvezda,* February 21, 1967.

Chapter Seven: The Balance of Power as System and Policy

THE BALANCE of power, like power itself, is an ambiguous symbol. When used in reference to an international system the term is especially subject to plural usages. One tack taken when confronted by this ambiguity has been to confine the term exclusively to the classical balance of power, that is, a state system having five or more essential actors whose decision-makers follow a prescription to thwart any actor from dominating the known political universe. In addition, the explicit requirement is often attached, that one actor consciously perform the function of balancer. There is much by way of clarity to commend such a tack. For purposes of analyzing Soviet perspectives, however, it is excessively restrictive. The concern here is with the manner in which, in the Soviet view, a balancing process operates in the contemporary international system and the contingencies which influence its operation; hence I will be less confining in my usage of "balance of power."

One may properly differentiate among international systems according to, first, the degree to which the balancing *process* is consciously manipulated by the decision-makers of the major actors[1] and, second, the extent to which the system tends toward stability. (Among Western specialists, equilibrium has generally been considered conducive to and even equivalent

[1] Inis L. Claude, Jr. has distinguished between automatic, semi-automatic, and manually operated equilibrating processes. (*Power and International Relations*, p. 43.) By semi-automatic, Professor Claude refers to a system in which "the automatism of the system is supplemented by the calculated operations of the unique participant, the state committed to the process of equilibrium" (p. 48).

to stability; some, however, argue that stability requires that one side possess preponderant power.) These two criteria are not identical. One can hypothesize a set of circumstances in which a system will tend to be stable regardless of the extent to which the decision-makers of the participant units consciously endeavor to maintain the system[2]—which in the contemporary era primarily means keeping the resort to violence within limits. Similarly, all the skills and efforts of Castlereagh, Talleyrand, and Metternich could not circumvent the stability-destroying secular trends of the nineteenth century, such as the rise of nationalism and democracy, uneven demographic changes, and technological innovations.

There is a sense in which any international system is a balance-of-power system by virtue of its being a system, that is, a series of variables which are sufficiently interrelated that they cohere. I have spoken throughout as though there were, in the Soviet view, an international *system*—and properly so. The phrase distribution (or correlation) of power, *sootnoshenie sil,* implies a degree of interdependence which is descriptive of a system. To be sure, it implies a highly nonintegrative system—nothing, certainly, like the Hegelian *Rechtsstaat*, nor the rigidly hierarchical order which Soviet authors have said characterized international relations under imperialism. At the same time, the last years of Khrushchev's tenure saw an increased recognition in Soviet literature of the systemic attributes of international relations. Even if "the view came to prevail in the post-Stalin years that international law was the totality of elements common to both capitalist and socialist

[2] Some Western scholars, for instance, read the record of the 18th-century balance system as one in which the Invisible Hand—largely taking the form of the level of weapons technology—operated, and devalue the role ascribed to conscious manipulation of the quadrille in maintaining the system.

superstructures;"[3] and by 1960 it had become "impossible, of course, to deny the important influence of military technology on the interdependence of the two systems;"[4] it remained the case that for the better part of the Khrushchev years the focus of analysis was primarily on the two systems and that these were socio-economic as well as state systems.

Dating roughly from the Twenty-second C.P.S.U. Congress, and continuing through the first three years after Khrushchev's ouster, however, there was increasingly an overt recognition of the existence of a "*world political system*"[5] which involve, in one view, "the following main types of relations":

(1) relations of socialist states among themselves;

(2) relations between socialist states and the economically underdeveloped countries of Asia, Africa, and Latin America;

(3) relations between economically underdeveloped countries;

(4) relations between socialist and imperialist states;

[3] Alexander Dallin, *Soviet Union at the United Nations*, p. 7.

[4] Iu. Krasin and I. Kurbatkin, Review of John H. Herz's *International Politics in the Atomic Age, in Mirovaia ekonomika*, No. 5 (May 1960), p. 144.

[5] I. Lemin, "Leninskii printsip mirnogo sosushchestvovaniia i sovremennost' " [The Leninist Principle of Peaceful Coexistence and Modern Times], *Mirovaia ekonomika*, No. 4 (April 1963), p. 7, italics added. For a reference to "the system of international relations," see V. G. Trukhanovskii, ed., *Istoriia mezhdunarodnykh otnoshenii i vneshnei politiki SSSR* [History of International Relations and Foreign Policy of the U.S.S.R.], Vol. III (1945-1963gg.) (Moscow: Izdatel'stvo "Mezhdunarodnye otnosheniia," 1964), p. 3. For similar remarks after Khrushchev's ouster, see AN IMEMO, *Stroitel'stvo kommunizma . . .*, p. 476; and Lemin's remarks at an international conference of Marxists on the occasion of the 50th anniversary of the publication of Lenin's *Imperialism*. "Mezhdunarodnaia konferentsiia marksistov," *Mirovaia ekonomika*, No. 7 (July 1967), especially p. 69.

(5) relations between imperialist states and underdeveloped countries;

(6) relations of imperialist states among themselves.[6]

Another, earlier, view was expressed by Galkin, who designated "the systems of political relations" as those,

> (1) between the world Socialist community and the imperialist bloc;
>
> (2) between imperialist countries and the oppressed nations or newly independent states;
>
> (3) between the imperialist Powers themselves;
>
> (4) between the Socialist countries;
>
> (5) between the Socialist countries and the oppressed nations or states recently freed from oppression.[7]

The extent of interrelationship was further emphasized by the definitions of international relations noted in a previous connection as:

> . . . the aggregate of the economic, legal, ideological and military contacts and ties between classes and nations in the world arena, between states and systems of states, between the main economic formations and their alliances, between the most influential political forces and organizations.[8]
>
> . . . a whole complex of economic, political, ideological, juridical, diplomatic and military ties and interrelationships between peoples, states, and systems of states, between the

[6] Lemin, "Leninskii . . . ," p. 7.

[7] A. Galkin, "Some Aspects of the Problem of Peace and War," *International Affairs*, No. 11 (November 1961), p. 30.

[8] N. Inozemtsev, "Results and Prospects of the Development of International Relations," *International Affairs*, No. 11 (November 1961), p. 15.

basic social, economic and political forces and organizations active in the world.[9]

The two definitions appear to illustrate or at least suggest a change in emphasis. The first (1961) definition adverted to economic formations and their alliances, while the latter (1962) did not; the latter, on the other hand, admitted, among other things, "*political* . . . systems of states." Paralleling the much publicized argument advanced in the Soviet Union, that in the words of the Party Program, "socialism counterposes to capitalism *a new type of international relations*,"[10] a consciousness of present-day international relations as an autonomous system with its own set of rules was developing.

Even prior to this, however, the use of *sootnoshenie sil* as a theoretical construct in the loosest sense, suggested that the implicit model of international reality for the Soviet observer was that of a system. But Soviet thinking about international relations diverged sharply from the assumptions of many Western theorists who also conceptualize international reality as a system. The latter have tended to assume the natural and necessary outcome of a multi-sovereignty system as stability at an equilibrium point. To impose order on the data, Western writers of such variegated theoretical positions as Hans Morgenthau, Morton Kaplan, George Liska, and Harold Lasswell have found an equilibrium model useful or even indispensable. That such an attitude is widespread is readily comprehensible. The Westerner's world-view is greatly colored by attitudes which lead him to regard the postwar world as an aberration. Stability, peace, and gradualism are to the Westerner words de-

[9] AN IMEMO, *Mezhdunarodnye otnosheniia* . . . , Vol. 1, p. xxvi, italics omitted.

[10] Saikowski and Gruliow, eds., *Current Soviet Policies*, p. 13, italics in original. But see the significant statement by Korionov, below, p. 268.

scribing normalcy in both its connotations: the expected and the desired.[11]

If these attitudes are readily comprehensible, they are not necessarily commendable. By taking equilibrium as the beginning rather than the end of analysis, expectations about the behavior of those who act in the name of states are created which may have little relation to reality. In particular, it may result in a failure to distinguish between a power-balancing, equilibrating policy that is an automatic, visceral response to a situation, and a consciously conceived policy of power-balancing—formulated, perhaps, as a result of centuries of participation in a state system. Moreover, it may obscure the fundamental differences between parametrically stable contexts and those in which disequilibrating tendencies—"positive feedback," in communications theory parlance—are highly probable.

Soviet observers, by contrast, have not been *predisposed* to assume stability and equilibrium as the natural or necessary outcome of state competition. Instead, doctrinal predispositions and experience alike induced expectations of violence, revolution, qualitative change, and disequilibrium. (Conceivably, these dispositions in the world-view might have longer durability than a belief in the inevitability of *the* revolution. Expectation of the latter might atrophy while the expectations of qualitative change and disequilibrating tendencies persist.)[12] The contemporary epoch, it was authoritatively asserted, was revo-

[11] Not every Western theorist, naturally, can be pegged in this fashion. For a colorful statement of the opposite view, see Nicholas Spykman, *America's Strategy in World Politics* (New York: Harcourt, Brace, 1942), p. 25: "A political equilibrium is neither a gift of the gods nor an inherently stable condition. . . . There is a tendency to look upon peace as normal and war as abnormal. . . ."

[12] See below, pp. 257-69.

lutionary in its essence: it was "an epoch of socialist and national-liberation revolutions." The trend was away from equilibrium, and that trend was permanent and irreversible.

Yet to have said this is to have said very little, for it merely expressed in one fashion core assumptions of the Soviet world view underlying a belief in the inevitability of "the revolution" and the inevitable displacement of the capitalist system of international relations. Were we to limit our analysis to this, we would have bypassed much of what was interesting in the Soviet perspective under Khrushchev—the complexity, relative sophistication, and apparently inescapable dilemma of Soviet thought.

Soviet observers of the Khrushchev period rather skillfully differentiated between stability-maintaining elements in the milieu or structure of the "capitalist" international system, and those in the international situation obtaining in the early 1960s. Those schooled in the Leninist tradition have always been keenly aware of the difference for the stability of a political system between a struggle in which the prize at stake is only the share of the pie to be divided, and a struggle in which the loser is obliged to yield that which he already has. It was just this latter pattern, it will be recalled, that Lenin depicted as the main destabilizing element in international relations in the late nineteenth and early twentieth centuries and which marked the beginning of "imperialism—the highest stage of capitalism." More specifically, Gen. S. N. Krasil'nikov, in the introduction to a Russian edition of Henry Kissinger's *Nuclear Weapons and Foreign Policy,* pointed out: "The comparative stability of the 'Vienna system' is explained by the weakness of the bourgeois revolutionary and national movements in the states of Europe, and also the significant force of feudal society in Russia, Austria, and other countries."[13]

Soviet commentators were attuned to another element of nineteenth-century international relations, tending to keep conflict within manageable limits, namely, the homogeneity of the component actors' socio-economic systems and ideologies. This theme was rather muted in Soviet writings in the early 1960s, presumably because of the officially expressed view that differences in ideology would not necessarily engender war. One suspects, however, that no Soviet observer would quarrel with this observation from I. Lemin:

> . . . it goes without saying that one capitalist country, struggling with another, does not intend to annihilate the other's capitalist system. But it endeavors to take away the other's markets, sources of raw materials, colonies, and 'spheres of influence,' to annex the other's territories, to expunge it from the numbers of the 'great powers' and generally from the ranks of independent states, to turn the other into its tributary and vassal.[14]

Conventional wisdom in the West has held that a basic rule of the balance-of-power game was that the essential actors were not to be eliminated from the ranks of the great powers, much less from the ranks of the independent states. If in the Soviet view the nineteenth-century power game, under conditions of ideological homogeneity, was as intense as Lemin contended, one can evoke an image of the contemporary international process that is destabilizing, to say the least.

[13] *Iadernoe oruzhie i vneshniaia politika*, p. 209n.

[14] Lemin, "K voprosu o protivorechiiakh mezhdu kapitalisticheskimi stranami" [On the Problem of Contradictions Between Capitalist Countries], *Mirovaia ekonomika*, No. 8 (August 1960), p. 37.

Finally, Soviet observers pointed to the structural differences between international relations in the age of imperialism and in the modern international system. Consonant with their view that international relations were rigidly hierarchical when capitalism's dominance was unchallenged, a balance-of-power system in which equal powers combined to prevent the domination of Europe by a single power was inconceivable. In the perennial struggle for place characteristic of capitalism, a strictly temporary equilibrium might result at that instant just prior to the time when one power surpassed another in the hierarchy. Anything more than a temporary equilibrium was out of the question—if only because of the law of unevenness of development under capitalism.

There was, however, a sense in which a balance-of-power system operated, and on which Soviet analysts laid stress. The dominant power (England and subsequently the United States), taking advantage of its geographically-secured invulnerability, operated a balance-of-power system in which the dominant power functioned as holder of the balance in order to preserve or secure its dominant position in the international order. V. G. Trukhanovskii, the editor-in-chief of *Voprosy istorii*, expressed this concept succinctly in an account of English foreign policy:

> [What the balance of power meant was] the establishment of English control over European politics by a path of setting off one group of European states against another and thereby weakening both militarily.
>
> The part England played in the First World War is directly connected with the struggle for a 'balance of power' *profitable* to it. The English ruling circles attached to the war calculations for re-establishing the former leading role

> of England in world affairs. They had in mind re-establishing by military means the 'balance of power' which was gradually infringed upon by the growth of German might at the end of the XIXth and beginning of the XXth century and which traditionally secured for England the role of arbiter in European and world affairs. . . .[15]

By contrast, in the third stage of capitalism's general crisis, there was no dominant power. The same ICBM that prompted an international order dominated by two roughly equal powers precluded the possibility of a balance-of-power system controlled by a single holder of the balance.[16] Since no state was invulnerable, no state could effectively achieve control by "setting off one group of . . . states against another" *militarily*.

The Unity of Theory and Practice: The Collapse of the Khrushchevian Synthesis

This last point, that no state was invulnerable, was singularly important because it pointed to what may be described as the Khrushchevian effort to reunify revolutionary theory and practice in the atomic age. The dilemma that threatened to rupture the unity of theory and practice was as obvious as it was real: how could "socialism" be achieved without war? Khrushchev's answer, in its essentials, was that Soviet capacity to strike the homeland of the dominant imperialist power deprived imperialism of its capability to impede artificially—through the conscious use of international violence—the disequilibrating revolutionary tendencies inherent in the times.

[15] V. G. Trukhanovskii, *Vneshniaia politika Anglii na pervom etape obshchego krizisa kapitalizma (1918-1939gg.)*, p. 13, italics added.

[16] For an argument dating the development even earlier (to the end of World War II), see N. N. Iakovlev, *Noveishaia istoriia SShA* [A Recent History of the USA] (Moscow: Sotsekgiz, 1961), p. 452.

While stability would be maintained at the superstructural level, so to speak, through the deterrence of the United States, the revolution would proceed apace unimpeded at the base. The contemporary international system would be undermined through changes in the domestic political structure of the participant units; Khrushchev, "the greatest revisionist of all times," had no alternative, once interstate war was precluded, but to return to the Marxian conception of revolution as a phenomenon taking place *within* a state.

Several secondary calculations underlay the Khrushchevian grand design. Soviet observers asserted that in the postwar world, changes in relative power position stemmed primarily from developments within a state,[17] rather than—as was traditional in a multi-polar system—from the formation and shiftings of alliances.

Another major part of the calculus was the concept, much remarked on in the West, of national democracy. As with many other concepts pertaining to international relations, there were plural voices in 1960-61 in the Soviet ruling group, as well as among the specialists, regarding the nature of the concept and which countries most nearly approximated it. Common to all Soviet accounts in the early sixties, however, was a changing conception of the developmental process in the Afro-Asian world. These countries, Soviet observers proclaimed, had the option of bypassing capitalism and pursuing instead a

[17] The Soviet argument—continued after Khrushchev's ouster—that developing the Soviet Union most helps the international communist movement, a logical continuation of proletarian internationalism, is seen by the Chinese as evidence that the Soviet Union is reluctant to engage in struggle. It certainly must be comforting to reassure oneself and one's countrymen that, say, by raising the standard of living for the Soviet citizen, one is building communism globally.

"non-capitalist path"[18] of development, one not necessarily led by the proletariat alone.[19] As a result largely of these internal changes, Soviet observers anticipated that the lesser actors in the international system, especially the newly independent ones, would be drawn increasingly toward the socialist camp. Foreign-policy behavior of the underdeveloped countries would be determined largely by domestic considerations, the class ties of the ruling group[20] and the demand for rapid industrialization.[21] It would also be strongly influenced by bandwagon

[18] Whether the noncapitalistic path would lead to a socialist goal remained to be seen. One major trend in the last years of Khrushchev's years in power among the modernists was increasingly—in large part for immediate tactical purposes—to blur the distinction between "scientific socialism" and other kinds of socialism. As a result, it became unclear whether for some Soviet observers there was any difference between the noncapitalist and the socialist paths.

[19] Of the literature on national democracies see especially Donald S. Carlisle, "The Changing Soviet Perception of the Developmental Process in the Afro-Asian World," *Midwest Journal of Political Science*, Vol. VIII, No. 4 (November 1964), pp. 385-407, on which the above draws heavily.

[20] Stated most simply, the Soviet position postulated that

"Where the power is preserved in the hands of the most right wing circles of the bourgeoisie or even of the feudal elements, where the democratic movement is insufficiently powerful [there occurs] a policy of orientation toward [or] alliance with the most powerful capitalist states, a policy of support for imperialist *diktat.* By contrast, in those cases where the moderate, left, or democratic groups of the bourgeoisie possess power and the popular masses exert an active influence on the whole political situation, a foreign policy results in principles of neutralism, friendly ties with all countries and peaceful coexistence."

(Gantman et al., "Tekushchie problemy . . . ," *Mirovaia ekonomika*, No. 7 (July 1960), p. 15.

[21] It was assumed that the Soviet and Chinese models would draw the underdeveloped countries closer to the camp. On the different models see Donald S. Zagoria, "Some Comparisons Between the Rus-

tendencies; rather than pursue policy courses based on balance-of-power considerations, the elites of the underdeveloped countries, Soviet observers seem to have anticipated, would hasten to abandon moribund capitalism.[22]

Similarly, domestic pressure in the European states, especially the small, northern powers, would intensify demands for neutrality as the Soviet Union's relative strength grew. In the major imperialist powers, too, as we have seen, the "realistic forces," in the prevailing Soviet view, were gaining the upper hand. Those who realized that communism was the wave of the future would endeavor to achieve accommodation as painlessly as possible. A series of mutually reinforcing, self-fulfilling hypotheses would have been created and a "runaway inflation" would ensue.

Much could be said for the plausibility of the Khrushchevian vision, particularly as the world seemed to be taking shape until approximately 1960-61. It was widely accepted even in the West that it was only a matter of time before the Soviet Union overtook and surpassed the United States as a military, economic, and political power. Western international relations literature also lent some credence to Soviet expectations. A century ago, Lord Brougham argued that the maintenance of a system of equilibrium required the decision-makers place balancing of power above all other policy considerations. To do this, he observed, the decision-makers must "discourage sentiments in the people"—a phenomenon not likely to take place in an era of mass participation in foreign policy.[23] Annette

---

sian and Chinese Models," in A. Doak Barnett, *Communist Strategies in Asia* (New York: Praeger, 1963), pp. 11-33.

[22] Sokolovskii (1963 edn., p. 233) gives consideration to the possibility that nonsocialist countries would ally themselves with the socialist camp in case of war.

[23] Cited in Haas, "*The Balance of Power . . .*" pp. 471-74.

Baker Fox's study of small states' behavior in World War II,[24] moreover, as well as American behavior in the War of 1812, seems to indicate that small states are less likely to pursue balance-of-power policies than the great powers because they lack sufficient "security reserve."

There were several flaws, however, in the Khrushchevian view. The flaws, destroying the unity of theory and practice, were associated with the interrelated tasks of maintaining the present international system and establishing the future international relations of a new type. Evidence from the Soviet press, moreover, indicated that, particularly after the Cuban missile crisis, Soviet observers themselves were increasingly aware of the tenuousness of the Khrushchevian resynthesis.

For one thing, there was the question of world war, the prevention of which, in the Soviet reading, clearly constituted the core task of international system maintenance. As the Party Program stated authoritatively, "*The question of war and peace is the basic question of our time. . . . The chief thing is to prevent a thermonuclear war, not to allow it to break out.*"[25]

Soviet expectations of violence in the two arenas which Marxists-Leninists had traditionally thought contained the major seeds of *world* wars—interimperialist relations and relations between imperialist and socialist states—were generally quite low throughout the latter part of Khrushchev's term. Public utterances, by specialists and members of the Soviet elite, suggest that Soviet international relations commentators shared the view of Karl Deutsch and his associates, that the North Atlantic community had become a *security* community

[24] Annette Baker Fox, *The Power of Small States* (Chicago: The University of Chicago Press, 1959).

[25] Translated in Saikowski and Gruliow, eds., *Current Soviet Policies*, p. 13, italics in original.

in which war was virtually unthinkable.[26] They would similarly have agreed with Samuel P. Huntington[27] that the arena of global politics had ceased to be an arena characterized by a high expectation of violence—a "*military*" arena, in Lasswell and Kaplan's terminology[28]—and had become instead a "*civic*" arena in which the expectations of violence were low.

General war ceased to be "fatalistically inevitable"; in fact, it was highly unlikely. Nevertheless, neither was peace inevitable. Expectations of violence in the global arena were low but *not null*. As long as they were not null, the revolution was not inevitable. The sensible task, therefore, for all good revolutionaries was to decrease the chances of world war in such a way as not to seriously impede the revolutionary process.[29]

Soviet international relations observers in the latter years under Khrushchev further displayed an awareness that not all the inputs crucial to the maintenance of the international

[26] Karl W. Deutsch et al., *Political Community and the North Atlantic Area* (Princeton, N.J.: Princeton University Press, 1957).

[27] Samuel P. Huntington, "Patterns of Violence in World Politics," in Huntington, ed., *Changing Patterns of Military Politics* (New York: The Free Press of Glencoe, 1962), pp. 17-50, especially p. 17.

[28] Harold D. Lasswell and Abraham Kaplan, *Power and Society*, p. 252.

[29] The qualification is an important one. To suggest that at the margin, the value, "peace," takes precedence over "socialism" is not to argue that Soviet decision-makers will always forego "revolutionary gains" to enhance "peace." The only policy implication to be derived is that if, in the Soviet perception, the likelihood of central war can be decreased without sacrificing at least the aspiration to enhance other values, Soviet decision-makers will pursue a course designed to decrease the likelihood of central war. Surely, however, certain Western proposals designed to minimize the likelihood of war would, if effectuated, entail too great a sacrifice of values other than "peace" to warrant any expectation that the Soviet Union, under any conceivable leadership, would accept them.

system were either "objectively" determined by the world historical process or sufficiently subject, directly or indirectly, to the influence of history's chosen people (or more precisely—and this was part of the problem—the right-thinking elements among history's chosen people). Specifically the avoidance of general war was contingent, in part, on the behavior of the decision-makers in the leading capitalist power. As Khrushchev declared in the Central Committee Report to the Twenty-second Party Congress: "The threat of war is hard to avert unilaterally, just as a campfire is hard to put out if one is pouring water, another kerosene."[30]

Just as the billiard-ball model as a general theory with a single solution point collapsed when the motives and behavior of the decision-makers were treated—quite properly—as a variable input, so too did the Khrushchevian effort to resynthesize the unity of theory and practice under nuclear age conditions collapse when the "minds of men" were intruded in the equation. As Khrushchev recognized in 1963, "the policy, comrades, of the imperialist countries is after all determined by people. And these people also have brain cases and brains. The direction in which their brain bearings rotate is [however] another question."[31] This being the case, international politics in the Soviet perspective could no longer be considered a *closed* system, i.e., a system with a solution at a single point. The analytical model, and world history, were open-ended.

In addition to the atom bomb and the "subjective" foreign policy of the United States, the Soviet Union itself, by its very successes, undermined the Khrushchevian calculus. Funda-

[30] *Pravda*, October 17, 1961; trans. in *Current Digest*, Vol. XIII, No. 41 (November 8, 1961), at p. 3.

[31] Khrushchev, *Pravda*, July 20, 1963.

mentally the Soviet Union was confronted with the same dilemma that the German socialists of the Second International had been: the Soviet elite, by its own cognizance, had an immense stake in the maintenance of the international system, both for the benefits the Soviet Union secured in that system and because the violent destruction of the international system would destroy mankind or at least "halt progress and throw humanity back tens or perhaps hundreds of years."[32] The proletariat in the Marxist tradition were truly revolutionary because they had nothing to lose but their chains. For the Soviet Union during Khrushchev's tenure, however, "*gone* [were] *the days when the working men rising in struggle against capitalism had indeed nothing to lose but their chains. Through selfless, heroic struggle, the masses have won immense material, political and cultural gains, gains that are embodied in the socialist world system. Tomorrow the whole world and the civilization created by their labor will belong to the working people.*"[33]

The implication was clear: how can a system, in this case an international system, be overthrown in whose continuance one has an immense stake? How is the present system to be maintained until the arrival of the glorious future; how can a "glorious tomorrow" be achieved without destroying "today"? How, if today is destroyed, will there be a tomorrow? ("Nowadays, people ask not only *what* will the future be like, but *will* there be a future?"[34]) How, if tomorrow is achieved, can

[32] "The Policy of Peaceful Coexistence Proves its Worth," *World Marxist Review*, Vol. v, No. 12 (December 1962), p. 3. Many other statements expressing this sentiment might be cited. One of the earliest was N. Talensky, "The Character of Modern War," *International Affairs*, No. 10 (October 1960), pp. 23-27.

[33] "The Policy of Peaceful Coexistence . . . ," p. 6, italics added.

[34] Kariakin, "Allen Dulles Instead of Karl Marx," p. 87, italics in original.

it avoid looking very like today? Such was the nature of the Soviet dilemma.

The Soviet response in the early 1960s took several forms. One consequence of the collapse of general theory was a dramatic upsurge in the propensity for conceptual, methodological, and doctrinal innovation on the part of the international relations specialists. Substantively the response was reflected in a manifestly intensified inclination to discriminate among the patterns of interaction and patterns of behavior which would affect the likelihood of global conflict.

After many years of overt indiscrimination Soviet international relations commentary during Khrushchev's last years in power revealed a capacity to differentiate, in terms of the likelihood of violence, among potential occupants of the White House; between the White House and the Pentagon;[35] between those who regarded central war as an acceptable instrument of policy in the thermonuclear age and those who did not;[36] between those who admitted that "the hope to create 'positions of preponderant strength' [militarily had] collapsed for good" and those who had not;[37] and between stabilizing and destabilizing strategic policies and weapons systems.[38]

[35] Cf. the description of the Cuban crisis in Gantman et al., "Mirovaia politika . . . ," p. 6.

[36] E.g., V. Pechorkin, "About 'Acceptable War,'" *International Affairs*, No. 3 (March 1963), pp. 20-25.

[37] V. V. Kortunov, "Ideological Struggle in Conditions of the Peaceful Co-existence of the Two Systems," *International Affairs*, No. 8 (August 1963), p. 7.

[38] Note the comments of Marshal A. Yeremenko [Eremenko], "Absurd Plans, Ridiculous Hopes," *International Affairs*, No. 6 (June 1963), p. 19, on the proposal to create a NATO nuclear force: it will "give certain members of this bloc a more 'favourable' opportunity to touch off a world conflagration" but "there will be no accession in the West's military might." (Interestingly he states that "it might seem to some that . . . since there will be no accession in the West's military

Another kind of discrimination of interest to Western theorists concerned with balance theory—as well as, needless to say, to American foreign-policy elites—was taking place in the Soviet Union. In a manner analogous to the collective-security, balance-of-power debate that has upset Western theorists and policy-makers alike at several junctures throughout the half-century since World War I, Soviet decision-makers toward the end of Khrushchev's years in power were apparently attempting to grapple with the difficult theoretical and policy-relevant questions which arise when one no longer considered the most powerful capitalist state necessarily the most aggressive state. The relatively simple tactical task of identifying the capitalist groups with which to ally against the main enemy was supplanted by an infinitely more complex, if theoretically more interesting, issue. Just as the British foreign policy dialogue in the interwar period revolved around whether Britain should counter-weight status quo France, the strongest continental power after World War I, or firmly join with France in keeping Germany weak; just as American policy-makers have chosen between a policy that attempts to separate China from the Soviet Union, and one which attempts to separate the Soviet Union from China; just as the American policy-makers have been obliged to choose between attempting to further the split in the "socialist camp" in order to weaken its power position, and attempting to seek to avoid a split for fear that China and the Soviet Union would each act more aggressively—so, too, were Soviet decision-makers obliged to determine whether the main danger to Soviet values stemmed from the most *powerful* or from the most *aggres-*

---

might, why break a lance?" [*ibid.*]) On the MLF see Brzezinski, "Moscow and the M.L.F.: Hostility and Ambivalence," *Foreign Affairs*, Vol. XLIII, No. 1 (October 1964), pp. 126-34.

sive capitalist forces. With respect to choices among alternative elites within particular capitalist countries, Soviet commentary during Khrushchev's term in power seems to have been unanimous in opting—in direct contrast with the Chinese—for those viewed as more liberal and more realistic, as the 1960 and 1964 American elections bore witness. With respect to the proper handling of interstate contradictions, however, Soviet commentary suggested more ambivalence. A lengthy statement by "Sovetov" in mid-1963 illustrated the nature of the dilemma and probably bespoke an ongoing dialogue in Moscow:

> In connection with the intensification of the struggle and intrigues in the Atlantic alliance, the question now being asked in the West is: to whom, in these conditions will the Socialist countries give their support? For this fortune-telling historic precedent is being used to the full. It is recalled, for instance, that after the First World War the Soviet Union displayed good will towards the countries oppressed by the so-called peace system of Versailles. After Hitler's advent to power in Germany when the danger of fascism and war developed in Europe, the U.S.S.R. began to draw close to Britain and France against whom the revanchist threat was levelled.
>
> All kinds of rumours have also been circulated. At one time Western observers considered that in connection with the increasing split in the imperialist camp there was a 'noticeable rapprochement' between the U.S.S.R. and the U.S.A. since, apparently, the U.S.S.R. prefers to deal with one representative of the opposing bloc rather than a group of countries defending views which it is difficult to reduce to a common denominator. Against this, reports from unknown

sources have been widespread in the British and American press alleging that President de Gaulle, having forged the Bonn-Paris axis, intends to draw this axis closer to the countries of the world Socialist system.

To put the question in this way, however, is essentially illegitimate. *In the present situation there can be no question, in general, . . . of the Socialist countries giving preference or being more favourable to one or other imperialist grouping. No objective grounds for this exist. From the point of view of Socialist foreign policy the question today is not that of how much to interfere in the family quarrel in NATO, but how best to use the situation that has arisen in the interests of consolidating peace and the security of the peoples, in the interests of their national and social emancipation.*

To achieve these aims it is very important to understand the influence of the deepening split in the imperialist camp on the general, international situation. It is clear, on the one hand, that the discord among the imperialists weakens their possibility of pursuing an aggressive foreign policy towards the Socialist countries and the neutral states.

On the other hand, the consequence of the conflicts in the imperialist camp and the rivalry between France and the U.S.A. for the 'good will' of the Federal Republic of Germany is that the weight of the latter in NATO can become considerably stronger, leading to further increased aggressiveness on the part of the military bloc.[39]

In terms of conventional balance-of-power literature, it was instructive that Soviet analysis distinguished between an in-

[39] A. Sovetov, "Contradictions in the Western Bloc," *International Affairs,* No. 6 (June 1963), p. 8, italics added.

ternational system characterized by high tension and one which was not. "The leaders of the C.P.C.," the the C.P.S.U. charged in its July 14, 1963 letter, "consider it to their advantage to preserve and intensify international tension, especially in the relations between the U.S.S.R. and the U.S.A. They apparently believe that the Soviet Union should reply to provocations by provocations, . . . should accept the challenge of the imperialists to a competition in adventurism and aggressiveness. . . . To take to this road would be to jeopardize peace and the security of the peoples."[40] Contrary to Molotov, Mao, and others, the Soviet ruling group headed by Khrushchev[41] asserted that war was more likely under conditions of high tension, particularly because Khrushchev was relatively more troubled by the possibility of accidental war.[42]

There was *some* evidence of an appreciation of differences in kinds of balancing processes. In one possible pattern for the international system, each of the major actors—both assuming that a preponderance on the side of those it determines to be the peace forces would more likely deter the enemy than would equilibrium—would strive for overwhelming preponderance. Out of the mutual striving, shifts in the distribution of power around equilibrium would result. Soviet analysis recognized that such a pattern had occurred as a result of the American reaction to Soviet claims to have altered the distribution of power.

[40] *Pravda*, July 14, 1963.

[41] For a discussion of this well-documented divergence in perspectives see Tucker, *Soviet Political Mind* pp. 201-13.

[42] E.g., the statement of *Izvestiia* correspondent V. Matveyev [Matveev], "Danger of 'Accidental War,'" *International Affairs*, No. 9 (September 1962), p. 78. "Any technical device may fail, but a technical failure can lead to disaster only *in a climate of artificially heightened tension*," italics in original.

By contrast, after the Cuban missile crisis some Soviet commentators claimed to discern the development of a pattern that would involve another kind of balance process. Not only would war lose its relevance as a mode of foreign policy, but so too would the arms race, a fact, it was asserted, that influential circles in both camps were beginning to recognize. In Lemin's words, "Even in the ruling group of the capitalist camp the influence is growing of those who understand that in our age war *and the arms race* no longer can serve as an instrument of policy."[43] Each side, rather than engage in a mutually reinforcing weapons-technology race, would not pursue disequilibrating policies (in the strategic realm, at least), if the other side did not. Each side would seek to *deny* military preponderance to the other. N. M. Nikol'skii declared, "the distribution of power on the plane of the prevention of wars and their exclusion from the life of mankind—such is the principled new posing of the question of the significance of the distribution of power in international relations."[44] Power balancing qua strategic policy would not necessarily entail the abandonment of preponderance as a goal; the preponderance would be of another sort and achieved by different means.[45] In the words of one article, itself an echo of official Party pronouncements, the socialist camp's goal remained "the attainment of a maximal preponderance of forces over the camp of imperialism,"[46] to be achieved by "implacable struggle with

[43] I. Lemin, "Leninskii printsip mirnogo sosushchestvovaniia i sovremennost'," p. 19, italics added.

[44] N. M. Nikol'skii, *Osnovnoi vopros sovremennosti*, p. 236.

[45] It may be reasonably anticipated that intra-elite disputes over resource allocations will be structured in terms of the ways of achieving preponderance.

[46] V. Korionov, "Leninizm i mirovoi revoliutsionnyi protsess" [Leninism and the World Revolutionary Process], *Mirovaia ekonomika*, No.

capitalism by new forms," "that is, in the sphere of material production on the paths of economic competition."[47] Nevertheless, the resulting balancing process would differ substantially from one in which the two main protagonists persisted in endeavors to secure weapons-technology breakthroughs. Indeed, statements such as those by Nikol'skii and Lemin conveyed an impression that some international relations commentators toward the end of Khrushchev's term were in the process of reappraising the previously unquestioned tenet that the achievement of "an invincible preponderance of power" was the goal of Soviet policy. Such statements may also provide a partial explanation for Khrushchev's exaggerated claims with respect to the distribution of power. By claiming that minimum deterrence, coupled with the Soviet Union's rapid economic growth, signified the possession of a preponderance (but not an "invincible preponderance," which would necessitate revolutionary activism) of power, he may have been trying to restructure Soviet attitudes, to encourage key Soviet elites to adjust to a world of mutual vulnerability, a world in which world war was no longer an instrument of foreign policy, a world in which a military policy of "second best" was sufficient.

The aspiration to reunify theory and practice, however, had not dissipated by the end of the Khrushchev regime. As an

---

6 (June 1963), p. 17. The importance of Korionov's article is underlined by the fact that it was a paper presented at a "scientific conference" of the Institute of World Economy and International Relations in connection with the beginning of open polemics with the Chinese.

[47] *Ibid.*, pp. 16 and 11. One does not have the impression that before the Cuban missile crisis, any Soviet observers were construing "peaceful economic competition" as excluding efforts to secure strategic breakthroughs, but rather as ruling out use of general war as an instrument for determining the global *kto-kogo.*

article by Gen. Talenskii, shortly before Khrushchev's ouster, bore witness, there was an evident reluctance on the part even of those closest to Khrushchev to reconcile themselves to a world in which the atom bomb does not "observe the class principle" and where Soviet security and the contingent nature of the future was "directly dependent on the good will and designs of the other side, which is a highly subjective factor."[48] Consequently, Talenskii argued by implication, Soviet decision-makers would be obliged to pursue policies which would create the necessary minimal requirement for the restoration of the "class principle" to its proper, dominant, place among the causal forces of history, namely the creation of the functional equivalent of the pre-atomic era. "*There is only one reasonable alternative to a race in anti-missile systems,*" he warned; it is "*the early implementation of general and complete disarmament.*"[49]

While the choice of balancing patterns had clearly not been resolved by October 1964, the atom bomb and the interdeterminancy of the international system had induced an awareness among Soviet decision-makers of the contingent nature of tomorrow. By 1963-64 it had begun to appear that the Sino-Soviet split cast doubt on the unquestioned *desirability* of creating the international system which they expected would replace the one obtaining in the third stage of capitalism's general crisis. Just as the Sino-Soviet split greatly lessened Soviet confidence in the distribution of world power between socialism and capitalism, so too did it provoke serious *overt* misgivings about the nature of international relations under socialism. Toward the end of Khrushchev's tenure in power it

[48] "Anti-Missile Systems and Disarmament," *International Affairs,* No. 10 (October) (Russian edn. to press September 21, 1964), p. 17.

[49] *Ibid.*, p. 19, italics in original.

was evident that Khrushchev, at least, saw no possibility of a major reconciliation with Communist China in the policy-relevant future. Instead, it appeared that the U.S.S.R. had resigned itself to a long struggle to maintain its position of dominance in the socialist camp(s) and in the international communist movement(s). Soviet expectations, given this operative assumption, seemed increasingly in 1963-64 to be that relations among socialist states would be little different from relations among imperialist states or between camps. Just prior to Khrushchev's removal, *Pravda*, in a statement evidently reflecting Khrushchev's determination to reach a final parting of the ways with the Chinese, authoritatively characterized "the Chinese leaders' . . . struggle against the U.S.S.R. [and] other socialist countries . . . [as] not [differing] *in its bitterness, its scope and methods, from the 'cold war' of imperialism against socialism.*"[50] The use of the term "cold war" —which equated the perceived intensity of Chinese enmity to the Soviet Union with the alleged enmity of the American imperialists—provided an indication of Soviet, or at least Khrushchevian, expectations concerning the nature of intracamp relations for much of the policy-relevant future. One also encountered occasional statements that provide a more precise indication of the parameters of conflict within the camp, parameters which seemed to be very wide indeed. In particular, Soviet spokesmen felt constrained to deny the possibility of "all-out thermonuclear war" between the Soviet Union and the Chinese People's Republic and to rule out the possibility of a *renversement des alliances*[51] involving an alliance of the United States and the Soviet Union. But within these limits, any options were possible.

[50] *Pravda*, September 2, 1964.

[51] Inozemtsev, "Edinstvo zapada?" p. 65.

Under such conditions, especially when combined with low Soviet expectations of central war between the capitalist and socialist camps, the world system of socialist states no longer appeared to be considered *automatically* desirable. As Korionov said, this time in *International Affairs,*

> The new world system of Socialist states is now in the making. Entirely new, previously unknown relations are being established between them, and these relations are a prototype of the relations soon to be established all over the world. . . . *Will this be a truly fraternal alliance of the nations, completely free of hostility and mistrust, or a system of states still tainted with mistrust between peoples, without real fraternal mutual assistance and help for each other, a system with trends to isolation and autarchy?*[52]

Korionov's question was in effect answered by Ponomarev, who declared that "*traces of the abnormal, ugly relations between nations born of capitalism remain for some time after the socialist revolution.*"[53] Indeed, Ponomarev hinted at a realization that "socialism," with its consequent national "oneness of will and action," might engender a more virulent nationalism than found in noncommunist societies—with the result that the international relations of a new type might be even more hazardous than international relations during the third stage of capitalism's general crisis:

> Socialism brings with it an unprecedented consolidation of the nations. The crystallization of the socio-political unity of

[52] V. G. Korionov, "Proletarian Internationalism—Our Victorious Weapon," p. 13, italics added.

[53] B. Ponomaryov [Ponomarev], "Proletarian Internationalism—a Powerful Force in the Revolutionary Transformation of the World," *World Marxist Review*, Vol. VII, No. 8 (August 1964), p. 66, italics added.

> a nation is accompanied by a powerful surge of patriotism. It can be said that only under socialism does a nation truly feel it is a single whole and acquire a oneness of will and action. This firm unity of society, of the nation, is an achievement of socialism, striking proof of its superiority over capitalism which disunites people.
>
> However, one should not ignore the danger of a resurgence of nationalist sentiment under certain circumstances as a by-product of socialist patriotism. Nationalism is deeply rooted in the consciousness and psychology of definite social strata. It adapts itself to the new conditions, parasitizing on the lofty feeling of patriotism.[54]

The global socialist tomorrow had, in the Soviet appraisal, lost much of its luster. It was no longer historically necessary; nor was it necessarily the case that the international relations of a new type would be greatly at variance with the post-imperialist, nonsocialist international system of the sixties. On the other hand, Soviet spokesmen clearly recognized a stake in the maintenance of the latter system. Small wonder, therefore, that by October 1964 some Soviet commentators and policy-makers increasingly were having misgivings as to whether the displacement of the contemporary international system was a game that was worth the candle.

KHRUSHCHEV's successors were considerably more circumspect, especially after September 1965, than Khrushchev had been in giving vent to statements which revealed a commitment to the maintenance of the international system. Peaceful coexistence was no longer characterized as the general line of Soviet foreign policy; and was instead relegated to a posi-

[54] *Ibid.*

tion of parity with proletarian internationalism.[55] Moreover, the Khrushchevian conception of international politics as a non-zero sum game, which underlay Khrushchev's assertion that peaceful coexistence in the atomic age had a new content, was obscured—apparently intentionally—by characterizations of peaceful coexistence as a policy observed consistently throughout the Soviet Union's 50-year history.[56] The shift in symbols was accompanied by a shift in behavior. The collectivity of leadership was clearly prepared to pursue "possessive" goals more actively than Khrushchev—in part, presumably, because following the immediate aftermath of the Cuban missile crisis, Soviet leaders (like their American counterparts) were less fearful of escalation and more confident in the stability of the deterrent than Khrushchev had been. Soviet behavior and the analysis of the specialized press, however, revealed a preoccupation with limited moves and shifts in the global distribution of power which would result in incremental gains in power and/or security[57] terms for the Soviet Union, and not with the articulation of a grand design.

Consonant with the increased separation of international relations and the world historical process that characterized Soviet commentary after Khrushchev's ouster, neither his successors nor the international relations specialists writing after October 1964 were particularly forthcoming in explaining the manner in which the transformation of the present interna-

[55] V. Trukhanovsky, "Proletarian Internationalism and Peaceful Coexistence," *International Affairs*, No. 8 (August 1966), pp. 54-59.

[56] *Ibid.*, p. 57.

[57] The United States bombing of North Vietnam in February 1965, a scant four months after the new ruling group's accession to power, tended to preclude any overt tension between the goals of enhancing security and enhancing power and to encourage the traditional equation of the most powerful capitalist state and the most threatening.

tional system would be accomplished. It is open to question how much a Kosygin or a Brezhnev was preoccupied by such matters. The one method, in any event, that seemed to offer any prospect for achieving the reunification of theory and practice—the establishment of a highly effective anti-missile system—was a matter to which members of the ruling group were unlikely publicly to address themselves at length. Nor was there consensus in Moscow on what might be expected of an anti-missile system. Talenskii, who had warned in October 1964 that "general and complete disarmament" was the "only alternative" to an anti-missile missile race, in 1965 attacked the "dangerous illusion" that "it is possible to find acceptable forms of nuclear war."[58] In 1966, furthermore, in conditions considerably less favorable to the expression of a modernist perspective than a year before, he reiterated that "the salvation of mankind is not in the search of a dependable shelter, for in the age of megaton nuclear weapons no such shelter can be created for all people. The only way to avert the horrors of a world thermonuclear holocaust is to prevent any nuclear war and any military conflict which might lead to it."[59] On the other hand, the directly opposed position was expressed by Col. Rybkin in September 1965, when he asserted that "there are opportunities for creating and developing new means of conducting war that are capable of reliably countering an enemy's nuclear blows"[60]

Moreover, the dimensions of the post-Khrushchevian calculus which justified continued revolutionary optimism remained essentially the same as Khrushchev's: *in the long run* the Soviet

[58] "The Late War," *International Affairs*, No. 5 (May 1965), p. 15.

[59] N. Talensky, "June 22: Lessons of History," *International Affairs*, No. 6 (June 1966), p. 46.

[60] Cited in Kolkowicz, "The Red 'Hawks' . . . ," p. 46.

Union would outstrip the United States. The national liberation movement—"zig-zags" and "waverings" notwithstanding[61]—was, moreover, an objectively anti-imperialist phenomenon, and there was every reason to assume that *in the long run* most of the new states would pursue noncapitalist paths of development. *In the long run*, the socialist alliance system would prove more viable than the Western alliance. What was novel in post-Khrushchevian commentary was the heightened emphasis on the magnitude of the task of building an international relations of a new type and on the duration of the struggle. Statements affirming the inevitability of the revolution seemed increasingly to represent little more than routine affirmations of marginal significance at best.[62] Khrushchev's naive Twenty-first Congress estimation of 1970 as the time when the Soviet Union would catch up with the United States, a subject of implicit critique in specialist literature already in 1963, was quickly abandoned after October 1964, to be replaced by more conservative and realistic estimates of Soviet growth and sophisticated calculations of American growth rates. With regard to the transformation of the decolonized world, similarly, the focus was on overcoming "enormous difficulties." "Revolution generally and an anti-imperialist one in particular," it was stressed, is no picnic—"not a stroll along a smooth sidewalk."[63] In their moments of greatest candor, furthermore, Soviet specialists revealed few illusions about the nature of relations among socialist states or the proximity of "international relations of a new type." The nature of relations among socialist states for the present—and at least for as long into the future

[61] I. Lemin, "Velikaia Oktiabr'skaia sotsialisticheskaia revoliutsiia . . . ," p. 16.

[62] See especially the statement by Sanakoev, "The World Socialist System . . . ," p. 62.

[63] Marinin, "Sotsialisticheskii internationalizm . . . ," p. 14.

as the "Mao group" controlled the levers of power in China—was shaped, in the Soviet view, primarily by the fact that the dominant faction in China regarded the Soviet Union as "'Enemy Number One.'"[64] There were even hints that, for some, Rumania's independent course had had perhaps almost as sobering an effect on expectations concerning future relations among socialist states as the Sino-Soviet split. (The latter, after all, had involved questions of ideology.) In any event, there was little to suggest that the idealized socialist tomorrow was in any way imminent. "In our time and in the foreseeable future the world system of socialism can develop only as a union of sovereign states."[65] There were, in fact, intimations—the evidence permits no stronger word—that Soviet spokesmen were in the process of redefining the nature of "socialism" in such a way that countries pursuing a noncapitalist path—whether ruled by a Leninist party and guided by "scientific socialism" or not—with close linkages to the Soviet Union would be regarded as socialist, while other states, *whether or not ruled by Leninist parties and guided by scientific socialism,* which were not linked with the Soviet Union, would not be so regarded.[66] By this ploy, China would no longer be des-

[64] Lemin, "Velikaia Oktiabr'skaia sotsialisticheskaia revoliutsiia . . . ," p. 17.

[65] Butenko, "O zakonomernostiakh . . . ," p. 89.

[66] For a statement that "in the past few years several African countries have embarked on the road to Socialism," see V. Granov, "The War and the Post-War World," *International Affairs*, No. 4 (April 1965), p. 43.

An article in *Pravda* (July 4, 1967) by L. Deliusin and L. Kiuzadzhian, entitled "A Threat to Socialism in China," stated that

"in such a backward country as China, with its medieval survivals, socialism cannot be built without relying on the support of the world proletariat and its chief achievement—the socialist commonwealth—without making use of the creative experience of states that are eco-

ignated a socialist country, while certain forms of African socialism would become explicitly acceptable. Socialism for Soviet "Marxist-Leninists" would become a term of approbation to characterize any nonimperialist power with which the Soviet Union had good relations. The goal of system transformation would, as a result, itself be transformed into an instrument for legitimating changes within the context of the contemporary international system favorable to the Soviet Union. Khrushchev, by introducing the third stage of capitalism's general crisis, had created the doctrinal conditions for regarding the Leninist past as irrelevant to post-imperialist, atomic-age international politics. His successors, by elongating the revolutionary time perspective into centuries, seemed, in shaping present-day Soviet foreign policy behavior, to preclude a major role for a commitment to building a global communist future.

---

nomically, politically, and culturally more advanced. For an underdeveloped country, rejection of cooperation with the Socialist countries means rejection of advance along the path of social and economic progress, renunciation of the achievement of socialist ideals."

For an English translation see *Current Digest*, Vol. XIX, No. 27 (July 26, 1967), p. 9.

Chapter Eight: Post-imperialism and the Transformation of Soviet Foreign Policy

THE TIME is not long past when Soviet Marxist-Leninists viewed international relations as playing an essentially secondary role in the world historical process, and when Soviet specialists on international affairs (in their public commentary, at least) functioned almost exclusively as ideologues. As the preceding chapters of this study have demonstrated, however, the years since the Twentieth C.P.S.U. Congress have witnessed a significant transformation in Soviet perspectives on international relations. This transformation involved the role of the international relations specialist in Soviet society and the systematic study of international relations, on the one hand, and the substance of Soviet international relations perspectives, on the other.

Thus, to recapitulate briefly, during the Khrushchev years, the period dating from the Twentieth Congress—at which the dominant faction of the Presidium gave impetus to the revitalization of the social sciences, including international relations—to 1962 was one in which international relations became a legitimate area of inquiry for specialists below the apex of the Party and government apparatuses. The Institute of World Economy and International Relations was reconstituted in April 1956. In 1957 publication of its journal, *Mirovaia ekonomika i mezhdunarodnye otnosheniia*, was resumed. Rudimentary requisites for research—bibliographies, yearbooks of world affairs, and other standard reference works—became available. The scope of available information relevant to international relations inquiry was broadened considerably. After 1962 one could speak of the existence in the Soviet Union of international relations as a self-conscious discipline. At that time Soviet writers began to depict international relations as a "young science arising 'at the intersection' of a number of social sciences"[1] and to delineate the boundaries of the subject matter with which international relations should rightly be concerned. Finally, during the last two years of Khrushchev's rule there were indications of the onset of another stage in the development of international relations studies. The difference in sophistication between specialist analysis and more general commentary became, in several instances, more noticeable; the importance of methodology was stressed; increasingly the emphasis was on the international relations specialist's analytic and policy-prescriptive roles, rather than his role as ideologue. By October 1964, however, such a pattern had by no means become dominant.

There were major changes in the substance of Soviet perspectives, as well. Not surprisingly, in their analysis of the international system, Soviet commentators, rather than portray states as the sole international actors, depicted the international arena as populated by a plurality of types of corporate actors. By the end of Khrushchev's tenure in power, however, states appeared to have taken precedence over the "world systems" of capitalism and socialism as the main actors in the international arena. In part, the change reflected Soviet adjustment to the passing of rigid bipolarity and to the divisive tendencies within the two camps. Additionally, Soviet observers seemed to attach somewhat greater significance than previously to the role of institutions in the determination of actor-capability. The latter development, moreover, was also manifested in a greater disposition to write as though such diverse supranational entities as the United Nations, the Vatican, and the

[1] AN IMEMO, *Mezhdunarodnye otnosheniia . . .* , Vol. I, p. xxvi.

Common Market were international actors—notwithstanding the lack of United Nations and Vatican conformity to previous Soviet notions of the constituent elements of power.

Perhaps the most striking aspect of the Soviet description, in Khrushchev's last years, of the hierarchical structure of the modern international system was that it diverged fundamentally from conventional Bolshevik expectations about power relations, and in the name of creative Marxism-Leninism. In particular, it was no longer the case that in the "new, third stage of capitalism's general crisis" the international system was a rigidly hierarchical order headed by a single dominant power. Rather, the leading states were the two world powers. Their competition provided the framework against which, in the views of some Soviet observers, even small, formally independent states, although economically tied to imperialism and politically linked to the United States, could not always be considered dependent countries. In the early 1960s, moreover, Soviet observers, responding to the increased assertiveness of the second-level great powers in the two camps, began to show increased concern over the danger of catalytic war, thus recognizing that the question of war and peace was no longer solely a matter of relations between the leaders of the imperialist and socialist camps.

The main contradiction in the world, nevertheless, continued to consist of the relationships between the imperialist and socialist camps, and it was to this relationship that Soviet observers looked in analyzing the global distribution of power. Here an interesting progression was noted. Prior to 1959 the term of reference used in describing the balance of power as situation was "distribution of power" (usually *sootnoshenie sil*, occasionally *rasstanovka sil*). In 1959—although formulations involving the generic phrase "distribution of power" prevailed quantitatively—formulations containing *pereves sil* (favorable balance or preponderance of power) appeared. After late 1961 the focal term of reference became *ravnovesie sil* (equilibrium). This progression corresponded to changing Soviet appraisals of the existing as well as the ontological reality, that is, to changes in the Soviet perception of the distribution of power, as well as Soviet expectations of the imminence of revolutionary advance. The shifts in formulation had distinct limits. At the height of revolutionary optimism in 1958-60, Soviet observers continued to accord the United States world-power status. In 1962-64, while acknowledging that a reversal in socialist fortunes had occurred, they similarly continued to insist on the Soviet Union's position as a world power, while at the same time integrating the temporary reversal into their perception of the world historical process by elongating their time perspective.

The evolution of Soviet views about American foreign policy behavior was especially profound. The analysis of American capabilities was increasingly explicit and detailed. The depiction of the decision-making process reflected a shift in focus from Wall Street to Washington and seemed to be engendered by a belated recognition that the Keynesian revolution had indeed transformed the relation between the political system and the economy, and an awareness that the enhanced role of international relations had greatly augmented the position of the state and, especially the institution of the presidency. It was with respect to the evolving characterization of the motives of the majority in the American ruling group ("the realists") that the most dramatic change in Soviet perspectives on American foreign policy was to be seen. Khrushchev, especially, professed to detect a "reappraisal of values" within the American ruling group, and thus in effect to assert that the motives of American imperialism had changed. In the atomic age and under conditions of mutual deterrence, security in the Khrushchevian perspective was the primary value of the dominant, realistic element within the American leadership. As a result, the United States, while doubtless the major adversary, was no longer the main enemy, largely because the realistic elements could be expected to act to prevent the outbreak of general war.

Khrushchev's "prettification" of American imperialism was tied directly to his effort to sustain a belief in the inevitability of the revolution under atomic age conditions; to sustain, in other words, the expectation that the modern international system would in fact be transformed into a socialist "international relations of a new type." The dilemma posed by the constraints Soviet decision-makers considered operative in the atomic age—"the atomic bomb does not observe the class principle"—was as simple as it was intractable. In doctrinal terms the dilemma constituted a challenge to the unity of theory and practice. How could the triumph of socialism be gained without general war? How could the creation of "international relations of a new type" be accomplished while avoiding the violent destruction of the existing international system? Khrushchev's answer contemplated that Soviet missiles would deter the outbreak of general war and deprive imperialism of its capacity to impede artificially (through the "export of counter-revolution") processes taking place within states as a result of the disequilibrating tendencies inherent in a revolutionary epoch. The plausibility of such a vision, however, relied, among other things, on the behavior of the decision-makers in the leading capitalist power; that is, on a contingency which was neither "objectively" determined by the "world historical process" nor sufficiently subject to the influence of right-thinking communists. Under nuclear age conditions, therefore, the unity of theory and practice was ruptured. On Soviet observers' own terms, international relations could no longer be considered a closed system, i.e., a general theory with a predictable solution at a single point.

Developments in the three years following Khrushchev's ouster were not as dramatic as those of the early sixties. Especially after early 1965 Khrushchev's successors showed little enthusiasm for affirming the most clearly revisionist statements to which Khrushchev and the modernist specialists had given voice. Khrushchev's successors, for a plurality of reasons, were not heard repudiating the slogan, "workers of the world unite, you have nothing to lose but your chains." Token obeisance, at least, was generally rendered the Clausewitz dictum that war was the continuation of politics by other means. The Khrushchev doctrine, that peaceful coexistence was the general line of Soviet foreign policy, was abandoned. Nor were the three years separating Khrushchev's ouster and the Fiftieth Anniversary of Soviet rule characterized by major conceptual and methodological innovations among the specialists, to whom, with the collapse of general theory, one would expect to look increasingly for such innovations in Soviet international relations perspectives as might occur.

At the same time, it was evident in the fall of 1967 that at the elite level, as well as among the specialists, there remained an interest in encouraging systematic specialist analysis of international relations and a recognition by some that techniques—such as game theory and computer applications—developed in the West had a place in Soviet analysis, as well as in Soviet foreign policy. Moreover, despite the fact that Khrushchev's successors were noticeably less prone to engage in explicit doctrinal innovation than Khrushchev, the trend of

Soviet analysis of the structure of the international system, the analysts' projections for the future development of the international system, and perhaps even of American foreign policy, continued in the direction that Soviet commentary had been headed in the last years in which Khrushchev was in power. That direction had been toward a closer approximation of reality, and to a view of international politics in many ways similar to that of the Western post-billiard ball consensus. The emphasis of post-Khrushchevian commentary has been on the state and the state system; the tendency has been increasingly to separate the world historical process from the analysis of world politics. Several specialists, moreover, were increasingly candid about the nature of the world system of socialist states and less inclined to blur the concepts "socio-economic system" and "state system." Similarly, the changes in the Soviet depiction of the global hierarchy were largely to be accounted for by the capacity of Soviet observers to react to changes in the international order. The gap between the world powers and other great powers narrowed, and the border separating the lesser-ranked great powers and the major independents became more ill-defined. In a like manner, Khrushchev's claims about the global distribution of power were consciously reduced, while at the same time the Khrushchev calculus, with its attention to situational aspects of power, was retained. Even post-Khrushchevian commentary on American foreign policy —which after the American bombing of North Vietnam moved away from Khrushchev's benign assumption that the "realists" constituted the majority within the American ruling group, while continuing to emphasize the role of Washington (rather than Wall Street)—can be considered a step toward a more realistic appraisal of American foreign policy. Certainly post-Khrushchev utterances about the rate of historical development were more realistic. In a sense, the Soviet commentary at this time retained the insight that ours is a revolutionary epoch while simultaneously pushing the time when the international relations of a new type would be created so far into the future as to be of little if any operative significance for Soviet foreign policy in the late 1960s.

All things considered, there has been a marked tendency for Soviet perspectives on international relations to converge with American analysis. For both, international relations was no longer a closed system with a solution at a single point. Instead, both entertained open-ended perspectives on the process of world politics. American and Soviet perspectives on the basic structure of the modern international system were basically similar. Even Soviet analysis of the internal politics of American foreign policy—at least the more acute examples thereof—seemed to accept the basic assumptions about the locus of decision-making within a capitalist state. Soviet commentary revealed the same preoccupation with the political significance of technology, especially weapons technology, generally found among American international relations specialists and an analogous attention to the constraints imposed on the behavior of states by the atomic age.

THE INCREASING parallelism of Soviet and American depictions of the modern international system suggests the bearing of this study on the conventional wisdom regarding the influence of ideology on Soviet behavior. In the conventional wisdom, ideology performs plural functions. One such function is as the language of politics. So conceived, ideology serves as a medium of communication among the elite and as a vehicle for the transmission of information in two directions: upward to the ruling group, and downward to party subordinates, specialists in the Academy of Sciences, and society at large. A second function is as a guide to analysis. Communist ideology is said to provide the Soviet observer with a frame of reference, a means of orientation in a variegated social and political universe. Some Western specialists have stressed the extent to which the ideological preconceptions of Soviet specialists and decision-makers have enabled the latter to appraise acutely international reality, perhaps more so than their Western counterparts,[2] while others, by contrast, have stressed the degree to which ideologically derived predispositions distort Soviet images of global reality. In both instances, ideology is seen as a major determinant of Soviet foreign policy behavior. Thus those who tend to regard ideology as a guide to analysis are among those prone to allot a third function to ideology, that is, as a guide to action. In addition to providing a general policy orientation, it has been contended, specific policy prescriptions flow directly from core assumptions of the ideology —for example, "smash the old apparatus." Communist ideology further serves as a guide to action by defining, albeit somewhat imprecisely, Soviet goal orientation. Yet a fourth function accorded ideology relates to its role in *legitimation.* It supplies a justification for the C.P.S.U.'s dominant position in Soviet society, serves to justify changes in policy, and—because truth is historically contingent—permits doctrinal innovation in the light of changed circumstances under the guise of "creative Marxism-Leninism."

[2] See, for instance, Brzezinski, *The Soviet Bloc,* pp. 383-408, *Ideology and Power,* passim; Adam B. Ulam, *The New Face of Soviet Totalitarianism* (Cambridge, Mass.: Harvard University Press, 1963), pp. 65-90; *The Unfinished Revolution* (New York: Vintage Books, 1964), passim; and Vernon Aspaturian, "The Challenge of Soviet Foreign Policy," in Morton A. Kaplan, ed., *The Revolution in World Politics* (New York: John Wiley and Sons, Inc., 1962), pp. 209-32.

In part, these functions are considered characteristic attributes of any ideology. To an important extent, however, they stem from distinctive features in Soviet ideology. Enumerations vary, but one inventory of the salient characteristics (that given by Brzezinski and Samuel P. Huntington in *Political Power: USA/USSR*[3]) may be taken as representative. For Brzezinski and Huntington the crucial features of Soviet ideology consist in its "conscious" and "purposive" nature. In their view Soviet ideology is

> a set of political ideas that are overt, systematic, dogmatic, and embodied in a set of institutions. . . . The Soviet political ideas [they explain], are overt in the sense that there are certain officially proclaimed 'texts' which contain the basic doctrines and guides to action. They are systematized in the sense that these texts are regularly revised and brought up to date in the light of both experience and the needs of ruling elite. They are institutionalized in the sense that they have been proclaimed to be the official ideology of the Soviet state, binding upon every citizen, embodied in the ruling Communist Party, and articulated by appointed 'ideologues.' They are dogmatized in the sense that, until any of its tenets have been officially revised or repudiated, the ideology is to be accepted without reservation by anyone who wishes to describe himself as a Communist.[4]

It has also been contended that reference to ideology in explanations of Soviet behavior is particularly appropriate in the case of foreign policy. Two arguments, both having wide currency, have been advanced to buttress this view. One argu-

[3] (New York: The Viking Press, 1964), pp. 17-70.
[4] *Ibid.*, p. 19.

ment[5] admits that internally—unlike the Soviet Union during the period of collectivization, "the second revolution," and mass purges—a complex large-scale industrial society, with its attendant day-to-day administrative task orientation,[6] is not conducive to the maintenance of revolutionary zeal. It asserts that such, however, is not the case with Soviet foreign policy. Rather, foreign policy successes are seen, in this view, as providing the basis for the maintenance of *elan* in circumstances where, even in Marxist terms, ideology is largely irrelevant to the Soviet domestic context. Foreign policy serves as a surrogate for rapid industrialization: the international arena becomes the barricade to be stormed. "As Soviet society changes, so will Marxism-Leninism. . . . Linked to real science, . . . Marxism-Leninism can evolve into a more effective doctrine of domestic control while maintaining its revolutionary virtue in terms of international affairs."[7] It has been further suggested that the erosion of ideology will progress considerably more slowly in the realm of Soviet foreign policy than domestically because, as Adam Ulam puts it, "while the Soviet citizen, including the indoctrinated party member, has numerous occasions to discover the contradictions or irrelevancies of Marxism in his daily life, he enjoys no such tangible experience insofar as the world outside the USSR is concerned."[8]

[5] The argument has been well developed in the works of Adam Ulam. See *The New Face*, pp. 65-90 and *The Unfinished Revolution*, pp. 278-99. Cf. Brzezinski and Huntington, *Political Power USA/USSR*, p. 69 and Kurt London, *The Making of Foreign Policy* (Philadelphia: J. B. Lippincott, 1965), p. 11.

[6] Indeed, assuming there were changes over time in the occurrence of the two terms *bor'ba* (struggle) and *problemy* (problems), such shifts in relative frequency might provide a simple and parsimonious measure of ideology erosion.

[7] Brzezinski and Huntington, *Political Power USA/USSR*, p. 69.

[8] *The New Face*, p. 74.

There were, to be sure, dimensions to the conventional interpretation of the influence of ideology on Soviet behavior, which were borne out by the evidence presented in previous chapters of this book. The very nature of the study—the translation, as it were, of Soviet concepts from the argot of Marxism-Leninism into the language of international politics—lent credence to the notion that in the Soviet Union under Khrushchev and in the three years since his involuntary retirement, ideology functioned as the language of politics, and by and large, the language of analysis as well. In this respect, the period analyzed evidenced obvious continuity with prior periods in Soviet history. The jargon remained essentially Bolshevik in form. The central terms employed were primarily those of long standing in Marxist-Leninist discourses—"the general crisis of capitalism," "contradictions," "the correlation of forces," "ruling circles," and the like. The framework of analysis continued to reveal demonstrable ideological overtones. Soviet commentators shared with their Bolshevik predecessors an ideologically influenced propensity to view the international environment, and consequently the international system, as characterized by qualitative, disequilibrating, revolutionary change. Moreover, while the analysis of the "world historical process" during Khrushchev's tenure in office was in horizontal, international-political terms (again, actually an element of continuity, since a similar disposition may be seen in Lenin's *Imperialism* and in Stalin's thought), it was, significantly, to the analysis of the *world historical process* that Soviet observers in the Khrushchev years largely addressed themselves. Soviet commentators, before and after Khrushchev's ouster, in their analysis and like their Bolshevik predecessors, considered the primary focus of the class struggle to be the international arena. Like Stalin, they manifested a strong proclivity to regard the state—the institutionalized expression of a class—as the main actor in the international arena. They continued to perceive international politics as hierarchically based and structured largely in terms of power, and yielded little in their contempt for the smaller powers in the international order. As with Lenin and Stalin, also, the centrality of the distribution of power in the Khrushchevian appraisal was readily seen. Other instances in which ideology at least colored the framework of analysis might be mentioned but the persisting influence of ideology in this regard should be clear.

Nevertheless, the weight of the evidence presented in prior chapters of this book would seem to indicate that in matters touching on the Soviet Union's external relations, there have been important changes in the roles of ideology, coupled with the alterations in core doctrinal positions. It was, moreover, the ideological high priests who were in large measure the instigators of that process. Thus the developing differentiation in sophistication and technique between the writings of the specialists and general commentary clearly suggest that the specialists increasingly were extricating themselves from the confines of Marxism-Leninism, and hence that ideology was playing a lesser role in influencing specialists in their analyses. To put the matter somewhat differently, Soviet specialists, rather than let Lenin do their thinking for them, found they could utilize Lenin to legitimate their thinking no matter how un-Leninist those thoughts might be. As one frequent contributor to the Soviet international relations dialogue candidly recognized, "in Lenin's works there is such a wealth of wisdom that each new epoch will find something *new* in them."[9]

[9] K. Ivanov, "The National-Liberation Movement and the Non-capitalist Path of Development," *International Affairs*, No. 9 (September 1964), p. 35, italics in original.

It was equally apparent from the radical alterations in doctrine undertaken by Khrushchev that he, the leading "ideology-action generalizer," was decreasingly influenced by substantive doctrinal elements of Marxism-Leninism. During the last years of the Khrushchev period, one was hardly likely to promote analytical clarity by utilizing the term "Bolshevik" and "Soviet" interchangeably. To do so would place one in the awkward position of subsuming under the rubric "Bolshevik" persons—specialists and generalists alike—who, among other things, (a) explicitly denied that the workers had nothing to lose but their chains, (b) accused another "socialist" state of conducting a "cold war" policy in its relations with the Soviet Union, and (c) questioned the relevance in the atomic age of the Clausewitz dictum that war is the continuation of politics.

The extent to which doctrine served to guide post-Khrushchev analysis was a bit more problematical, since, as we have seen, Khrushchev's successors were notably more reluctant than Khrushchev to engage in wholesale doctrinal alteration. A single answer was in all likelihood not possible for all the members of the ruling group. Nevertheless, the elongation of Soviet revolutionary time perspectives and the growing separation of the realms of world politics and the world historical process tend strongly to suggest that, while members of the post-Khrushchev ruling group were scarcely disinclined to use Lenin instrumentally, Lenin did little of their thinking for them. The limited role of ideology in influencing post-Khrushchevian Soviet analysis of modern world politics is perhaps best seen in the remarkable parallelism of Soviet and Western appraisals of the basic structural outlines of the international system, a phenomenon not to be inferred from the writings of those disposed to argue that Leninism on balance enhances

Soviet insight into international realities, or those who assume that it seriously distorts Soviet analysis.

Given the diminished role of ideology in analysis, it follows almost by definition that ideology served less as a guide to action than it had in previous Soviet analysis and that the conscious and purposive dimensions of Soviet ideology had been lessened. There were other elements, too, in the change in Soviet international relations perspectives that suggest the same conclusion. Indeed, this is only to recall a central point made earlier: what I have characterized as the collapse of general theory—that (on Soviet observers' own terms) international relations was no longer an analytically closed system with a single predictable solution point—resulted in the rupture of the unity of theory and practice. Moreover, it was less clear for the ruling group in the last years of Khrushchev's years in power than for previous Soviet regimes, that ideology determined Soviet goal orientation. Overt misgivings among Soviet spokesmen were encountered, which concerned the nature of future relationships among socialist states—the basis of the predicted international relations of a new type. At the same time, Soviet commentators manifested a more benign posture toward the international system in the "new, third stage of capitalism's general crisis" than they had showed toward the prior international system when imperialism allegedly determined the rules of the international game.

Similarly, Khrushchev's successors, while generally inclined to a less benign view of the contemporary international system, were probably as disenchanted with the prospects for relations among states ruled by purportedly Marxist-Leninist parties, and at least during 1966-67 more tolerant of candor concerning the nature of relations within the contemporary world system of socialist states. Given the time perspective of the post-Khrushchevian ruling group, furthermore, almost any policy could be, and apparently was, justified in terms of its contribution to building what was actually an ambiguous communist future.

Both for the ruling group and the specialist, ideology continued to serve a major legitimating function. Specialists throughout the period analyzed, continued generally to invoke the proper authorities when they introduced new facts and concepts, thereby minimizing the personal risks of innovation. They and the generalists continued to follow the time-honored Soviet practice of pronouncing the legitimating symbols "creative Marxism-Leninism" when discarding *specific*, awkward Leninist dictums. For the specialist in the 1960s, however, only the most token ideology was requisite for publication. Moreover—and this was crucial—the ideological high priests under Khrushchev created the doctrinal legitimation for regarding *Leninism* as irrelevant to atomic age international politics by declaring that the period when the nature of imperialism determined the style of international politics had been historically transcended. Invoking the mantle of Marxism-Leninism, Soviet commentators in the Khrushchev period, and Khrushchev in particular, legitimated the disavowal of Leninism as a guide to analysis and action.

The collapse of general theory, coupled with conflict within the ruling group and an evolution in the nature of party-specialist relations, caused a major discrepancy between Soviet reality in the sixties and what have been commonly described as distinctive aspects of Soviet ideology. In particular, the notion that in the absence of authoritative revision or repudiation, the ideology was to be accepted without reservation by all Soviet communists, clearly fails to characterize adequately the experience of Soviet international relations commentators in the sixties. It was no longer merely the case that a single leader or even a small coterie of leaders monopolized the capacity for doctrinal innovation. As a result, the notion of a general line had limited relevance to Soviet reality; the clarity which had in the past so typified Soviet ideology was gone. Furthermore, with respect to conventional assertions about the conscious and purposive nature of Soviet ideology, the significance of the fact of ideological devolution becomes particularly striking when one bears in mind the considerable encouragement, especially after 1962, that members of the elite gave to the specialist study of international relations. As a result, one witnesses the strange spectacle of the very persons ostensibly most committed to the maintenance of ideology encouraging developments the end product of which was bound to, and in fact did, result in a significant decentralization in the capacity for doctrinal innovation, a process that ran at cross purposes with a desire to utilize foreign policy gains to maintain the regime's unchallenged position in Soviet society and to maintain institutionalized revolutionary zeal.

INSTEAD, in the period analyzed, ideology came to have a pertinence for Soviet studies which differed from that indicated by the Western conventional wisdom, one which was of relevance for an explanation of the phenomenon to which this study has been addressed, namely, the evolution of Soviet perspectives on international relations and the systematic study thereof. In the classical Marxian conception, only the proletariat, because it lacked a stake in the system, was free of ideology and therefore able to appreciate the necessity of violent transformation of the system. Given the Soviet Union's level of development and world-power status, its decision-makers explicitly recognized their stake in the maintenance of the international system. Those who have argued that foreign policy would become a substitute for industrialization misjudged by assuming it would be the high priests who would be the last to lose the faith. They also erred in assuming that changes in the international system, because they were somehow more distant, would be less likely to induce changes in individual or collective beliefs than would internal developments. In the atomic age, in fact, international politics acquired an intense immediacy for Soviet decision-makers. As Robert Conquest has observed, "the existence of the hydrogen bomb, perhaps even without the current American superiority, [was] a threat so palpable and clear that it [could] not be evaded."[10] As the C.P.S.U. stated authoritatively in 1963, the atomic bomb does not observe the class principle, and as a result, whether Soviet commentators explicitly (as was done after the Cuban missile crisis) recognized or not, the days were gone when the workers of the world had nothing to lose but their chains. Consequently, it is to structural changes in the Soviet Union's position in the international system that one must look, first of all, for an explanation of the evolution of Soviet perspectives on the international system.

International structure provides a partial explanation for the differences between the utterances (and underlying attitudes)

[10] *Russia After Khrushchev* (New York: Columbia University Press, 1965), p. 60. Nevertheless, it would convey an excessively rigid picture of the mentality of those in the Soviet Union directly concerned with international relations to say of them that "the 50-megaton blast is just about the power required to penetrate the ideological carapace—the 'bone curtain' around the apparatchik mind . . ." (*ibid.*). For, judged by overt formulations, as we have seen, Soviet commentators proved reasonably adaptive (with the exception of intra-socialist camp relations) in responding to the impact of other relatively subtler, environmental changes in the structure of the international system.

of Khrushchev and his successors, by pointing to the diminished salience of the atomic age under conditions of greater deterrent stability, a stability that engenders an international politics as usual attitude among decision-makers, East and West. But an explanation focusing on the international environment fails to account for the different rate at which the assimilation of modernist perspectives took place among Soviet commentators. Differences in role, status, and recruitment patterns account for much of the differentiation, with those directly involved in international relations—i.e., Khrushchev and the members of the Institute of World Economy and International Relations—most drawn to views similar to those of their Western counterparts. For the military, with a role-engendered responsibility for war-waging, for those (like Shelepin) whose recruitment pattern suggest a vested interest in the tightening of all screws, and for those high-status ideologues under Stalin (like Deborin and Ivashin) who were shunted aside by a younger generation of specialists, by contrast, the realities of the atomic age have engendered fewer "imperatives."

Finally, the essentially idiosyncratic phenomenon of the personality and beliefs of the particular ruler must be pointed to —especially in view of the impact which the key political figure or figures still has in the Soviet system. Khrushchev's boldness in repudiating doctrine was not totally to be explained by structural (international or national) explanations. It was part of Khrushchev's heritage for his successors, however, that he encouraged the emergence of a generation of specialists less cowed by dogma and created the doctrinal legitimation for regarding Leninism as irrelevant in the atomic age by defining the nature of the epoch as the third post-imperialist stage of capitalism's general crisis.

In one sense, the partial regression to conservative symbols suggests that his successors have not wished to carry out the further dismantling of Leninism. In another sense, however, Khrushchev had already done their dirty work for them. By their very inattention to the relation of the modern period to the world historical process and their overt elongation of the revolutionary process into a period spanning perhaps hundreds of years, Khrushchev's successors indicated that they had reduced the constraints imposed on themselves by past doctrine—though not necessarily by past experience—and had undertaken no major commitment to the future. Like the decision-makers of other great powers, Soviet rulers found themselves 50 years after the Revolution aware of the burdens of power and preoccupied not with grand syntheses, but rather with the tasks—the achievement of which may be facilitated by specialist advice—of maintaining and enhancing, under atomic age conditions, the Soviet Union's position within the contemporary international system.

Selected Bibliography

No effort has been made to achieve all-inclusiveness in the bibliography. It includes only those non-Soviet sources which were important to the development of my thinking during the writing of this book, and those Soviet sources which represent important pieces of evidence. Speeches, official statements, and other items readily found in *Pravda* and *Izvestiia*—which are usually available in English in the *Current Digest of the Soviet Press* and frequently elsewhere—have not been itemized.

Non-Soviet Sources: Books and Articles

Binder, Leonard. "The Middle East as a Subordinate International System," *World Politics*, Vol. x, No. 3 (April 1958), pp. 408-29.

Bociurkiw, Bohdan R. "The Post-Stalin 'Thaw' and Soviet Political Science," *The Canadian Journal of Economics and Political Science*, Vol. xxx, No. 1 (February 1964), pp. 22-48.

Bromke, Adam and Philip E. Uren, eds. *The Communist States and the West*. New York: Frederick A. Praeger, 1967.

Brzezinski, Zbigniew K. "Communist Ideology and International Affairs," *Journal of Conflict Resolution*, Vol. iv, No. 3 (September 1960), pp. 266-91.

———. *Ideology and Power in Soviet Politics*. New York. Frederick A. Praeger, 1962.

———. "Moscow and the M.L.F.: Hostility and Ambivalence," *Foreign Affairs*, Vol. xliii, No. 1 (October 1964), pp. 126-34.

———. "Russia and Europe," *Foreign Affairs*, Vol. xlii, No. 3 (April 1964), pp. 428-44.

Brzezinski, Zbigniew K. *The Soviet Bloc: Unity and Conflict.* Cambridge, Mass.: Harvard University Press, 1960.

Brzezinski, Zbigniew and Samuel P. Huntington. *Political Power: USA/USSR.* New York: The Viking Press, 1964.

Burin, Frederic S. "The Communist Doctrine of the Inevitability of War," *American Political Science Review*, Vol. LVII, No. 2 (June 1963), pp. 334-54.

Carlisle, Donald S. "The Changing Soviet Perception of the Developmental Process in the Afro-Asian World," *Midwest Journal of Political Science*, Vol. VIII, No. 4 (November 1964), pp. 385-407.

Claude, Inis L. "National Interests and the Global Environment: A Review," *The Journal of Conflict Resolution*, Vol. VIII, No. 3 (September 1964), pp. 292-96.

———. *Power and International Relations.* New York: Random House, 1962.

Conquest, Robert. *Power and Policy in the USSR: The Study of Soviet Dynastics.* New York: St. Martin's Press, 1961.

Crane, Robert D., ed. *Soviet Nuclear Strategy.* Washington, D.C.: The Center for Strategic Studies, Georgetown University, 1963.

Dallin, Alexander. "Recent Soviet Historiography," in *Russia Under Khrushchev*, ed. Abraham Brumberg. New York: Frederick A. Praeger, 1962.

———. "The Soviet Stake in Eastern Europe," *The Annals,* Vol. 317 (May 1958), pp. 138-39.

———. *The Soviet Union at the United Nations: An Inquiry into Soviet Motives and Objectives.* New York: Frederick A. Praeger, 1962.

Dallin, Alexander et al. *The Soviet Union, Arms Control, and Disarmament: A Study of Soviet Attitudes.* New York: School of International Affairs, Columbia University, 1964.

Deutsch, Karl W. et al. *Political Community and the North Atlantic Area.* Princeton, N.J.: Princeton University Press, 1957.

Dinerstein, Herbert S. "Soviet Doctrine on Developing Countries: Some Divergent Views." RAND Paper P-2725. Santa Monica, Calif.: RAND Corporation, March 1963.

———. *War and the Soviet Union.* 2nd edn. revised. New York: Frederick A. Praeger, 1962.

Fainsod, Merle. *Smolensk Under Soviet Rule.* Cambridge, Mass.: Harvard University Press, 1958.

Farrell, R. Barry, ed. *Approaches to Comparative and International Politics.* Evanston, Ill.: Northwestern University Press, 1966.

Fejtö, François. *The French Communist Party and the Crisis of International Communism.* Cambridge, Mass.: The M.I.T. Press, 1967.

Fischer, George. *Science and Politics: The New Sociology in the Soviet Union.* Cornell Research Papers in International Studies, No. 1. Ithaca, N.Y.: Center for International Studies, Cornell University, 1964.

Fox, Annette Baker. *The Power of Small States.* Chicago, Ill.: The University of Chicago Press, 1959.

Fox, William T. R. "Les fondements moraux et juridiques de la politique étrangère américaine," in *La politique étrangère et ses fondements*, ed. J. B. Duroselle. Paris: A. Colin, 1954.

———. *The Super-powers.* New York: Harcourt, Brace, and Co., 1944.

Fox, William T. R., ed. *Theoretical Aspects of International Relations.* Notre Dame, Ind.: University of Notre Dame Press, 1959.

Fox, William T. R. and Annette Baker Fox. "The Teaching of

International Relations in the United States," *World Politics,* Vol. XIII, No. 3 (April 1961), pp. 339-59.

Gallagher, Matthew P. *The Soviet History of World War II.* New York: Frederick A. Praeger, 1963.

Garthoff, Raymond L. "The Concept of the Balance of Power in Soviet Policy Making," *World Politics,* Vol. IV, No. 1 (October 1951), pp. 85-111.

———. *Soviet Strategy in the Nuclear Age.* New York: Frederick A. Praeger, 1958.

Gehlen, Michael P. *The Politics of Coexistence.* Bloomington, Ind.: Indiana University Press, 1967.

Grosser, Alfred. "L'étude des relations internationales, spécialité américaine?" *Revue française de science politique,* Vol. VI, No. 3 (July-September 1956), pp. 634-51.

Gruliow, Leo, ed. *Current Soviet Policies II: The Documentary Record of the 20th Party Congress and Its Aftermath.* New York: Frederick A. Praeger, 1957.

———. *Current Soviet Policies III.* New York: Columbia University Press, 1960.

Gulick, Edward Vose. *Europe's Classical Balance of Power.* Ithaca, N.Y.: Cornell University Press, 1955.

Haas, Ernst B. "The Balance of Power: Prescription, Concept and Propaganda," *World Politics,* Vol. V, No. 4 (July 1953), pp. 442-77.

———. "The Comparative Study of the United Nations," *World Politics,* Vol. XII, No. 2 (January 1960), pp. 298-332.

Herz, John H. *International Politics in the Atomic Age.* New York: Columbia University Press, 1959.

Hoffmann, Stanley H. "International Relations: The Long Road to Theory," *World Politics,* Vol. XI, No. 3 (April 1959), pp. 346-77.

Hoffmann, Stanley H., ed. *Contemporary Theory in Inter-*

national Relations. Englewood Cliffs, N.J.: Prentice-Hall, Inc., 1960.

Hollander, Paul, "The Dilemmas of Soviet Sociology," *Problems of Communism*, Vol. XIV, No. 6 (November-December 1965), pp. 34-46.

Horelick, Arnold and Rush, Myron. *Strategic Power and Soviet Foreign Policy*. Chicago: The University of Chicago Press, 1966.

Hudson, G. F., Richard Lowenthal, and Roderick MacFarquhar, eds. *The Sino-Soviet Dispute*. New York: Frederick A. Praeger, 1960.

Huntington, Samuel P. *The Common Defense*. New York: Columbia University Press, 1961.

———. "Patterns of Violence in World Politics," *Changing Patterns of Military Politics*, ed. Samuel P. Huntington. New York: The Free Press of Glencoe, Inc., 1962.

Kaplan, Morton A. *System and Process in International Relations*. New York: John Wiley & Sons, 1957.

Keep, John and Liliana Brisby, eds. *Contemporary History in the Soviet Mirror*. New York: Frederick A. Praeger, 1964.

Kolkowicz, Roman. "The Red 'Hawks' on the Rationality of Nuclear War." Memorandum RM 4899PR. Santa Monica, Calif.: RAND Corporation, 1966.

———. *The Soviet Military and the Communist Party*. Princeton, N.J.: Princeton University Press, 1967.

Labedz, Leopold. "Sociology as a Vocation," *Survey*, No. 48 (July 1963), pp. 57-65.

Laqueur, Walter Z. "Orientalists in Moscow," *Soviet Survey*, No. 34 (October-December 1960), pp. 3-7.

Leites, Nathan. "Kremlin Thoughts: Yielding, Rebuffing, Provoking, Retreating." Memorandum RM-3618-ISA. Santa Monica, Calif.: RAND Corporation, 1963.

Leites, Nathan. *A Study of Bolshevism*. Glencoe, Ill.: The Free Press, 1953.

Linden, Carl A. *Khrushchev and the Soviet Leadership, 1957–1964*. Baltimore, Md.: The Johns Hopkins Press, 1966.

London, Kurt L. "The 'Socialist Commonwealth of Nations': Pattern for Communist World Organization," *Orbis*, Vol. III, No. 4 (Winter 1960), pp. 424-43.

Lowenthal, Richard. "The End of an Illusion," *Problems of Communism*, Vol. XIV, No. 1 (January-February 1963), pp. 1-10.

———. "The Revolution Withers Away," *Problems of Communism*, Vol. XII, No. 1 (January-February 1965), pp. 10-17.

Meyer, Alfred G. *Leninism*. 2nd edn. New York: Frederick A. Praeger, 1962.

Modelski, George, "Agraria and Industria: Two Models of the International System," *World Politics*, Vol. XIV, No. 1 (October 1961), pp. 118-43.

———. *The Communist International System*. Center of International Studies, Woodrow Wilson School of Public and International Affairs, Research Monograph No. 9. Princeton, N.J.: Princeton University Press, 1960.

Morgenthau, Hans J. *Politics Among Nations*. 3rd edn. New York: Alfred A. Knopf, 1960.

Niebuhr, Reinhold. *The Structure of Nations and Empires*. New York: Charles Scribner's Sons, 1959.

Organski, A.F.K. *World Politics*. New York: Alfred A. Knopf, 1958.

Ploss, S. I. "The Uncertainty of Soviet Foreign Policy," *World Politics*, Vol. XV, No. 3. (April 1963), pp. 455-64.

Robson, William A. *The University Teaching of Social Sciences: Political Science*. London: UNESCO, 1954.

Rubinstein, Alvin Z. "Selected Bibliography of Soviet Works

on the United Nations, 1946-59," *American Political Science Review*, Vol. LIV, No. 4 (December 1960), pp. 985-91.

———. *The Soviets in International Organizations*. Princeton, N.J.: Princeton University Press, 1964.

Saikowski, Charlotte and Leo Gruliow, eds. *Current Soviet Policies IV*. New York: Columbia University Press, 1962.

Shulman, Marshall D. "The Communist States and Western Integration," *International Organization*, Vol. XVII, No. 2 (Summer 1963) pp. 649-62.

———. "Bloc Reactions to the Common Market," *Problems of Communism*, Vol. XII, No. 5 (September-October 1963), pp. 47-54.

———. *Stalin's Foreign Policy Reappraised*. Cambridge, Mass.: Harvard University Press, 1963.

Singer, J. David. "International Conflict: Three Levels of Analysis," *World Politics*, Vol. XII, No. 3 (April 1960), pp. 453-61.

———. "The Level-of-Analysis in International Relations," *World Politics*, Vol. XIV, No. 1 (October 1961), pp. 77-92.

———. "Soviet and American Foreign Policy Attitudes: Content Analysis of Elite Articulations," *Journal of Conflict Resolution*, Vol. VIII, No. 4 (December 1964), pp. 424-35.

Skilling, Gordon. "In Search of Political Science in the U.S.S.R.," *The Canadian Journal of Economics and Political Science*, Vol. XXIX, No. 4 (November 1963), pp. 519-29.

Sokolovskii, V. D., ed. *Soviet Military Strategy. A translation of Voennaia strategiia*. 1st. edn., with an introduction, annotations, and supplementary materials by Herbert S. Dinerstein, Leon Goure, and Thomas Wolfe. A RAND Corporation Research Study. Englewood Cliffs, N.J.: Prentice-Hall, Inc., 1963.

Spykman, Nicholas. *America's Strategy in World Politics.* New York: Harcourt, Brace, and Co., 1942.

Thornton, Thomas P. "Communist Attitudes Toward Asia, Africa and Latin America," *Communism and Revolution: The Strategic Uses of Political Violence,* ed. Cyril E. Black and Thomas P. Thornton. Princeton, N.J.: Princeton University Press, 1964.

———. *The Third World in Soviet Perspective.* Princeton, N.J.: Princeton University Press, 1964.

Tucker, Robert C. *The Soviet Political Mind.* New York: Frederick A. Praeger, 1963.

Veto, Miklos. "Kremlin and Vatican," *Survey,* No. 48 (July 1963), pp. 163-72.

Waldo, Dwight. *Political Science in the United States of America.* Paris: UNESCO, 1956.

Waltz, Kenneth N. *Man, the State, and War.* New York: Columbia University Press, 1959.

Whitaker, Urban G., Jr. "Actors, Ends, and Means: A Coarse-Screen Macro-Theory of International Relations," *International Politics and Foreign Policy,* ed. James N. Rosenau. Glencoe, Ill.: The Free Press of Glencoe, Inc., 1961.

Wohlstetter, Albert. "The Delicate Balance of Terror," *Foreign Affairs,* Vol. XXXVII, No. 2 (January 1959), pp. 211-34.

Wolfe, Thomas W. "Shifts in Soviet Strategic Thought," *Foreign Affairs,* Vol. XLII, No. 3 (April 1964), pp. 475-86.

———. *Soviet Strategy at the Crossroads.* Cambridge, Mass.: Harvard University Press, 1964.

Wolfers, Arnold. *Discord and Collaboration.* Baltimore, Md.: The Johns Hopkins Press, 1962.

———. "Political Theory and International Relations," *The Anglo-American Tradition in Foreign Affairs,* ed. Arnold

Wolfers and Laurence W. Martin. New Haven, Conn.: Yale University Press, 1957.

Wright, Quincy. *The Study of International Relations.* New York: Appleton-Century-Crofts, 1955.

Yaresh, Leo. "The Problems of Periodization," *Rewriting Russian History*, ed. Cyril E. Black. New York: Frederick A. Praeger, 1956.

Zagoria, Donald S. *The Sino-Soviet Conflict: 1956–1961.* Princeton, N.J.: Princeton University Press, 1962.

———. "Some Comparisons Between the Russian and Chinese Models," *Communist Strategies in Asia*, ed. A. Doak Barnett. New York: Frederick A. Praeger, 1963.

Zimmerman, William. "Sokolovskii and his Critics: A Review," *Journal of Conflict Resolution*, Vol. VIII, No. 3 (September 1964), pp. 322-28.

Soviet Sources: Books

Airapetian, M. E. and G. A. Deborin. *Etapy vneshnei politiki SSSR* [The Stages of USSR Foreign Policy]. Moscow: Sotsekizdat, 1961.

Akademiia Nauk SSSR: Institut Istorii. *Sovetskii Soiuz v Organizatsii Ob"edinennykh Natsii* [The Soviet Union in the United Nations]. Moscow: Izdatel'stvo "Nauka," 1965.

Akademiia Nauk SSSR: Institut Mirovoi Ekonomiki i Mezhdunarodnykh Otnoshenii. *Ekonomicheskie problemy stran Latinskoi Ameriki* [Economic Problems of Latin America]. Moscow: Izdatel'stvo AN SSSR, 1963.

———. *Dvizhushchie sily vneshnei politiki SShA* [The Moving Forces of the U.S. Foreign Policy]. Moscow: "Nauka," 1965.

———. *Stroitel'stvo kommunizma i mirovoi revoliutsionnyi*

protsess [The Construction of Communism and the World Revolutionary Process]. Moscow: Izdatel'stvo "Nauka," 1966.

———. *Gorodskie srednie sloi sovremennogo kapitalisticheskogo obshchestva* [The Urban Middle Strata of Modern Capitalist Society]. Moscow: Izdatel'stvo AN SSSR, 1963.

———. *Mezhdunarodnye otnosheniia posle vtoroi mirovoi voiny* [International Relations Since the Second World War]. Vol. I, 1945-1949; Vol. II, 1950-1955; and Vol. III, 1956-64. Moscow: Gospolitizdat, 1962, 1963, 1965.

———. *Polozhenie sel'skogo khoziaistva i krest'ianstva v koloniiakh i drugikh slaborazvitykh stranakh* [The Situation in Agriculture and the Peasantry in Colonial and Other Underdeveloped Countries]. Moscow: Izdatel'stvo AN SSSR, 1958.

Arzumanian, A. *Krizis mirovogo kapitalizma na sovremennom etape* [The Crisis of World Capitalism in its Contemporary Stage]. Moscow: Izdatel'stvo AN SSSR, 1962.

Baryshnikov, V. N. *'Taivanskii vopros' v Kitaisko-Amerikanskikh otnosheniiakh* [The Taiwan Question and Chinese-American Relations]. Moscow: unpublished dissertation, AN SSSR, Institut Ekonomiki Mirovoi Sotsialisticheskoi Sistemy [Otdel Istorii], 1965.

Baturin, M. and S. Tarov. *Vneshniaia politika Sovetskogo Soiuza na sovremennom etape* [The Foreign Policy of the Soviet Union in the Contemporary Stage]. Moscow: Izdatel'stvo IMO, 1962.

Dalin, S. A. *Voenno-gosudarstvennyi monopolisticheskii kapitalizm v SShA* [Military-State Monopoly Capitalism in the USA]. Moscow: Izdatel'stvo Nauk, 1961.

XXIII s"ezd Kommunisticheskoi Partii Sovetskogo Soiuza: Stenograficheskii otchet [The 23rd Congress of the Communist Party of the Soviet Union: Stenographic Record]. Moscow: Politizdat, 1966.

Deborin, G. A., ed. *Mezhdunarodnye otnosheniia i vneshniaia politika Sovetskogo Soiuza, 1945–1949 gg.* [International Relations and the Foreign Policy of the Soviet Union, 1945-49]. Moscow: Izdatel'stvo IMO, 1958.

Diplomaticheskii slovar' [Diplomatic Dictionary]. Vol. I, A-I; Vol. II, K-P; and Vol. III, R-Ia. Ed. A. A. Gromyko et al. Moscow: Gospolitizdat, 1961, 1961, 1964.

Dmitriev, Boris [Piadyshev, B.]. *Pentagon i vneshniaia politika SShA* [The Pentagon and U.S. Foreign Policy]. Moscow: Izdatel'stvo IMO, 1961.

Durdenevskii, V. N. *Sovetskaia literatura po mezhdunarodnomu pravu* [Soviet Literature on International Law]. Moscow: Gosiurizdat, 1959.

Egorov, V. M., comp. *Mezhdunarodnye otnosheniia* [International Relations]. Moscow: Izdatel'stvo IMO, 1961.

Iakovlev, N. N. *Franklin Ruzvel't: chelovek i politik* [Franklin Roosevelt: The Man and the Politician]. Moscow: Izdatel'stvo "Mezhdunarodnye Otnosheniia," 1965.

Iakovlev, A. N. *Ideologiia Amerikanskoi "imperii"* [The Ideology of American "Empire"]. Moscow: Izdatel'stvo "Mysl'," 1967.

———. *Ideinaia nishcheta apologetov 'kholodnoi voiny'* [The Ideological Bankruptcy of the Apologists of the 'Cold War']. Moscow: Sotsekgiz, 1961.

Il'ichev, L. F. *Obshchestvennye nauki i kommunizm* [The Social Sciences and Communism]. Moscow: Isdatel'stvo AN SSSR, 1963.

Institut Mezhdunarodnykh Otnoshenii. *Istoriia mezhdunarodnykh otnoshenii i vneshnei politiki SSSR* [History of International Relations and the Foreign Policy of the USSR].

Vol. III, 1945-1963. Ed. V. G. Trukhanovskii. Moscow: Izdatel'stvo "Mezhdunarodnye otnosheniia," 1964.

———. *Mirnoe sosushchestvovanie—Leninskii kurs vneshnei politiki Sovetskogo Soiuza* [Peaceful Coexistence—The Leninist Course of Soviet Foreign Policy]. Ed. and with an introduction by A. A. Gromyko. Moscow: Izdatel'stvo IMO, 1962.

Istoriia diplomatii [History of Diplomacy]. Vol. I ed. V. A. Zorin et al. 2nd edn. revised. Moscow: Gospolitizdat, 1959.

Istoriia diplomatii [History of Diplomacy]. Vol. II, 1871-1914, ed. A. A. Gromyko et al. 2nd edn. revised. Moscow: Gospolitizdat, 1963.

Koval'skii, N. *Vatikan i mirovaia politika* [The Vatican and World Politics]. Moscow: Izdatel'stvo IMO, 1964.

Krasin, Iu. *Mirnoe sosushchestvovanie—forma klassovoi bor'by* [Peaceful Coexistence—a Form of Class Struggle]. Moscow: Gospolitizdat, 1961.

Kuusinen, Otto et al., eds. Fundamentals of Marxism-Leninism. 1st edn. Moscow: Foreign Languages Publishing House, n.d.

———. Fundamentals of Marxism-Leninism. 2nd edn. revised. Moscow: Foreign Languages Publishing House, 1963.

———. *Osnovy Marksizma-Leninizma* [Fundamentals of Marxism-Leninism]. 1st edn. Moscow: Gospolitizdat, 1959.

———. *Osnovy Marksizma-Leninizma* [Fundamentals of Marxism-Leninism]. 2nd edn. Moscow: Gospolitizdat, 1962.

Lan [Kaplan], V. I. *SShA v voennye i poslevoennye gody* [The U.S. in the War and Post-war years]. Moscow: Izdatel'stvo "Nauka," 1964.

Lebedev, V. Z., ed. *O sovremennoi sovetskoi diplomatii* [Concerning Contemporary Soviet Diplomacy]. Moscow: Izdatel'stvo IMO, 1963.

Lenin, V. I. *Sochineniia* [Works]. Vol. XXI. 4th edn. Moscow: Gospolitizdat, 1952.

Leonidov, A. *Politika voennykh monopolii* [Policy of the Military Monopolies]. Moscow: Voenizdat, 1961.

Leont'ev, L.A. *Leninskoe issledovanie imperializma* [Leninist Research on Imperialism]. Moscow: Izdatel'stvo "Nauka," 1964.

Levin, D. B. *Diplomatiia: ee sushchnost', metody i formy* [Diplomacy: Its Essence, Methods, and Forms]. Moscow: Sotsekgiz, 1962.

Khrushchev, N. S. *K pobede razuma nad silami voiny!* [To the Victory of Reason Over the Forces of War!] Moscow: Politizdat, 1964.

———. *K pobede v mirnom sorevnovanii s kapitalizmom!* [To Victory in the Peaceful Competition with Capitalism!] Moscow: Gospolitizdat, 1955.

———. *Kommunizm—mir i schast'e narodov* [Communism—Peace and Happiness of the Peoples]. Vol. I, January-September 1961. Moscow: Gospolitizdat, 1962.

———. *Kommunizm—mir i schast'e narodov* [Communism—Peace and Happiness of the Peoples]. Vol. II, October-December 1961. Moscow: Gospolitizdat, 1962.

———. *Mir bez oruzhiia—mir bez voin* [World Without Arms—World Without War]. Vol. I, January-July 1959. Moscow: Gospolitizdat, 1960.

———. *Mir bez oruzhiia—mir bez voin* [World Without Arms—World Without War]. Vol. II, January-July 1959. Moscow: Gospolitizdat, 1960.

———. *O vneshnei politike Sovetskogo Soiuza, 1960 god.* [On the Foreign Policy of the Soviet Union, 1960]. Vol. I, January-May. Moscow: Gospolitizdat, 1961.

———. *O vneshnei politike Sovetskogo Soiuza, 1960 god.* [On

the Foreign Policy of the Soviet Union, 1960]. Vol. II, June-December. Moscow: Gospolitizdat, 1961.

———. *Predotvratit' voinu, otstoiat' mir!* [Prevent War, Defend the Peace!]. Moscow: Gospolitizdat, 1963.

———. *Za mir, za razoruzhenie, za svobodu narodov!* [For Peace, For Disarmament, For Freedom of the Peoples!]. Moscow: Gospolitizdat, 1960.

Kissinger, G. [H.]. *Iadernoe oruzhie i vneshniaia politika* [Nuclear Weapons and Foreign Policy]. Condensed translation with an introduction by S. N. Krasil'nikov. Moscow: Izdatel'stvo Inostranlit, 1959.

Menshikov, S. M. *Ekonomicheskaia politika pravitel'stva Kennedi* [The Economic Policy of the Kennedy Government]. Moscow: Izdatel'stvo "Mysl'," 1964.

Mezhdunarodnye ekonomicheskie organizatsii [International Economic Organizations]. Moscow: Izdatel'stvo IMO, 1960.

Morozov, G. I. *Organizatsiia Ob"edinennykh Natsii* [The United Nations Organization]. Moscow: Izdatel'stvo IMO, 1962.

Nikol'skii, N. M. *Osnovnoi vopros sovremennosti* [The Basic Question of Our Times]. Moscow: Izdatel'stvo "Mezhdunarodnye otnosheniia," 1964.

Popova, E. I. *SShA: bor'ba po voprosam vneshnei politiki* [The USA: The Struggle over Questions of Foreign Policy]. Moscow: Izdatel'stvo "Mezhdunarodnye otnosheniia," 1966.

Pukhovskii, N. V. *O mire i voine* [Concerning Peace and War]. Moscow: Izdatel'stvo "Mysl'," 1965.

Rybkin, E. I. *Voina i politika* [War and Politics]. Moscow: Voenizdat, 1959.

Sheinin, Iu. M. *Nauka i militarizm v SShA* [Science and

Militarism in the USA]. Moscow: Izdatel'stvo AN SSSR, 1963.

Sobakin, V. K. *Kollektivnaia bezopasnost'—garantiia mirnogo sosushchestvovaniia* [Collective Security—Guarantee of Peaceful Coexistence]. Moscow: Izdatel'stvo IMO, 1962.

Sokolovskii, V. D., ed. *Voennaia strategiia* [Military Strategy]. 1st edn. Moscow: Voenizdat, 1962.

Sokolovskii, V. D., ed. *Voennaia strategiia* [Military Strategy]. 2nd edn. corrected and enlarged. Moscow: Voenizdat, 1963.

Stroitel'stvo kommunizma i obshchestvennye nauki [The Social Sciences and the Construction of Communism]. Moscow: Izdatel'stvo AN SSSR, 1962.

Trukhanovskii, V. G. *Vneshniaia politika Anglii na pervom etape obshchego krizisa kapitalizma (1919–1939 gg.)* [English Foreign Policy in the First Stage of the General Crisis of Capitalism (1919-1939)]. Moscow: Izdatel'stvo AN SSSR, 1962.

Ul'ianovskii, R. A. *Neokolonializm SShA i slaborazvitye strany Azii* [U. S. Neocolonialism and the Underdeveloped Countries of Asia]. Moscow: Izdatel'stvo Vostochnoi Literatury, 1963.

Urlanis, B. Ts. *Voiny i narodonaselenie Evropy* [Wars and the Population of Europe]. Moscow: Sotsekizdat, 1960.

Voprosy gosudarstvennogo kapitalizma v imperialisticheskikh i razvivaiushchikhsia stranakh na sovremennom etape [Questions of State Capitalism in Imperialist and Developing Countries at the Contemporary Stage]. Moscow: Izdatel'stvo Moskovskogo universiteta, 1966.

Voprosy Marksistkoi sotsiologii [Questions of Marxist Sociology]. Leningrad: Izdatel'stvo LGU, 1962.

Vsesoiuznoe soveshchanie o merakh uluchsheniia podgotovki

nauchno-pedagogicheskikh kadrov po istoricheskim naukam [All-Union Conference on Measures of Improving the Preparation of Scientific-Pedagogical Cadres in the Historical Sciences]. Moscow: Izdatel'stvo "Nauka," 1964.

Zorin, Val. *Monopolii i politika SShA* [Monopolies and U.S. Politics]. Moscow: Izdatel'stvo IMO, 1960.

SOVIET SOURCES: ARTICLES FROM THE JOURNAL, *Mirovaia ekonomika i mezhdunarodnye otnosheniia*

Akademiia Nauk SSSR: Institut Mirovoi Ekonomiki i Mezhdunarodnykh Otnoshenii. "Ob imperialisticheskoi 'integratsii' v Zapadnoi Evrope ('obshchii rynok')" [Concerning Imperialist 'Integration' in Western Europe ('The Common Market')], supplement to No. 9 (September 1962), 3-16.

———. "O sozdanii 'obshchego rynka' i Evratom" [Concerning the Creation of the 'Common Market' and Euratom], No. 1 (July 1957), pp. 83-96.

———. "Uchenie V. I. Lenina ob imperializme i sovremennosti" [V. I. Lenin's Doctrine of Imperialism and Today] No. 5 (May 1967), pp. 3-22.

Aleksandrov, D. and O. Nakropin. "Mirnoe sosushchestvovanie i sovremennost'" [Peaceful Coexistence and the Contemporary World], No. 12 (December 1961), pp. 26-51.

Alekseev, E. et al. "Tekushchie problemy mirovoi politiki" [Current Problems of World Politics], No. 7 (July 1962), pp. 3-32.

Artemov, B. "O sovetsko-amerikanskikh otnosheniakh" [On Soviet-American Relations], No. 11 (November 1958), pp. 15-26.

Arzumanian, A. "Krizis mirovogo kapitalizma" [Crisis of World Capitalism], No. 12 (December 1961), pp. 3-25.

——. "Novyi etap obshchego krizisa kapitalizma" [New Stage in the General Crisis of Capitalism], No. 2 (February 1961), pp. 3-19.

——. "Sovremennyi kapitalizm i klassovaia bor'ba" [Contemporary Capitalism and the Class Struggle], No. 2. (February 1963), pp. 3-14.

Bagramov, L. et al. "Tekushchie problemy mirovoi politiki" [Current Problems of World Politics], No. 1 (January 1961), pp. 3-35.

Bolkhovitinov, N. "Doktrina Monro: legendy i deistvitel'nost" [The Monroe Doctrine: Legend and Reality], No. 9 (September 1960), pp. 14-26.

Butenko, A. "O zakonomernostiakh razvitiia sotsializma kak obshchestvennogo stroia i kak mirovoi sistemy" [Concerning the Law-Governed Development of Socialism as a Social System and as a World System], No. 11 (November 1966), pp. 84-91.

Cheprov, I. and Ia. Iudin, "Nesostoiatel'nost politiki voennykh blokov" [The Bankruptcy of the Policy of Military Blocs], No. 4 (April 1959), pp. 68-80.

"XXII s"ezd KPSS i zadachi dal'neishego izucheniia problemy mirovogo razvitiia" [The Twenty-second Congress of the CPSU and the Tasks of Further Studying the Problems of World Development], No. 3 (March 1962), pp. 3-19.

Editorial "Nashi zadachi" (Our Tasks), No. 1 (July 1957), pp. 3-6.

Epstein, S. "Gruppy davleniia" [Interest Groups], review of Stanislaw Ehrlich, *Grupy nacisku*, No. 8 (August 1963), pp. 150-151.

Galkin, A. A. et al. "Tekushchie problemy mirovoi politiki" [Current Problems of World Politics], No. 7 (July 1959), pp. 3-43.

Galkin, A. A. et al. "Tekushchie problemy mirovoi politiki" [Current Problems of World Politics], No. 1 (January 1960), pp. 3-32.

Galkin, A. "Vneshniaia politika umiraiushchego imperializma" [The Foreign Policy of Moribund Imperialism] No. 6 (June 1962), pp. 3-16.

Gantman, V. et al. "Tekushchie problemy mirovoi politiki" [Current Problems of World Politics], No. 7 (July 1960), pp. 3-33.

———. "Tekushchie problemy mirovoi politiki" [Current Problems of World Politics], No. 1 (January 1962), pp. 3-23.

———. "Tekushchie problemy mirovoi politiki" [Current Problems of World Politics], No. 1 (January 1963), pp. 3-23.

Gantman, V., Nikonov, A. and D. Tomashevskii. "Mirovye voiny XX veka i dialektika istorii" [World Wars of the Twentieth Century and the Dialectic of History], No. 8 (August 1964), pp. 3-15 and No. 9 (September 1964), pp. 30-44.

Georgiev, A. "Konferentsiia chitatelei v Minske" [Conference of Readers in Minsk], No. 12 (December 1963), p. 143.

Gerasimov, G. "Teoriia igr i mezhdunarodnye otnosheniia" [The Theory of Games and International Relations], No. 7 (July 1966), pp. 101-108.

Iakovlev, N. "Opyt vtoroi mirovoi voiny i ego otsenka ideologami vneshnei politiki SShA" [The Experience of World War II and its Appraisal by U.S. Foreign Policy Ideologists], No. 10 (October 1959), pp. 28-35.

Inozemtsev, N. "'Atomnaia diplomatiia' SShA: proekty i deistvitel'nost' " [U.S. Atomic Diplomacy: Schemes and Reality], No. 3 (March 1958), pp. 29-43.

———. "Edinstvo zapada?" [Western Unity?], No. 3 (March 1963), pp. 63-65.

Iudin, Iu. "Monopolii SShA i politika Vashingtona" [U.S. Monopolies and the Policy of Washington], No. 8 (August 1963), pp. 36-49.

Iur'ev, N. "Uzel imperialisticheskogo sopernichestva v Kongo" (The Knot of Imperialist Rivalry in the Congo), No. 1 (January 1963), pp. 24-35.

Kisilev, V. "Rabochii klass i natsional'no-osvoboditel'nye revoliutsii" [The Working Class and National Liberations Revolutions], No. 10 (October 1963), pp. 93-98.

Kolesov, N. "Semiletnii plan i mezhdunarodnoe rabochee dvizhenie" [The Seven-year Plan and the International Labor Movement], No. 5 (May 1959), pp. 3-13.

Kolikov, N. "Osnovnye sily sovremennogo revoliutsionnogo protsessa" [Fundamental Forces of the Contemporary Revolutionary Process], No. 3 (March 1966), pp. 3-18.

Kon, I. "Problemy mezhdunarodnykh otnoshenii v sovremennoi burzhuaznoi sotsiologii" [Problems of International Relations in Contemporary Bourgeois Sociology], No. 2 (February 1960), pp. 56-69.

———. "Sushchestvuet li atlanticheskaia tsivilizatsiia?" [Does an Atlantic Civilization Exist?] No. 1 (January 1958), pp. 8-18.

"Konferentsiia na temu 'Amerikanskaia' "pomoshch" stranam Azii' " [Conference on the Topic 'American "Aid" to Asian Countries'], No. 1 (January 1958), pp. 95-134.

"Konferentsiia zhurnala 'Mirovaia ekonomika i mezhdunarodnye otnosheniia' v Tbisili" [Conference of the Journal 'World Economy and International Relations' in Tbisili], No. 12 (December 1959), pp. 142-44.

Kononeko, A. " 'Lokal'nye voiny' v politike i strategii SShA" ['Local Wars' in U.S. Policy and Strategy], No. 10 (October 1959), pp. 16-25.

Korionov, V. "Leninizm i mirovoi revoliutsionnyi protsess" [Leninism and the World Revolutionary Process], No. 6 (June 1963), pp. 5-17.

Larionov, V. "Razvitie sredstv vooruzheniia i strategicheskie konseptsii SShA" [The Development of the Means of Armament and U.S. Strategic Concepts], No. 6 (June 1966), pp. 74-81.

Lemin, I. "K voprosu o protivorechiakh mezhdu kapitalisticheskimi stranami" [To the Problem of Contradictions Between Capitalist Countries], No. 8 (August 1960), pp. 25-40.

———. "Leninskii printsip mirnogo sosushchestvovaniia i sovremennost' " [The Leninist Principle of Peaceful Coexistence and Today], No. 4 (April 1963), pp. 3-15.

———. "Marks i voprosy vneshnei politiki" [Marx and Questions of Foreign Policy], No. 5 (May 1958), pp. 20-33.

———. "Mezhdunarodnye otnosheniia na novom etape obshchego krizisa kapitalizma" [International Relations at a New Stage of the General Crisis of Capitalism], No. 4 (April 1961), pp. 3-18.

———. "Velikaia Oktiabr'skaia sotsialisticheskaia revoliutsiia i mirovaia politika," [The Great October Socialist Revolution and World Politics], No. 6 (June 1967), pp. 3-17.

Leonidov, A. "Tainyi soiuz voennykh monopolii i ego rol' v mirovoi politike" [Secret Alliance of War Monopolies and Its Role in World Politics], No. 11 (November, 1958) pp. 27-46 and No. 3 (March 1959), pp. 68-82.

Leont'ev, L. "Marks i kapitalizm nashikh dnei" [Marx and the Capitalism of Our Days], No. 5 (May 1958), pp. 3-19.

Marinin, M. "Chelovechestvo mozhet i dol'zhno zhit' bez voin" [Mankind Can and Must Live Without Wars], No. 8 (August 1960), pp. 3-14.

Marinin, M. "Leninizm i segodniashnii mir" [Leninism and Today's World], No. 4 (April 1962), pp. 3-20.

———. "Nekotorye osobennosti nyneshnego etapa mezhdunarodnykh otnoshenii" [Some Unique Features of the Contemporary Stage of International Relations], No. 6 (June 1958), pp. 3-14.

Mel'nikov, D. "Novaia epokha v mezhdunarodnykh otnosheniiakh" [A New Epoch in International Relations], No. 11 (November 1965), pp. 3-13.

———. "Sotsialisticheskii internatsionalizm i politika voinstvuiushchego imperializma" [Socialist Internationalism and Militant Imperialism], No. 6 (June 1966), pp. 3-18.

———. "Obostrenie mezhimperialisticheskikh protivorechii na sovremennom etape" [Aggravation of Inter-imperialist Contradictions in the Contemporary Stage], No. 6 (June 1963), pp. 18-33.

Mil'shtein, M. and A. Slobodenko. "Problema sootnosheniia politiki i voiny v sovremennoi imperialisticheskoi ideologii" [The Problem of the Correlation of Politics and War in Present Imperialist Ideology], No. 9 (September 1958), pp. 58-73.

Mirskii, G. "Tvorcheskii Marksizm i problemy natsional'no-osvoboditel'nykh revoliutsii" [Creative Marxism and the Problems of National-Liberation Revolutions], No. 2 (February 1963), pp. 63-68.

Morozov, G. "Organizatsiia Ob"edinennykh Natsii i zadachi sokhraneniia mira" [The United Nations Organization and the Tasks of Preserving Peace], No. 10 (October 1960), pp. 14-26.

———. "Usovershenstvovanie struktury OON — nazrevshaia zadacha" [Perfecting the Structure of the UN—an Urgent Task], No. 8 (August 1961), pp. 31-44.

"Nauchnaia zhizn'" [Scientific Life], No. 2 (February 1960), pp. 152-55.

Nazarov, N. "Ideinye korni revisionizma v voprosakh mezhdunarodnykh otnoshenii" [Ideological Roots of Revisionism in Questions of International Relations], No. 7 (July 1958), pp. 18-30.

"'Obshchii Rynok' i ego rol' v ekonomike i politike sovremennogo imperializma" ['The Common Market' and its Role in the Economy and Politics of Contemporary Imperialism], No. 7 (July 1959), pp. 108-16, No. 8 (August 1959), pp. 104-17, No. 9 (September 1959), pp. 86-106, and No. 10 (October 1959), pp. 73-83.

"Obsuzhdeniia zhurnala 'Mirovaia ekonomika i mezhdunarodnye otnosheniia'" [Discussions of the Journal 'World Economy and International Relations'], No. 8 (August 1962), p. 156.

"Osnovnaia zadacha sovremennosti" [The Fundamental Task of Modern Times], No. 1 (January 1958), pp. 3-7.

Popov, K. "Plany i perspektivy 'Obshchego Rynka'" [Plans and Prospects of the 'Common Market'], No. 7 (July 1959), pp. 108-10.

Popov, V. A Review of V. G. Trukhanovskii, Vneshniaia politika Anglii na pervom etape obshchego krizisa kapitalizma (1918-1939 gg.), No. 1 (January 1963), p. 154.

Rubinshtein, M. "Nauka i mezhdunarodnye otnosheniia" [Science and International Relations], No. 6 (June 1958), pp. 36-46.

———. "Torzhestvo Leninizma" (The Triumph of Leninism), No. 4 (April 1959), pp. 3-15.

Rumiantsev, A. M. "Reshaiushchii faktor razvitiia chelovecheskogo obshchestva" [The Decisive Factor in the Development of Human Society], No. 1 (January 1966), pp. 3-15.

Rysakov, P. "Severo-Atlanticheskii blok i strany severnoi Evropy" [The North Atlantic Bloc and the Countries of Northern Europe], No. 3 (March 1962), pp. 78-89.

Sheinin, Iu. Review of Herman Kahn, *On Thermonuclear War*, No. 5 (May 1962), pp. 147-52.

———. Review of Herman Kahn, *Thinking About the Unthinkable*, No. 1 (January 1963), pp. 141-46.

Terekhov, V. and Shastitko, V. "Mezhdunarodnoe sotsialisticheskoe razdelenie truda" [International Socialist Division of Labor], No. 7 (July 1963), pp. 87-93.

Trofimenko, G. "Bor'ba v SShA po voprosam vneshnei politiki" [Struggle Within the U.S.A. on Questions of Foreign Policy], No. 9 (September 1958), pp. 106-16.

———. "Realizm i vneshniaia politika SShA" [Realism and Foreign Policy of the U.S.A.], No. 3 (March 1960, pp. 29-42.

Ul'ianovskii, R. "Amerikanskaia strategiia v Indii" [American Strategy in India], No. 5 (May 1963), pp. 27-38.

Varga, N. "Marks i kapitalizm ego vremeni" [Marx and the Capitalism of His Time], No. 3 (March 1958), pp. 3-13.

———. "'Obshchii Rynok' i mirovoi kapitalisticheskii rynok" [The 'Common Market' and the World Capitalist Market], No. 7 (July 1959), pp. 110-12.

———. "Teoreticheskie problemy ekonomiki 'Obshchego Rynka'" [Theoretical Problems of the Economy of the 'Common Market'], No. 10 (October 1962), pp. 49-59.

Soviet Sources: Articles from the Journal, *International Affairs* (Moscow)

Airapetyan [Airapetian], M. "The Periodization of the History of Soviet Foreign Policy," No. 2 (February 1958), pp. 63-70.

Airapetyan [Airapetian], M. and G. Deborin. "The Guiding

Force of Socialist Foreign Policy," No. 11 (November 1959), pp. 34-39.

Anatolyev [Anatol'ev], G. and B. Marushkin. "Through the Distorting Glass," Review of George Kennan, *The Decision to Intervene*, No. 1 (January 1959), pp. 104-106.

Baturin, M. "Peace and the Status Quo," No. 1 (January 1958), pp. 71-76.

Bogush, E. "Karl Marx on the Foreign Policy of the Working Class," No. 5 (May 1958), pp. 19-25.

"Conference of Leningrad Readers," No. 7 (July 1958), p. 127.

Editorial "Imperialist Aggression in the Congo," No. 8 (August 1960), pp. 64-65.

———. "An Imperative Demand," No. 1 (January 1958), pp. 3-8.

Fedoseyev [Fedoseev], P. "Sociological Theories and the Foreign Policy of Imperialism," No. 3 (March 1957), pp. 10-22.

Galkin, A. "The 'Paradoxes' of Western Foreign Policy," No. 2 (February 1960), pp. 51-56.

———. "Some Aspects of the Problem of War and Peace," No. 11 (November 1961), pp. 29-35.

Gerasimov, G. "The First Strike Theory," No. 3 (March 1965), pp. 39-45.

Glagolev, I. and V. Larionov. "Soviet Defence Might and Peaceful Coexistence," No. 11 (November 1963), pp. 27-33.

Gonionsky [Gonionskii], S. "The Unburied Corpse of the Monroe Doctrine," No. 10 (October 1960), pp. 60-66.

Granov, V. "The War and the Post-War World," No. 4 (April 1965), pp. 42-48.

"How the Vatican is Run," No. 3 (March 1963), pp. 114-15.

"The Ideological Struggle and Present International Relations," No. 8 (August 1963), pp. 3-41.

Ilyichov [Il'ichev], L. "The Sputniks and International Relations," No. 3 (March 1958), pp. 7-17.

Inozemtsev, N. "Results and Prospects of the Development of International Relations," No. 11 (November 1961), pp. 15-21.

Ivanov, K. "International Relations and the Collapse of Colonialism," No. 5 (May 1957), pp. 11-21.

———. "Present-day Colonialism and International Relations," No. 4 (April 1962), pp. 36-45.

———. "Present-day Colonialism: Its Socio-economic Aspect," No. 2 (February 1960), pp. 34-41.

———. "The U.S.A.—Prop of a Collapsing Colonialism," No. 4 (April 1958), pp. 45-54.

Ivashin, I. "Comments on 'A Letter to the Editors,'" No. 1 (January 1957), pp. 164-65.

———. "The October Revolution and International Relations," No. 11 (November 1966), pp. 48-52.

Korionov, V. "The Crisis of 'The Position of Strength' Policy," No. 3 (March 1958), pp. 31-35.

———. "Proletarian Internationalism—Our Victorious Policy," No. 8 (August 1963), pp. 12-17.

Korovin, E. "Proletarian Internationalism in World Relations," No. 2 (February 1958), pp. 23-30.

Korovin, E. et al. "A Letter to the Editor," No. 12 (December 1956), pp. 98-99.

———. "Conquest of Outer Space and Some Problems of International Relations," No. 11 (November 1959), pp. 88-96.

Kortunov, V. V. "Ideological Struggle in Conditions of the Peaceful Co-existence of the Two Systems," No. 8 (August 1963), pp. 6-12.

Leonidov, A. "The Strategy of 'Psychological Warfare,'" No. 4 (April 1959), pp. 30-37.

Lvov [L'vov], M. "U.N.: Rostrum, Forum, Arena," No. 11 (November 1963), pp. 10-15.

Matveyev [Matveev], V. "Danger of 'Accidental War,'" No. 9 (September 1962), pp. 77-78.

"The Nature and Specific Features of Contemporary International Relations," No. 10 (October 1962), pp. 93-98.

Nikolayev [Nikolaev], Y. "Soviet-French Relations—an Important Factor of World Politics," No. 12 (December 1966), pp. 10-16.

"The Only True Road," No. 1 (January 1962), pp. 8-12.

"Our Idea of a World Without Arms," No. 7 (July 1962), pp. 49-64.

Pechorkin, V. "About Acceptable War," No. 3 (March 1963), pp. 2-25.

Pechorkin, V. "Crisis of Imperialism's Military Doctrine," No. 7 (July 1962), pp. 32-37.

"The Periodization of the History of Soviet Foreign Policy," No. 5 (May 1958), pp. 71-75.

Polyakov [Poliakov], V. "Strange Objectivity," Review of Herbert Nicholas, *The United Nations as a Political Organization*, No. 6 (June 1963), pp. 89-90.

"Readers Discuss Our Journal," No. 3 (March 1958), pp. 123-24.

"Reports and Discussions," No. 3 (March 1957), p. 163.

"Review of Letters," No. 1 (January 1957), p. 161.

"Review of Letters," No. 5 (May 1957), pp. 135-36.

Sanakoyev [Sanakoev], Sh. "The Decisive Factor in World Development," No. 2 (February 1961), pp. 3-10.

Sovetov, A. "Contradictions in the Western Bloc," No. 6 (June 1963), pp. 3-8.

———. "Leninist Foreign Policy and International Relations," No. 4 (April 1960), pp. 3-9.

Sovetov, A. "New Trends and the Realities," No. 8 (August 1963), pp. 42-48.

———. "The Soviet Union and Present International Relations," No. 1 (January 1966), pp. 3-9.

Talensky [Talenskii], N. "The 'Absolute Weapon' and the Problems of Security," No. 4 (April 1962), pp. 22-27.

———. "Anti-Missile Systems and Disarmament," No. 10 (October 1964), pp. 15-19.

———. "The Character of Modern War," No. 10 (October 1960), pp. 23-27.

———. "A Guardian of Peace and Security," No. 2 (February 1958), pp. 15-22.

———. "Military Strategy and Foreign Policy," No. 3 (March 1958), pp. 26-30.

———. "The Soviet Disarmament Programme and Its Critics," No. 11 (November 1959), pp. 7-11.

———. "The Technical Problems of Disarmament," No. 3 (March 1961), pp. 60-63.

———. "June 22: Some Lessons of History," No. 6 (June 1966), pp. 45-48.

Timofeveyev [Timofeveev], T. "Inter-State Relations and Social Contradictions," No. 2 (February 1960), pp. 12-17.

Trukhanovsky [Trukhanovskii], V. "From the Korean War to the Paris Agreements," No. 10 (October 1964), pp. 99-101.

Tunkin, G. "The Soviet Union and International Law," No. 11 (November 1959), pp. 40-47.

Viskov, S. "The Crisis of Imperialism's Foreign Policy," No. 1 (January 1962), pp. 20-26.

Volodin, M. "U.N. in a Changed World," No. 9 (September 1962), pp. 6-9.

Yeremenko [Eremenko], A. "Absurd Plans, Ridiculous Hopes," No. 6 (June 1963), pp. 15-18.

Yeremenko [Eremenko], A. "For Peace on Earth," No. 1 (January 1962), pp. 27-31.

Yermonski [Ermonskii], A. and O. Nakropin. "General Line of Soviet Foreign Policy," No. 9 (September 1966), pp. 76-84.

Yevgenyev [Evgenenev], G. "Lobbying in the U.S.A.," No. 6 (June 1963), pp. 93-94.

Zaslavsky [Zaslavskii], D. "What Will Happen Ten Years Hence?" No. 6 (June 1957), pp. 78-85.

ARTICLES FROM OTHER SOVIET SOURCES

Arab-ogly, E. "Victims of the Capitalist Moloch," *World Marxist Review*, Vol. v, No. 8 (August 1962), pp. 47-52.

Arzumanian, A. A. "Vazhnye voprosy razvitiia mirovoi ekonomiki" [Important Problems of the Development of the World Economy], *Vestnik Akademii Nauk SSSR*, No. 8 (August 1962), pp. 14-22.

"Building a United Anti-Imperialist Front," *World Marxist Review*, Vol. vi, No. 1 (January 1963), pp. 69-84.

"Conference of Marxist Sociologists," *World Marxist Review*, Vol. v, No. 2 (February 1962), pp. 79-84.

Dragilev, M. S. "Ob osobennosti novogo, tret'ego etapa obshchego krizisa kapitalizma" [Concerning the Unique Features of the New, Third Stage of the General Crisis of Capitalism], *Voprosy istorii*, No. 4 (April 1962), pp. 18-33.

"XX s"ezd komunisticheskoi partii Sovetskogo Soiuza i zadachi izucheniia sovremennogo Vostoka" [The Twentieth Congress of the Communist Party of the Soviet Union and the Tasks of Studying the Modern Orient], *Sovetskoe vostokovedenie*, No. 1 (January 1956), pp. 3-12.

Editorial "Reshit' problemu reorganizatsii OON" [Resolve the Problem of the Reorganization of the UN], *Kommunist,* No. 4 (March 1961), pp. 12-15.

———. "Vydaiushchiesia dokumenty sovremennosti" [Signal

Documents of Our Time], *Voprosy istorii*, No. 2 (February 1961), pp. 3-13.

Furaev, V. K. "O sostoianii i perspektivakh izucheniia istorii otnoshenii mezhdu SSSR i SShA v Sovetskoi istoriograficheskoi nauke" [On the Prospects for the Study of the History of the Relations between the U.S.S.R. and the U.S.A. in Soviet Historiography]. Unpublished conference paper, March 23, 1965.

Il'ichev, Leonid. "Metodologicheskie problemy estestvoznaniia i obshchestvennykh nauk" [Methodological Problems of the Natural and Social Sciences], *Kommunist*, No. 16 (November 1963), pp. 59-64.

———. "Metodologicheskie problemy estestvoznaniia i obshchestvennykh nauk" [Methodological Problems of the Natural and Social Sciences], *Vestnik Akademii Nauk SSSR*, No. 11 (November 1963), pp. 3-46.

Karyakin [Kariakin] Y. [Yu], "Allen Dulles Instead of Karl Marx," *World Marxist Review*, Vol. v, No. 4 (April 1962), pp. 82-87.

Kaz'min, N. "Tesnee sviazat' s zhizn'iu prepodavanie obshchestvennykh nauk v vuzakh" [Link the Training of the Social Sciences in Higher Schools More Closely with Life], *Kommunist*, No. 6 (April 1961), pp. 18-28.

Khrushchev, N. S. "Za novye pobedy mirovogo kommunisticheskogo dvizheniia" [For New Victories of the World Communist Movement], *Kommunist*, No. 1 (January 1961), pp. 3-37.

Korionov, V. "Lippman protiv Lippmana" [Lippmann vs. Lippmann], *Kommunist*, No. 9 (June 1962), pp. 121-25.

Kremnyev [Kremnev], Mikhail. "The Non-aligned Countries and World Politics," *World Marxist Review*, Vol. vi, No. 4 (April 1963), pp. 29-35.

Malinovskii, R. "Programma KPSS i voprosy ukrepleniia vooruzhennykh sil SSSR" [The CPSU Program and Questions of Strengthening the Armed Forces of the USSR], *Kommunist*, No. 7 (May 1962), pp. 11-12.

"Meeting of Representatives of Communist and Workers' Parties, Moscow, 1960: Statement," *World Marxist Review,* Vol. III, No. 12 (December 1960), pp. 3-28.

"Mezhdunarodnaia tribuna kommunistov" [International Forum of Communists], *Kommunist*, No. 4 (March 1963), pp. 94-95.

Mitin, M. "Nerushimoe edinstvo sotsialisticheskikh stran" [The Indissoluble Unity of the Socialist Countries], *Kommunist*, No. 2 (January 1961), pp. 11-12.

Nevsky, Gen. A. [pseudo.] "Modern Armaments and Problems of Strategy," *World Marxist Review,* Vol. VI, No. 3 (March 1963), pp. 30-35.

"Ob organizatsii Instituta Mirovoi Ekonomiki i Mezhdunarodnykh Otnoshenii" [Concerning the Organization of the Institute of World Economy and International Relations], *Vestnik Akademii Nauk SSSR*, No. 6 (June 1956), pp. 117-118.

"O merakh po ulushcheniiu podbora i podgotovki propagandistskikh kadrov" [Concerning Measures for Improvement of the Selection and Preparation of Propaganda Cadres], *Partinaia zhizn'*, No. 10 (May 1961), pp. 29-33.

"O reorganizatsii Instituta Prava v Institute Gosudarstva i Prava" [Concerning the Reorganization of the Institute of Law into the Institute of State and Law], *Vestnik Akademii Nauk SSSR*, No. 8 (August 1960), pp. 116.

Pavlov, V. I. Review of A. M. Rumiantsev, ed., *Sovremennoe osvoboditel'noe dvizhenie i natsional'naia burzhuaziia*, in *Narody Azii i Afriki*, No. 5 (May 1961), pp. 219-26.

"The Policy of Peaceful Coexistence Proves its Worth," *World Marxist Review,* Vol. v, No. 12 (December 1962), pp. 3-8.

Ponomarev, Boris N. "Zadachi istoricheskoi nauki i podgotovka nauchno-pedagogicheskikh kadrov v oblasti istorii" [The Tasks of Historical Science and the Preparation of Scientific-pedagogical Cadres in History], *Voprosy istorii,* No. 1 (January 1963), pp. 3-35.

Ponomaryov [Ponomarev], B. "Proletarian Internationalism—a Powerful Force in the Revolutionary Transformation of the World," *World Marxist Review,* Vol. III, No. 8 (August 1964), pp. 59-70.

Potekhin, I. "Narody Azii i Afriki—brat'ia" [The Peoples of Asia and Africa are Brothers], *Aziia i Afrika segodnia,* No. 3 (March 1962), pp. 4-5.

"Problems of Modern Capitalism," *World Marxist Review,* Vol. v, No. 12 (December 1962), pp. 58-79.

"Problemy razvitiia mirovoi sotsialisticheskoi sistemy" [Problems of the Development of a World Socialist System], *Vestnik Nauk SSSR,* No. 11 (November 1966), pp. 86-89.

"Rezoliutsiia XXII s"ezd kommunisticheskoi partii Sovetskogo Soiuza" [Resolutions of the Twenty-second Congress of the Communist Party of the Soviet Union], *Kommunist,* No. 16 (November 1961), pp. 3-19.

Strumilin, S. "Mir cherez 20 let" [The World Twenty Years From Now], *Kommunist,* No. 13 (September 1961), pp. 25-36.

Suslov, M. "XXII s"ezd KPSS i zadachi kafedr obshchestvennykh nauk" [The Twenty-second C.P.S.U. Congress and the Tasks of the Departments of Social Sciences], *Kommunist,* No. 3 (February 1962), pp. 15-46.

Talenskii, N. "Neoproverzhimyi vyvod istorii" [The Indisputable Conclusion of History], *Kommunist*, No. 7 (May 1960), pp. 31-41.

Timofeev, T. "Leninskii kurs mirovogo kommunisticheskogo dvizheniia i ego protivniki" [The Leninist Course of the World Communist Movement and its Opponents], *Kommunist*, No. 13 (September 1963), pp. 33-42.

Ustinov, V. A. "O primenenii elektronnykh matematicheskikh mashin v istoricheskoi nauke" [Concerning the Application of Electronic Computers to History], *Voprosy istorii,* No. 8 (August 1961), pp. 3-7.

Ustinov, V. A. "Primenenie elektronnykh matematicheskikh mashin v istoricheskoi nauke" [The Application of Electronic Computers in History], *Voprosy istorii,* No. 8 (August 1962), pp. 97-117.

"V Institute Vostokovedeniia" [In the Institute of Eastern Studies], *Voprosy istorii,* No. 3 (March 1957), pp. 196-201.

"Vsesoiuznoe soveshchanie istorikov" [All-Union Meeting of Historians], *Voprosy istorii,* No. 2 (February 1963), pp. 3-75.

"Za torzhestvo tvorcheskogo Marksizma-Leninizma" [For Creative Marxism-Leninism], *Kommunist,* No. 11 (July 1963), pp. 3-36.

Zubok, L. "V. I. Lenin ob Amerikanskom imperializme i rabochem dvizhenii SShA," [V. I. Lenin on American Imperialism and the Worker Movement of the U.S.], *Novaia i noveishaia istoriia,* No. 2 (went to press, March 1, 1963), pp. 50-64.

Non-Soviet Communist Sources

Anonymous Czech literary figure. "The Art of Survival," *Survey*, No. 51 (April 1964), pp. 77-86.

Carrillo, Santiago. "Some International Problems of the Day,"

World Marxist Review, Vol. vi, No. 5 (May 1963), pp. 4-10.

"A Comment on the Statement of the Communist Party of the U.S.A.," *Peking Review*, Vol. vi, Nos. 10-11 (March 15, 1963), pp. 58-62.

"The Differences Between Comrade Togliatti and Us," *Peking Review*, Vol. vi, No. 1 (January 4, 1963), pp. 3-21.

Heyden, G. and A. Kosing. "The Dialectics of Politics," *World Marxist Review*, Vol. vi, No. 3 (March 1963), pp. 23-29.

Kardelj, Edvard. *Socialism and War*. London: Methuen and Co., 1961.

Mao Tse-tung. *On the Protracted War*. Peking: Foreign Languages Press, 1954.

Marx, Karl and Friedrich Engels. *The Russian Menace to Europe*. Glencoe, Ill.: The Free Press, 1952.

Maurer, I. G. "The Inviolable Foundation of the Unity of the International Communist Movement," *World Marxist Review*, Vol. vi, No. 11 (November 1963), pp. 12-20.

"No One Can Save the Indian Reactionaries from their Political Bankruptcy," *Peking Review*, Vol. vi, No. 35 (August 30, 1963), pp. 6-8, 10.

Observer. "What Kennedy's 'State of the Union' Message Reveals," *Peking Review*, Vol. vi, No. 4 (January 25, 1963), pp. 5-7.

Oesterling, Kjeld and Norman Freed. *Peace, Freedom and You*. Prague: Peace and Socialism, 1963.

"Peaceful Coexistence—Two Diametrically Opposed Policies," *Peking Review*, Vol. vi, No. 51 (December 20, 1963), pp. 6-18.

"A Proposal Concerning the General Line of the International Communist Movement," the June 14, 1963 Letter of C.P.C. Central Committee in Reply to the March 30, 1963 Letter of the C.P.S.U. Central Committee, *Peking Review*, Vol. vi, No. 25 (June 21, 1963), pp. 6-22.

Index

STUDIES OF THE RUSSIAN INSTITUTE

PUBLISHED BY COLUMBIA UNIVERSITY PRESS

THAD PAUL ALTON, *Polish Postwar Economy*

JOHN A. ARMSTRONG, *Ukrainian Nationalism*

ABRAM BERGSON, *Soviet National Income and Product in 1937*

EDWARD J. BROWN, *The Proletarian Episode in Russian Literature, 1928-1932*

HARVEY L. DYCK, *Weimar Germany and Soviet Russia, 1926-1933: A Study in Diplomatic Instability*

RALPH TALCOTT FISHER, JR., *Pattern for Soviet Youth: A Study of the Congresses of the Komsomol, 1918-1954*

MAURICE FRIEDBERG, *Russian Classics in Soviet Jackets*

ELLIOT R. GOODMAN, *The Soviet Design for a World State*

DAVID GRANICK, *Management of the Industrial Firm in the USSR: A Study in Soviet Economic Planning*

THOMAS TAYLOR HAMMOND, *Lenin on Trade Unions and Revolution, 1893-1917*

JOHN N. HAZARD, *Settling Disputes in Soviet Society: The Formative Years of Legal Institutions*

DAVID JORAVSKY, *Soviet Marxism and Natural Science, 1917-1932*

DAVID MARSHALL LANG, *The Last Years of the Georgian Monarchy, 1658-1832*

GEORGE S. N. LUCKYJ, *Literary Politics in the Soviet Ukraine, 1917-1934*

HERBERT MARCUSE, *Soviet Marxism: A Critical Analysis*

KERMIT E. MC KENZIE, *Comintern and World Revolution, 1928-1943: The Shaping of Doctrine*

CHARLES B. MC LANE, *Soviet Policy and the Chinese Communists, 1931-1946*

JAMES WILLIAM MORLEY, *The Japanese Thrust into Siberia, 1918*

ALEXANDER G. PARK, *Bolshevism in Turkestan, 1917-1927*

MICHAEL BORO PETROVICH, *The Emergence of Russian Panslavism, 1856-1870*

OLIVER H. RADKEY, *The Agrarian Foes of Bolshevism: Promise and Default of the Russian Socialist Revolutionaries, February to October, 1917*

OLIVER H. RADKEY, *The Sickle Under the Hammer: The Russian Socialist Revolutionaries in the Early Months of Soviet Rule*

ALFRED J. RIEBER, *Stalin and the French Communist Party, 1941-1947*

ALFRED ERICH SENN, *The Emergence of Modern Lithuania*

ERNEST J. SIMMONS, editor, *Through the Glass of Soviet Literature: Views of Russian Society*

THEODORE K. VON LAUE, *Sergei Witte and the Industrialization of Russia*

ALLEN S. WHITING, *Soviet Policies in China, 1917-1924*

PUBLISHED BY TEACHERS COLLEGE PRESS

HAROLD J. NOAH, *Financing Soviet Schools*

PUBLISHED BY PRINCETON UNIVERSITY PRESS

PAUL AVRICH, *The Russian Anarchists*

JOHN M. THOMPSON, *Russia, Bolshevism, and the Versailles Peace*

LOREN R. GRAHAM, *The Soviet Academy of Sciences and the Communist Party, 1927-1932*

ROBERT A. MAGUIRE, *Red Virgin Soil: Soviet Literature in the 1920's*

T. H. RIGBY, *Communist Party Membership in the U.S.S.R., 1917-1967*

WILLIAM ZIMMERMAN, *Soviet Perspectives on International Relations, 1956-1967*

BOOKS WRITTEN UNDER THE AUSPICES OF THE INSTITUTE OF WAR AND PEACE STUDIES COLUMBIA UNIVERSITY

Defense and Diplomacy, by Alfred Vagts, 1956. King's Crown Press.

Inspection for Disarmament, ed., Seymour Melman, 1958. Columbia University Press

Theoretical Aspects of International Relations, ed., William T. R. Fox, 1959. University of Notre Dame Press.

Man, the State, and War, by Kenneth N. Waltz, 1959. Columbia University Press.

The Common Defense: Strategic Programs in National Politics, by Samuel P. Huntington, 1961. Columbia University Press.

Changing Patterns of Military Politics, ed., Samuel P. Huntington, 1962. Free Press.

Strategy, Politics, and Defense Budgets, by Warner R. Schilling, Paul Y. Hammond, and Glenn H. Snyder, 1962. Columbia University Press.

Political Power: USA/USSR, by Zbigniew Brzezinski and Samuel P. Huntington (jointly with the Russian Institute), 1964. Viking Press.

Political Unification: A Comparative Study of Leaders and Forces, by Amitai Etzioni. 1965. Holt, Rinehart and Winston.

Stockpiling Strategic Materials, by Glenn H. Snyder, 1966. Chandler Publishing Company.

The Politics of Military Unification, by Demetrios Caraley, 1966. Columbia University Press.

NATO and the Range of American Choice, by Annette B. Fox and William T. R. Fox, 1967. Columbia University Press.

To Move a Nation: The Politics of Foreign Policy in the Administration of John F. Kennedy, by Roger Hilsman (jointly with the Washington Center of Foreign Policy Research, Johns Hopkins University), 1967. Doubleday and Company.

Foreign Policy and Democratic Politics, by Kenneth N. Waltz (jointly with the Center for International Affairs, Harvard University), 1967. Little, Brown and Co.

A World of Nations, by Dankwart A. Rustow, 1967. Prentice-Hall.

Asia and United States Policy, by Wayne A. Wilcox, 1967. Prentice-Hall.

Western European Perspectives on International Affairs, by Donald J. Puchala and Richard L. Merritt (jointly with the Yale Political Data Program), 1968. Praeger.

The American Study of International Relations, by William T. R. Fox, 1968. University of South Carolina Press.

How Nations Behave, by Louis Henkin (jointly with the Council on Foreign Relations), 1968. Praeger.

Alliances and Small Powers, by Robert L. Rothstein, 1968. Columbia University Press.